THE
METAPHYSICAL
POETS

THE
METAPHYSICAL
POETS

DONNE, HERBERT, VAUGHAN
TRAHERNE

BY

J. B. LEISHMAN

NEW YORK
RUSSELL & RUSSELL · INC
1963

FIRST PUBLISHED, 1934

REISSUED, 1963, BY RUSSELL & RUSSELL, INC.

L. C. CATALOG NO: 63—9323

PRINTED IN THE UNITED STATES OF AMERICA

PREFACE

THE following book, the result of several years' teaching experience, is an attempt to communicate to others, especially to those who are not already familiar with it, something of the pleasure and interest I have found in the study of seventeenth-century poetry. I have tried to give a full and representative selection from the work of Donne, Herbert, Vaughan, and Traherne, together with such biographical information, such illustration of contemporary movements, ideas, feelings, intuitions, and such elucidatory comment, as seem to me necessary for the complete enjoyment of the poems I have chosen, and may, I hope, be useful to the reader in the course of further travels into this most fascinating land.

My special thanks are due to my friends Professor V. de S. Pinto, Mr. Geoffrey Tillotson, and Mr. John Butt, who read the whole of my work in manuscript, and who made many valuable suggestions. On Walton's *Lives* of Donne and Herbert Mr. Butt's authority is unrivalled, and his generous help has saved me from many errors.

Messrs. P. J. & A. E. Dobell have kindly given me permission to include extracts from Traherne.

My debt to Professor Grierson's edition of Donne's poems and to his invaluable commentary I have often acknowledged, and indeed it will be everywhere apparent.

J. B. L.

CONTENTS

INTRODUCTION

THE seventeenth century, so much of which is reflected in
the work of Donne, Herbert, Vaughan, and Traherne, is
one of the most varied and interesting periods in our social,
political, and literary history. In many ways it differs intensely from that shorter and more unified period, the Age of
Elizabeth. 'The Age of Elizabeth'! The title is on the whole
a happy one, for it emphasizes that enthusiastic patriotism,
that strong feeling of national unity developed during the
long struggle with Spain, which is perhaps the most characteristic feature of the age. Then, too, it was during the Age of
Elizabeth that the Renaissance, that great intellectual fer-
ment due partly, though not entirely, to the rediscovery of the
glories of ancient literature, reached its fullest expansion in
England. Men's horizons were immeasurably widened, and
the world seemed full of boundless possibilities:

> Right well I wote, most mighty Soveraine,
> That all this famous antique history
> Of some th' aboundance of an ydle braine
> Will judged be, and painted forgery,
> Rather then matter of just memory;
> Sith none that breatheth living aire does know
> Where is that happy land of Faery,
> Which I so much doe vaunt, yet no where show,
> But vouch antiquities, which no body can know.
>
> But let that man with better sence advize,
> That of the world least part to us is red;
> And daily how through hardy enterprize
> Many great Regions are discovered,
> Which to late age were never mentioned.
> Who ever heard of th' Indian Peru?
> Or who in venturous vessell measured
> The Amazon huge river, now found trew?
> Or fruitfullest Virginia who did ever vew?
>
> Yet all these were, when no man did them know,
> Yet have from wisest ages hidden beene;
> And later times thinges more unknowne shall show.
> Why then should witlesse man so much misweene,
> That nothing is but that which he hath seene?

B

What if within the Moones fayre shining spheare,
What if in every other starre unseene
Of other worldes he happily should heare,
He wonder would much more; yet such to some appeare.[1]

Such, I think, is the kind of image which most of us have
formed of the Elizabethan Age, and indeed it is true that the
things I have mentioned are faithfully reflected in its literature
and give it a kind of unity. But there is something more. Not
all Elizabethan poetry is joyous and confident. That old
medieval spirit which loved to moralize on the vicissitudes
of fortune and to contrast the pomp and circumstance of
princes with the loneliness and corruption of the grave still
persisted—nay, the contrast between the world and the spirit
was often more acutely felt now that the attractions of the
world had been multiplied. Too often in speaking of the
Elizabethan Age we forget this strain of profound melancholy
in its literature—in Spenser's complaints of the misery of courts
and the unhappiness of those who put their trust in princes, in
Shakespeare's tragedies and in those sonnets where he celebrates the triumph of time over strength, beauty, and prosperity, and in Sir Walter Raleigh, who wrote in his *History of
the World*:

> ... the minde of man hath two Ports, the one alwaies frequented
> by the entrance of manifold vanities; the other desolate and
> over-growne with grasse, by which enter our charitable thoughts
> and divine contemplations.[2]

Then, too, in spite of the outward unity that was maintained
with such difficulty by the careful and compromising policy of
the queen, grave dissensions were being caused by religious
controversy. The protestant divines who had sought a refuge
in Germany and Switzerland from the persecutions of Mary
Tudor had returned, and were eager to establish the doctrine
and discipline of Geneva. And already the merchants were
grumbling about the high taxation. When the strong hands of
Elizabeth and her counsellors were removed all these controversies and differences increased under the imprudent governments of James and Charles, until they finally came to a head
in the Civil War.

About the turn of the century the balance shifts. We may
say that Elizabethan literature is on the whole a literature of
confidence, but I think we may also say that seventeenth-

---

[1] *Faerie Queene*, Proem to Bk. II.
[2] Bk. I, chap. vi, § ix; ed. 1634, p. 83.

century literature is on the whole a literature of disillusion. Both moods are characteristic of the Renaissance, which after all was but a fertilization of the medieval mind; but in a good deal of the imaginative literature of the seventeenth century— that is to say, of the pre-Augustan seventeenth century, which both preceded and overlapped the Restoration, so that to- wards the end of the century we are often aware of two worlds existing side by side—in a good deal of this literature that note of melancholy which the Elizabethans sometimes strike, and which those who have not reflected on the continuity of the Middle Ages and the Renaissance may have been tempted to call medieval, sounds more deeply and more persistently. In a lecture on Cowley Mr. Garrod applies to a good deal of 'metaphysical' poetry the suggestive phrase 'a poetry of books and thinking', and it is certainly true that a good deal of seventeenth-century poetry and prose was written by men who either in sorrow or contempt had turned aside from the troubles and confusions around them and had found inspira- tion either in books or in some intensely personal experience. The main stream of the national life does not seem to flow through this literature as it flows through that of the pre- ceding age, true as it is that this stream itself has been rather 'shorn and parcelled'. It is an age of lonely and divided souls. Vaughan and Traherne live obscurely in retirement, meditat- ing on God, on nature, and on the experiences of childhood. Herbert, after his hopes of state preferment have been dis- appointed, struggles to dedicate himself entirely to the claims of the religious life. Donne wrestles with his experience of love, and when he requires images or illustrations he draws them, not from the picturesque and popular mythology which had inspired earlier poets, but from those abstruse studies in divinity which he had pursued with no less eagerness than the love of woman. And in some of his poetry he treats this abstruse learning in a spirit similar to that of Burton and Sir Thomas Browne. Great readers and scholars, of immense but uncritical learning, they found that the knowledge they had so laboriously acquired had not, after all, shed much light on the great mysteries of existence, had not helped much to con- firm the truths which they considered most important. Hold- ing therefore to a few central convictions, they were disposed to regard all other knowledge as more or less on the same level of importance or unimportance, to play with it much as the Elizabethans had played with words, and to allow their imagination to suggest subtle analogies and resemblances. This is the source of much of what has been called 'metaphysical wit' —learned men, rather sceptical about the value of their learning, and playing with the conceptions and theories of philosophy, theology, and the science or pseudo-science of their day much as their predecessors had played with words. And Donne, like Herbert, is disappointed in his hopes of secular preferment, and after long years of lonely meditation and hope deferred he too enters the Church and allows his congregation to share in his lonely struggles, to profit by his knowledge of those dark places of the heart he had explored in earlier years, to enter his intense and passionate soul striving after settled faith and the subjugation of its 'sin of fear'.

If, to borrow a phrase from Johnson, there is sometimes mirth in the melancholy of seventeenth-century poetry, one often seems to detect some melancholy in its mirth. The impudent, cynical wit of Beaumont and Fletcher and of many of the earlier poets suggests a certain hollowness and absence of foundations.

In theory, as well as in practice, many of these poets rejected much that was characteristic in the work of their predecessors. About the turn of the century we perceive in the satires of Hall, Marston, Guilpin, and others, and of course in those of Donne himself; in the *Parnassus Plays* and in Jonson's Humour Comedies, a reaction, chiefly on the part of young templars and university men, against that dictatorship of literary taste and literary fashion which had been for so long exercised by the court; against the romantic platonism of Spenser and the conventional insincerities of so many of the sonneteers; against sugared conceits and reminiscences of Ovid, and against what seemed the degradation of poetry by those popular playwrights who wrote only to please the mob. Their various attacks on what they call 'wanton' poetry are usually accompanied by satirical portraits of the readers and admirers of that poetry, foolish courtiers like Gullio in the *Parnassus Plays*, whose worship of 'sweet Mr. Shakespeare' and admiration for *Romeo and Juliet, Venus and Adonis,* and *The Rape of Lucrece* is a theme for mirth—effeminate young men who treasure up their mistresses' ribbons and shoe-laces and write sonnets about them. Hall and Guilpin severely attack Nashe for having written *The Choice of Valentines,* one of the most licentious of Elizabethan poems, for the Earl of Southampton or some other noble patron; and in the *Parnassus Plays* we see poor Ingenioso (who represents Nashe) compelled by poverty to write such poetry as his foolish patron demands. It is true that the greatest genius among these young men who desired a change was himself writing love-poetry at this time; but it was very different from that which the sonneteers had written and which the courtiers admired—unconventional, unsentimental, cynical, passionate, absolutely realistic and sincere. The templars and university men were getting tired of court fashions and affectations, and wanted to satirize them or to see them satirized. Indeed, they were prepared to welcome a kind of literature very different from any that had yet appeared: something hard, satirical, and rather bitter. It was primarily for them that Ben Jonson wrote his comedies: they were his chosen audience; it was to them that he dedicated *Every Man Out Of His Humour* and *Volpone*. And however much they might differ from him in outlook and personal experience all the younger poets were profoundly influenced by Jonson—Jonson the scholar, the upholder of a dignified and strenuous conception of poetry, the despiser of mere sweetness and conventional ornament, the striver after classical terseness and grace, the champion of a more serious and intellectual kind of 'wit' than that which had pleased his predecessors, the apostle, in fact, of a poetry that cared only for the praises of connoisseurs.

There is a great difference between the witty, cynical, secular poetry of Carew and Suckling, their 'manifold vanities', and the 'divine contemplations' of Herbert and Vaughan; nevertheless, a careful reader will perceive that something like a common tradition has shaped the experiences which came to them through these 'two ports', and that the term 'metaphysical' may not inappropriately be applied to them all; for they drew their conceits from recesses of experience—not merely, as Johnson says, of learning—'not very much frequented by common readers of poetry'.

JOHN DONNE

I

FOR our knowledge of the facts of Donne's life we are chiefly indebted to Izaak Walton's beautiful biography. The author of the *Compleat Angler* was born at Stafford in 1593, came up to London where he was apprenticed to a member of the Ironmongers' Company, and by 1614 was in possession of 'half a shop' two doors west of Chancery Lane. This was in the parish of St. Dunstan's in the West, a living with which Donne was presented in 1624, from which date his acquaintance with Walton probably began; and it may well have been Donne who introduced him to Sir Henry Wotton and the other eminent persons, especially divines, with whom he became intimate. For business was not his chief interest; he was something of a scholar and a poet, and he won the friendship of many of the most distinguished churchmen of his day. He retired from business in 1643, and enjoyed forty years of uninterrupted leisure, spending most of his time at Winchester, partly with his friend Bishop Morley, and partly with his daughter who had married a prebendary of the Cathedral, in whose house he died at the great age of ninety in 1683.

His life of Donne was first published in 1640 as a preface to a collection of Donne's sermons, and again, considerably expanded and corrected, in 1658. Walton is chiefly concerned with Dr. Donne the preacher, and tells us comparatively little about Jack Donne the poet. Have we any other source of information? Of his youth, except for a few obscure allusions in the verse *Letters*, we know almost nothing beyond what Walton has told us, but from about 1600 our knowledge is supplemented by the large collection of letters published by his son in 1651, and by a few letters in other collections. The result is that during the period from 1600 to 1617, in which year his wife died, 'our knowledge', as Gosse says,

> of his emotions and movements becomes so precise, in the light of the documents published in these volumes, that we may now claim to follow Donne's career more minutely than that of any other Elizabethan or Jacobean man of letters, except, perhaps, Bacon.[1]

[1] *Life and Letters of John Donne*, vol. i, p. xvi.

Master *John Donne* [says Walton] was born in *London*, in the year 1573[1] of good and vertuous Parents: and, though his own Learning and other multiplyed merits may justly appear sufficient to dignifie both Himself and his Posterity: yet, the Reader may be pleased to know, that his Father was masculinely and lineally descended from a very antient Family in *Wales*, where many of his name now live, that deserve and have great reputation in that Countrey.

By his Mother he was descended of the Family of the famous and learned Sir *Thomas Moor*, sometime Lord *Chancellour* of *England*: as also, from that worthy and laborious *Judge Rastall*, who left Posterity the vast Statutes of the Law of this Nation most exactly abridged.

He had his first breeding in his Fathers house, where a private Tutor had the care of him, until the tenth year of his age; and, in his eleventh year, was sent to the University of *Oxford*; having at that time a good command both of the French and Latine Tongue. This and some other of his remarkable Abilities, made one then give this censure of him; *That this age had brought forth another* Picus Mirandula; of whom Story says, *That he was rather born, than made wise by study.*

There he remained for some years in *Hart-Hall*, having for the advancement of his studies Tutors of several Sciences to attend and instruct him, till time made him capable, and his learning expressed in publick exercises declared him worthy to receive his first degree in the Schools, which he forbore by advice from his friends, who being for their Religion of the Romish perswasion, were *conscionably* averse to some parts of the Oath that is alwaies tendered at those times; and not to be refused by those that expect the titulary honour of their studies.

About the fourteenth year of his age, he was transplanted from *Oxford* to *Cambridge*; where, that he might receive nourishment from both Soils, he staied till his seventeenth year; all which time he was a most laborious Student, often changing his studies, but endeavouring to take no degree, for the reasons formerly mentioned.

About the seventeenth year of his age, he was removed to *London*, and then admitted into *Lincolns-Inne*, with an intent to study the *Law*; where he gave great testimonies of his Wit, his Learning, and of his Improvement in that profession: which never served him for other use than an Ornament and Self-satisfaction.

His Father died before his admission into this Society; and being a Merchant, left him his portion in money (it was 3000 l.). His Mother and those to whose care he was committed, were watchful to improve his knowledge, and to that end appointed

[1] Actually 1572.

him Tutors both in the *Mathematicks*, and in all the other *Liberal Sciences*, to attend him. But with these Arts they were advised to instil into him particular Principles of the *Romish Church*; of which those Tutors profest (though secretly) themselves to be members.

They had almost obliged him to their faith; having for their advantage, besides many opportunities, the example of his dear and pious Parents, which was a most powerful perswasion, and did work much upon him, as he professeth in his Preface to his *Pseudo-Martyr*; a Book of which the Reader shall have some account in what follows.

He was now entered into the eighteenth year of his age; and at that time had betrothed himself to no Religion that might give him any other denomination than *a Christian*. And Reason, and Piety had both perswaded him, that there could be no such sin as *Schism*, if an adherence to some visible Church were not necessary.

About the nineteenth year of his age, he, being then un-resolv'd what Religion to adhere to, and, considering how much it concern'd his soul to choose the most Orthodox, did therefore (though his youth and health, promised him a long life) to rectifie all scruples that might concern that, presently lay aside all study of the Law: and, of all other Sciences that might give him a denomination; and begun seriously to survey, and consider the Body of Divinity, as it was then controverted betwixt the *Reformed* and the *Roman Church*. And as *Gods blessed Spirit did then awaken him to the search, and in that industry did never forsake him,* (they be his own words) *so he calls the same holy Spirit to witness this Protestation; that, in that disquisition and search, he proceeded with humility and diffidence in himself; and, by that which he took to be the safest way; namely, frequent Prayers, and an indifferent affection to both parties*; and indeed, truth had too much light about her to be hid from so sharp an Inquirer; and, he had too much ingenuity, not to acknowledge he had found her.

Being to undertake this search, he believed the *Cardinal Bellarmine* to be the best defender of the *Roman cause*, and therefore betook himself to the examination of his Reasons. The Cause was weighty: and wilful delays had been inexcusable both towards God and his own Conscience; he therefore proceeded in this search with all moderate haste, and about the twentieth year of his age, did shew the then *Dean* of *Gloucester* (whose name my memory hath now lost) all the Cardinals works marked with many weighty observations under his own hand; which works were bequeathed by him at his death as a Legacy to a most dear Friend.[1]

---

[1] World's Classics ed., pp. 23–6.

This study of Bellarmine could not, as Walton declares, have begun 'about the nineteenth year of his age', since Bellarmine's *Disputationes* were not published until 1593, when Donne was twenty-one. Moreover, Walton implies that this course of study and the conversion that followed it were speedily effected, but Donne, in the preface to his *Pseudo-Martyr*, 1610, implies that it was a slow and deliberate affair:

> They who have descended so lowe, as to take knowledge of me, and to admit me into their consideration, know well that I used no inordinate haste, nor precipitation in binding my conscience to any locall Religion. I had a longer worke to doe then many other men; for I was first to blot out, certaine impressions of the Romane religion, and to wrastle both against the examples and against the reasons, by which some hold was taken; and some anticipations early layde upon my conscience. . . . And although I apprehended well enough, that this irresolution not only retarded my fortune, but also bred some scandall, and endangered my spirituall reputation, by laying me open to many mis-interpretations; yet all these respects did not transport me to any violent and sudden determination, till I had, to the measure of my poore wit and judgement, survayed and digested the whole body of Divinity, controverted betweene ours and the Romane Church.[1]

And he declares that he proceeded with 'frequent praier, and equall and indifferent affections'. For although the wildness of his life, which in later years he bitterly regretted, and the impudent, cynical, worldly tone of most of the poetry he wrote at this time, have led many critics to suppose that in his youth Donne's interest in religion was almost purely intellectual, his third satire, which must also have been written about this time, will hardly allow us to take that view. Its rough lines—for Donne and his young contemporaries, who were now vigorously applying themselves to satire, believed that the model satirist was Persius, and that what seemed to them his chief characteristics, 'hardness of conceit and harshness of style', were to be imitated—its rough lines are penetrated by an intense eagerness for truth and contempt for indifference. We must seek for truth, he cries, but where is she to be found? Some seek her at Rome, because she was there a thousand years ago, others at Geneva, others at

---

[1] B2v–B3.

home, while some are content to suppose that all religions
are the same;

> . . . but unmoved thou
> Of force must one, and forc'd but one allow;
> And the right; aske thy father which is shee,
> Let him aske his; though truth and falsehood bee
> Neare twins, yet truth a little elder is;

[i.e. the true religion is apparently that which, in Dryden's words,
'rests upon the primitive at last': hence Donne's eager study of
the fathers of the Church.]

> Be busie to seeke her, beleeve mee this,
> Hee's not of none, nor worst, that seekes the best.
> To adore, or scorne an image, or protest,
> May all be bad; doubt wisely; in strange way
> To stand inquiring right, is not to stray;
> To sleepe, or runne wrong, is. On a huge hill,
> Cragged, and steep, Truth stands, and hee that will
> Reach her, about must, and about must goe.

In fact, we must simply admit that Jack Donne was a very
complex character, not to be explained by any simple formula,
and that while, in the splendid words of Sir Walter Raleigh,
one of the gates of his mind was 'always frequented by the
entrance of manifold vanities', the other was able to admit
'divine contemplations'.

Walton continues:

> About a year following he resolved to travel; and the Earl
> of *Essex* going first the *Cales*, and after the *Island voyages*, the
> first *Anno* 1596. the second 1597. he took the advantage of those
> opportunities, waited upon his Lordship, and was an eye-
> witness of those happy and unhappy employments.
>
> But he returned not back into *England*, till he had staid some
> years first in *Italy*, and then in *Spain*, where he made many
> useful observations of those Countreys, their Laws and manner
> of Government, and returned perfect in their Languages.[1]

At first sight this passage seems to mean that 'about a year
following', i.e. about 1594, Donne joined the Cadiz expedition,
which sailed in June 1596, and that after the return of the
Islands expedition in October 1597 he spent 'some years'
abroad, although we know that on March 1, 1602, he had been
secretary to Egerton for four years, i.e. since 1598—a sequence
of events that is manifestly absurd and impossible. The
mystery has recently been cleared up by Mr. John Sparrow

[1] p. 26.

('The Date of Donne's Travels' in *A Garland for John Donne*, Harvard, 1931), who on the one hand shows that there is strong evidence for believing that Donne's travels took place between November or December 1594 and June 1596, and on the other hand very plausibly suggests that Walton knew this, but that he sandwiched into his correct description of the sequence of events a clumsy and careless parenthesis about the Cadiz and Islands expeditions.

The Islands expedition was driven back to Plymouth by a terrible storm which Donne realistically described in a verse epistle to his friend Christopher Brooke. The companion piece to this poem, *The Calme*, is even finer, and must be quoted in full. To find in the description of some particular incident an opportunity for a display of 'wit' by means of ingenious comparisons, metaphors, and associations, discovering, as Johnson puts it, 'occult resemblances in things apparently unlike', is a favourite exercise of many seventeenth-century poets, and many excellent examples are to be found in Marvell's poem on Appleton House.

> Our storm is past, and that storms tyrannous rage,
> A stupid calme, but nothing it, doth swage.
> The fable is inverted, and farre more
> A blocke afflicts, now, then a storke before.
> Stormes chafe, and soone weare out themselves, or us;
> In calmes, Heaven laughs to see us languish thus.
> As steady'as I can wish, that my thoughts were,
> Smooth as thy mistresse glasse, or what shines there,
> The sea is now. And, as the Iles which wee
> Seeke, when wee can move, our ships rooted bee.
> As water did in stormes, now pitch runs out:
> As lead, when a fir'd Church becomes one spout.
> And all our beauty, and our trimme, decayes,
> Like courts removing, or like ended playes.
> The fighting place now seamens ragges supply;
> And all the tackling is a frippery.
> No use of lanthornes; and in one place lay
> Feathers and dust, to day and yesterday.
> Earths hollownesses, which the worlds lungs are,
> Have no more winde then the upper valt of aire.
> We can nor lost friends, nor sought foes recover,
> But meteorlike, save that wee move not, hover.
> Onely the Calenture together drawes
> Deare friends, which meet dead in great fishes jawes:
> And on the hatches as on Altars lyes
> Each one, his owne Priest, and owne Sacrifice.

Who live, that miracle do multiply
Where walkers in hot Ovens, doe not dye.
If in despite of these, wee swimme, that hath
No more refreshing, then our brimstone Bath,
But from the sea, into the ship we turne,
Like parboyl'd wretches, on the coales to burne.
Like *Bajazet* encag'd, the shepheards scoffe,
Or like slacke sinew'd *Sampson*, his haire off,
Languish our ships. Now, as a Miriade
Of Ants, durst th' Emperours lov'd snake invade,
The crawling Gallies, Sea-goales, finny chips,
Might brave our Pinnaces, now bed-ridde ships.
Whether a rotten state, and hope of gaine,
Or to disuse mee from the queasie paine
Of being belov'd, and loving, or the thirst
Of honour, or faire death, out pusht mee first,
I lose my end: for here as well as I
A desperate may live, and a coward die.
Stagge, dogge, and all which from, or towards flies,
Is paid with life, or pray, or doing dyes.
Fate grudges us all, and doth subtly lay
A scourge, 'gainst which wee all forget to pray,
He that at sea prayes for more winde, as well
Under the poles may begge cold, heat in hell.
What are wee then? How little more alas
Is man now, then before he was? he was
Nothing; for us, wee are for nothing fit;
Chance, or our selves still disproportion it.
Wee have no power, no will, no sense; I lye,
I should not then thus feele this miserie.[1]

But Donne was having adventures on land as well as at sea. And here we come to a very vexed question, that of the 'sincerity' of the *Elegies* and of the *Songs and Sonnets*. I may as well commit myself at the outset by declaring that while I hardly think we are justified in looking for a record of definite facts, of a definite sequence of events, I cannot bring myself to regard these poems as mere *jeux d'esprit*, or, to borrow a phrase which used to be applied to Shakespeare's Sonnets, as 'academic exercises'. Neither can I agree with those critics who are inclined to pick and choose, to regard the bitter and cynical poems as 'exercises' and the more tender and philosophic ones as 'sincere'. I confess I cannot see why we should not regard them all as equally sincere, even if we do not find them all

---

[1] *Poems*, ed. Grierson, 1912, vol. i, p. 178.

equally congenial. Wordsworth too has been subjected to the
same process of picking and choosing: when critics found in
him something they did not like they assumed that he could
not have meant what he said, or, like John Morley, roundly
declared that it was 'nonsense'. To-day, however, owing
largely to the patient and sympathetic work of Raleigh and
Bradley, this attitude to Wordsworth, like the 'academic exercise' view of Shakespeare's Sonnets, does not find much favour.
On the whole it seems wiser to assume as a matter of course
that great poets mean what they say.

There is much to be said for the view that certain of Donne's
Elegies seem to form a group and to record the experience of
an intrigue with some married woman during 1596 and 1597.
Here is an extract from the one entitled *Loves Warre*, which may
have been written before his departure with the Islands expedition in 1597:

> Till I have peace with thee, warr other men,
> And when I have peace, can I leave thee then?
> All other Warrs are scrupulous; Only thou
> O fayr free Citty, maist thyselfe allowe
> To any one . . .
> Here let mee warr; in these armes lett mee lye;
> Here lett mee parlee, batter, bleede, and dye.
> Thyne armes imprison me, and myne armes thee;
> Thy hart thy ransome is; take myne for mee.
> Other men war that they their rest may gayne;
> But wee will rest that wee may fight agayne.
> Those warrs the ignorant, these th'experienc'd love,
> There wee are alwayes under, here above.
> There Engins farr off breed a just true feare,
> Neere thrusts, pikes, stabs, yea bullets hurt not here.
> There lyes are wrongs; here safe uprightly lye;
> There men kill men, we'will make one by and by.
> Thou nothing; I not halfe so much shall do
> In these Warrs, as they may which from us two
> Shall spring. Thousands wee see which travaile not
> To warrs; But stay swords, armes, and shott
> To make at home; And shall not I do then
> More glorious service, staying to make men?[1]

The fifth elegy, *His Picture*, seems also to have been written
at this time.

> Here take my Picture; though I bid farewell,
> Thine, in my heart, where my soule dwels, shall dwell.

[1] p. 122.

'Tis like me now, but I dead, 'twill be more
When wee are shadowes both, then 'twas before.
When weather-beaten I come backe; my hand,
Perhaps with rude oares torne, or Sun beams tann'd,
My face and brest of hairecloth, and my head
With cares rash sodaine stormes, being o'rspread,
My body'a sack of bones, broken within,
And powders blew staines scatter'd on my skinne;
If rivall fooles taxe thee to'have lov'd a man,
So foule, and course, as, Oh, I may seeme than,
This shall say what I was: and thou shalt say,
Doe his hurts reach mee? doth my worth decay?
Or doe they reach his judging minde, that hee
Should now love lesse, what hee did love to see?
That which in him was faire and delicate,
Was but the milke, which in loves childish state
Did nurse it: who now is growne strong enough
To feed on that, which to disused tasts seemes tough.[1]

However, after his return from the Azores, his affection for her
seems to have cooled, for in the seventh elegy he exclaims con-
temptuously:

Natures lay Ideot, I taught thee to love,
And in that sophistrie, Oh, thou dost prove
Too subtile: Foole, thou didst not understand
The mystique language of the eye nor hand:
Nor couldst thou judge the difference of the aire
Of sighes, and say, this lies, this sounds despaire:
Nor by the'eyes water call a maladie
Desperately hot, or changing feaverously.
I had not taught thee then, the Alphabet
Of flowers, how they devisefully being set
And bound up, might with speechlesse secrecie
Deliver arrands mutely, and mutually.
Remember since all thy words us'd to bee
To every suitor; *I, if my friends agree;*
Since, household charmes, thy husbands name to teach,
Were all the love trickes, that thy wit could reach;
And since, an houres discourse could scarce have made
One answer in thee, and that ill arraid
In broken proverbs, and torne sentences.
Thou art not by so many duties his,
That from the worlds Common having sever'd thee,
Inlaid thee, neither to be seene, nor see,
As mine: who have with amorous delicacies

[1] p. 86.

Refin'd thee'into a blis-full Paradise.
Thy graces and good words my creatures bee;
I planted knowledge and lifes tree in thee,
Which Oh, shall strangers taste? Must I alas
Frame and enamell Plate, and drinke in Glasse?
Chafe waxe for others seales? breake a colts force
And leave him then, beeing made a ready horse?[1]

It is possible that certain of the *Songs and Sonnets* were inspired by the faithlessness of this lady—*The Curse*, for example, where he exclaims:

Who ever guesses, thinks, or dreames he knowes
Who is my mistris, wither by this curse;
   His only, and only his purse
   May some dull heart to love dispose,
And shee yeeld then to all that are his foes;
   May he be scorn'd by one, whom all else scorne,
   Forsweare to others, what to her he'hath sworne,
   With feare of missing, shame of getting, torne:

concluding, after two more vigorous stanzas,

          And all which shall
Be annex'd in schedules unto this by mee,
Fall on that man; For if it be a shee
Nature before hand hath out-cursed mee.[2]

And then there is that tremendous poem of concentrated hate, *The Apparition*:

When by thy scorne, O murdresse, I am dead,
   And that thou thinkst thee free
From all solicitation from mee,
Then shall my ghost come to thy bed,
And thee, fain'd vestall, in worse armes shall see;
Then thy sicke taper will begin to winke,
And he, whose thou art then, being tyr'd before,
Will, if thou stirre, or pinch to wake him, thinke
   Thou call'st for more,
And in false sleepe will from thee shrinke,
And then poore Aspen wretch, neglected thou
Bath'd in a cold quicksilver sweat wilt lye
   A veryer ghost then I;
What I will say, I will not tell thee now,
Lest that preserve thee'; and since my love is spent,
I'had rather thou shouldst painfully repent,
Then by my threatnings rest still innocent.[3]

But this mood of bitter hatred gives place to one of cynicism

[1] p. 89.   [2] p. 41.   [3] p. 47.

and disgust, as in that remarkable poem *Loves Alchymie*, where he rejects all the splendid hyperboles of the sonneteers, and declares that what is called love is nothing more than the brief satisfaction of a transient desire:

> Some that have deeper digg'd loves Myne then I,
> Say, where his centrique happinesse doth lie:
>   I have lov'd, and got, and told,
> But should I love, get, tell, till I were old,
> I should not finde that hidden mysterie;
>   Oh, 'tis imposture all:
> And as no chymique yet th'Elixar got,
>   But glorifies his pregnant pot,
>   If by the way to him befall
> Some odoriferous thing, or medicinall,
>   So, lovers dreame a rich and long delight,
>   But get a winter-seeming summers night.
>
> Our ease, our thrift, our honor, and our day,
> Shall we, for this vaine Bubles shadow pay?
>   Ends love in this, that my man,
> Can be as happy'as I can; If he can
> Endure the short scorne of a Bridegroomes play?
>   That loving wretch that sweares,
> 'Tis not the bodies marry, but the mindes,
>   Which he in her Angelique findes,
>   Would sweare as justly, that he heares,
> In that dayes rude hoarse minstralsey, the spheares.
>   Hope not for minde in women; at their best
>   Sweetnesse and wit, they'are but *Mummy*, possest.[1]

Sometimes his cynicism is more cheerful, as in *Loves Deitie*, where, after arguing that it is unreasonable that 'I must love her, that loves not mee', he comforts himself with the reflection that even if he did contrive to fall in love with a woman who loved him in return, she would, since there is no truth in women, most certainly be proving false to some other lover in doing so:

> Rebell and Atheist too, why murmure I,
>   As though I felt the worst that love could doe?
> Love might make me leave loving, or might trie
>   A deeper plague, to make her love mee too,
> Which, since she loves before, I'am loth to see;
> Falsehood is worse then hate; and that must bee,
>   If shee whom I love, should love mee.[2]

And in the famous poem *Goe, and catche a falling starre* his cynicism has become positively boisterous.

[1] p. 39.   [2] p. 54.

Goe, and catche a falling starre,
    Get with child a mandrake roote,
Tell me, where all past yeares are,
    Or who cleft the Divels foot,
Teach me to heare Mermaides singing,
    Or to keep off envies stinging,
            And finde
            What winde
Serves to advance an honest minde.

If thou beest borne to strange sights,
    Things invisible to see,
Ride ten thousand daies and nights,
    Till age snow white haires on thee,
Thou, when thou retorn'st, wilt tell mee
All strange wonders that befell thee,
            And sweare
            No where
Lives a woman true, and faire.

If thou findst one, let mee know,
    Such a Pilgrimage were sweet;
Yet doe not, I would not goe,
    Though at next doore wee might meet,
Though shee were true, when you met her,
And last, till you write your letter,
            Yet shee
            Will bee
False, ere I come, to two, or three.[1]

Then come a group of poems in which he celebrates not only
the inconstancy of women, but his own inconstancy, which
he has now adopted as a principle, and in which he glories.

Womans constancy

Now thou hast lov'd me one whole day,
To morrow when thou leav'st, what wilt thou say?
Wilt thou then Antedate some new made vow?
        Or say that now
We are not just those persons, which we were?   5
Or, that oathes made in reverentiall feare
Of Love, and his wrath, any may forsweare?
Or, as true deaths, true maryages untie,
So lovers contracts, images of those,
Binde but till sleep, deaths image, them unloose?   10
        Or, your owne end to Justifie,
For having purpos'd change, and falsehood; you
Can have no way but falsehood to be true?

[1] p. 8.

Vaine lunatique, against these scapes I could
Dispute, and conquer, if I would,   *15*
Which I abstaine to doe,
For by to morrow, I may thinke so too.[1]

In *Loves Diet* he tells how he clipped love's wings and kept him
within bounds by carefully watching himself and suppressing
all signs of undue affection, while subjecting those of his mistress to the worst possible interpretation. The poem concludes:

Thus I reclaim'd my buzard love, to flye
At what, and when, and how, and where I chuse;
Now negligent of sport I lye,
And now as other Fawkners use,
I spring a mistresse, sweare, write, sigh and weepe:
And the game kill'd, or lost, goe talke, and sleepe.[2]

He now declares that he hates constancy in women.

The Indifferent

I can love both faire and browne,
Her whom abundance melts, and her whom want betraies,
Her who loves lonenesse best, and her who maskes and plaies,
Her whom the country form'd, and whom the town,
Her who beleeves, and her who tries,
Her who still weepes with spungie eyes,
And her who is dry corke, and never cries;
I can love her, and her, and you and you,
I can love any, so she be not true.

Will no other vice content you?
Wil it not serve your turn to do, as did your mothers?
Or have you all old vices spent, and now would finde out others?
Or doth a feare, that men are true, torment you?
Oh we are not, be not you so,
Let mee, and doe you, twenty know.
Rob mee, but binde me not, and let me goe.
Must I, who came to travaile thorow you,
Grow your fixt subject, because you are true?

Venus heard me sigh this song,
And by Loves sweetest Part, Variety, she swore,
She heard not this till now; and that it should be so no more.
She went, examin'd, and return'd ere long,
And said, alas, Some two or three
Poore Heretiques in love there bee
Which thinke to stablish dangerous constancie.
But I have told them, 'since you will be true,
You shall be true to them, who'are false to you.'[3]

[1] p. 9.   [2] p. 55.
[3] p. 12. I have added the inverted commas in the last two lines.

He begs Cupid to let him remain a light o' love until old age:

Loves Usury

For every houre that thou wilt spare mee now,
   I will allow,
Usurious God of Love, twenty to thee,
When with my browne, my gray haires equall bee;
Till then, Love, let my body raigne, and let
Mee travell, sojourne, snatch, plot, have, forget,
Resume my last yeares relict: thinke that yet
   We'had never met.

Let mee thinke any rivalls letter mine,
   And at next nine
Keepe midnights promise; mistake by the way
The maid, and tell the Lady of that delay;
Onely let mee love none, no, not the sport;
From country grasse, to comfitures of Court,
Or cities quelque choses, let report
   My minde transport.

This bargaine's good; if when I'am old, I bee
   Inflam'd by thee,
If thine owne honour, or my shame, or paine,
Thou covet most, at that age thou shalt gaine.
Doe thy will then, then subject and degree,
And fruit of love, Love I submit to thee,
Spare mee till then, I'll beare it, though she bee
   One that loves mee.[1]

At one time, then, he really thought that there was such a thing as true love and faithfulness in woman, that there was something in the chivalrous devotion of Spenser and the sonneteers. Then he was deceived, was for a time inflamed with hatred and bitterness, but gradually developed a cynical philosophy of love; resolved to get what enjoyment out of it he could, but not to let it unduly disturb his peace of mind. Therefore he declares that he hates constancy: first, because he is not quite confident that his cynical philosophy is right; secondly, because if some apparently ideal woman should persuade him to discard it, he might discover later that after all she was no better than the rest, and so have to pass through the same bitter experience once again. And so he resolves never to let his affections be strongly engaged, not at any rate until he is an old man; then, even if disillusionment awaits him, and if it turns out that there was nothing more

[1] p. 13.

in love than what his cynical philosophy had supposed, he will
at least have the satisfaction of having got from love most of
the enjoyment it had to offer. *In utrumque paratus*, in fact.

Of course, one cannot speak with certainty, one cannot assume that either the experiences or the facts were exactly as
I have suggested; but it is at least probable that some such
dialectic lies behind the poems we have been considering. I
have offered the reader an hypothesis, a scaffolding, which he
may find useful, and which he is at full liberty to reject after
it has served its turn. For in the interpretation of poetry, while
it is absurd and unnecessary to ask, What was the precise, particular experience from which it arose? it is most important
to ask, and to try to answer, the question, What was the *kind* of
experience?

And yet, after all, perhaps both the bitterness and the cynicism were exaggerated; for in that very interesting poem *Negative Love* he seems to review his experiences, and to say that he
could never really decide which conception of love was the
right one. Some people, he says, declare that love is merely
sensual, others, that it is merely ideal; clearly, neither of these
views can be right, for it is obvious that both the senses and
the mind find some kind of satisfaction. I, for my part, am
content to say that I don't know what love is; and therefore,
since I don't know what I'm looking for, I can't be disappointed by not finding it:

> I never stoop'd so low, as they
> Which on an eye, cheeke, lip, can prey,
>> Seldom to them, which soare no higher
>> Then vertue or the minde to'admire,
> For sense, and understanding may
>> Know, what gives fuell to their fire:
> My love, though silly, is more brave,
> For may I misse, when ere I crave,
> If I know yet, what I would have.

> If that be simply perfectest
> Which can by no way be exprest
>> But *Negatives*, my love is so.
>> To All, which all love, I say no.
> If any who deciphers best,
>> What we know not, our selves, can know,
> Let him teach mee that nothing; This
> As yet my ease, and comfort is,
> Though I speed not, I cannot misse.[1]

¹ p. 66.

Before proceeding farther let us consider briefly the style of these poems. The most striking thing about them is their extraordinary realism, their freedom from all the conventional ornaments of poetry. There are very few metaphors or images or illustrations, and what few there are are drawn exclusively from the everyday life of the city or the court. Not only is there nothing of the splendid imagery of Shakespeare's sonnets —there are none of the conventional, though often charming, ornaments which we usually associate with Elizabethan poetry: no references to Greek or Latin legend or mythology, no shepherds and shepherdesses, no beds of roses, no flowery meads, silver fountains, gentle zephyrs. He does not, like the sonneteers, ransack heaven and earth for comparisons to describe the transcendent beauty of his mistress; he does not say that her beauty scorches him like the sun, or that her coldness freezes him like ice. For all these things he seems to have had a profound contempt. Most of the Elizabethan poets used to address complimentary verses to each other, but the only one whom Donne ever condescended to praise was that other great master of realism and despiser of the taste of his age, Ben Jonson. Donne is not concerned with what Petrarch, or Ronsard, or Spenser, or the courtly Italian Platonists may have said about love: indeed, he probably thought it mostly nonsense. He is concerned only with his own experience of it, which he tries to analyse and to describe in the simplest possible language and in an almost conversational tone. It is true that Donne was not the only Elizabethan to protest against the conventional love-poetry which had flourished so long; towards the end of Elizabeth's reign there was quite a considerable reaction against it, which is expressed in the satires of Hall, Marston, and others, in the *Parnassus Plays*, and in Jonson's early comedies; but it was Donne alone who created an entirely new kind of love-poetry, and who, discarding all the old conventions, dared—to borrow Hazlitt's famous words about Montaigne—to say as an author what he felt as a man. And this was because Donne himself was such an extraordinary person, with a quite modern passion for introspection and self-analysis. Like many modern writers he was fascinated and preoccupied by the problem of the interaction between body and mind; and throughout his life this problem never ceased to fascinate him—in his early life in connexion with love, in his later life in connexion with the final separation of soul and body in death. Just as we see Jack Donne insisting on the impossibility of a purely spiritual love between man and woman, and, despite his temporary cynicism, on the unsatisfactoriness of a merely sensual one, so later we see Dr. Donne, during an illness which at first seemed likely to be mortal, eagerly seizing and analysing the signs of approaching dissolution, and finally, when he knows that the hand of death is indeed upon him, sending for a painter to paint a portrait of him dressed in his shroud, keeping it by his bedside during the last days, and so concluding his last meditation on the relation between body and soul.

The most remarkable quality, then, of the poems we have been considering is their realism, their absolute freedom from convention. This, and not the metaphysical wit, which has hardly appeared yet, is Donne's great original contribution to English poetry, and it is this quality which is chiefly insisted upon by Thomas Carew in his noble elegy on Donne:

> The Muses garden with Pedantique weedes
> O'rspred, was purg'd by thee; The lazie seeds
> Of servile imitation thrown away;
> And fresh invention planted, Thou didst pay
> The debts of our penurious bankrupt age;
> Licentious thefts, that make poëtique rage
> A Mimique fury, when our soules must bee
> Possest, or with Anacreons Extasie,
> Or Pindars, not their owne; The subtle cheat
> Of slie Exchanges, and the jugling feat
> Of two-edg'd words, or whatsoever wrong
> By ours, was done the Greeke, or Latine tongue,
> Thou hast redeem'd, and open'd Us a Mine
> Of rich and pregnant phansie, drawne a line
> Of masculine expression . . .
> But thou art gone, and thy strict lawes will be
> Too hard for Libertines in Poetrie.
> They will repeale the goodly exil'd traine
> Of gods and goddesses, which in thy just raigne
> Were banish'd nobler Poems, now, with these
> The silenc'd tales o'th'Metamorphoses
> Shall stuffe their lines, and swell the windy Page,
> Till Verse refin'd by thee, in this last Age
> Turne ballad rime, Or those old Idolls bee
> Ador'd againe, with new apostasie.

Let us now return to the substance of the poems. The quotation of *Negative Love*, in which Donne seemed to be reviewing his experiences, was perhaps a little premature, for the prevailing tone of the preceding poems had been a cheerful cynicism and a resolve not to allow his affections to be deeply engaged. But now come a group of poems which suggest that he who in the words of Biron in *Love's Labour's Lost* had been

> loues whip,
> A verie Beadle to a humerous sigh:
> A Criticke, nay, a night-watch Constable,
> A domineering pedant ore the Boy

is himself about to fall deeply in love. The tone is still slightly bantering and sometimes cynical, but there is present what was absent in the other poems, genuine tenderness. In *The Prohibition* he tells his mistress that she is neither to love him nor hate him, since he can endure neither.

> Take heed of loving mee,
> At least remember, I forbade it thee;
> Not that I shall repaire my'unthrifty wast
> Of Breath and Blood, upon thy sighes, and teares,
> By being to thee then what to me thou wast;
> But, so great Joy, our life at once outweares,
> Then, least thy love, by my death, frustrate bee,
> If thou love mee, take heed of loving mee.
>
> Take heed of hating mee,
> Or too much triumph in the Victorie.
> Not that I shall be mine owne officer,
>   And hate with hate againe retaliate;
> But thou wilt lose the stile of conquerour,
> If I, thy conquest, perish by thy hate.
> Then, least my being nothing lessen thee,
> If thou hate mee, take heed of hating mee.
>
> Yet, love and hate mee too,
> So, these extreames shall neithers office doe;[1]
> Love mee, that I may die the gentler way;
> Hate mee, because thy love is too great for mee;
> Or let these two, themselves, not me decay;
> So shall I, live, thy Stage, not. triumph bee;[2]
> Lest thou thy love and hate and mee undoe,
> *To let mee live, O love and hate mee too.*[3]

In *The Blossome* the opening is tender and melancholy, and then comes witty, bantering dialectic. He will leave his heart

[1] 'These extremes shall by counteracting each other prevent either from fulfilling his function.' Grierson.

[2] 'Alive, I shall continue to be the stage on which your victories are daily set forth; dead, I shall be your triumph, a thing achieved once, never to be repeated.' Grierson.   [3] p. 67.

with her in London, although he is sure she does not know what
a heart is, and he hopes on his return to find it as whole and
unconcerned as its owner; for, after all, he fears this lady is
rather too Platonic for him—perhaps during his absence he
will have grown indifferent towards her, and be ready to offer
his heart to some one more to his taste.

Little think'st thou, poore flower,
Whom I have watch'd sixe or seaven dayes,
And seene thy birth, and seene what every houre
Gave to thy growth, thee to this height to raise,
And now dost laugh and triumph on this bough,
Little think'st thou
That it will freeze anon, and that I shall
To morrow finde thee falne, or not at all.

Little think'st thou poore heart
That labour'st yet to nestle thee,
And think'st by hovering here to get a part
In a forbidden or forbidding tree,
And hop'st her stiffenesse by long siege to bow:
Little think'st thou,
That thou to morrow, ere that Sunne doth wake,
Must with this Sunne, and mee a journey take.

But thou which lov'st to bee
Subtile to plague thy selfe, wilt say,
Alas, if you must goe, what's that to mee?
Here lyes my businesse, and here I will stay:
You goe to friends, whose love and meanes present
Various content
To your eyes, eares, and tongue, and every part.
If then your body goe, what need you a heart?

Well then, stay here; but know,
When thou hast stayd and done thy most;
A naked thinking heart, that makes no show,
Is to a woman, but a kinde of Ghost;
How shall shee know my heart; or having none,
Know thee for one?
Practise may make her know some other part,
But take my word, shee doth not know a Heart.

Meet mee at London, then,
Twenty dayes hence, and thou shalt see
Mee fresher, and more fat, by being with men,
Then if I had staid still with her and thee.

For Gods sake, if you can, be you so too:
>I would give you
There, to another friend, whom wee shall finde
As glad to have my body, as my minde.[1]

The Message is a beautiful song that might well have been
'married' to music by Dowland or Morley:

Send home my long strayd eyes to mee,
Which (Oh) too long have dwelt on thee;
Yet since there they have learn'd such ill,
>Such forc'd fashions,
>And false passions,
>>That they be
>>Made by thee
Fit for no good sight, keep them still.

Send home my harmlesse heart againe,
Which no unworthy thought could staine;
But if it be taught by thine
>To make jestings
>Of protestings,
>>And crosse both
>>Word and oath,
Keepe it, for then 'tis none of mine.

Yet send me back my heart and eyes,
That I may know, and see thy lyes,
And may laugh and joy, when thou
>Art in anguish
>And dost languish
>>For some one
>>That will none,
Or prove as false as thou art now.[2]

Was this the beginning of the attachment that was finally to
engage and settle his affections?—Perhaps—but let us return
to Izaak Walton.

II

At this point Walton's narrative may to some extent be
supplemented by a few casual allusions in the verse *Letters*.
There is one to a certain 'Mr. B.B.', evidently still a student at
Cambridge, whom Donne invites to join him at the Inns of

[1] p. 59.   [2] p. 43.

Court, and having come there, to profit by his friend's bad example and not to waste his time.

> Is not thy sacred hunger of science
> Yet satisfy'd? Is not thy braines rich hive
> Fulfil'd with hony which thou dost derive
> From the Arts spirits and their Quintessence?
> Then weane thy selfe at last, and thee withdraw
> From Cambridge thy old nurse, and, as the rest,
> Here toughly chew, and sturdily digest
> Th'immense vast volumes of our common law;
> And begin soone, lest my griefe grieve thee too,
> Which is, that that which I should have begun
> In my youthes morning, now late must be done;
> And I as Giddy Travellers must doe,
> Which stray or sleepe all day, and having lost
> Light and strength, darke and tir'd must then ride post.[1]

Since Mr. John Sparrow has, I think, proved that Donne's travels took place between December 1594 and June 1596, that is to say, two years after his admission to Lincoln's Inn in May 1592, we may assume that this poem was written after his return from the Islands expedition in October 1597, between which date and his engagement by Egerton in the following year Donne may well have resumed his study of the law. But no doubt, in spite of his repentant studiousness, the Court as well as the Inns of Court continued to claim part of his time and attention—the Court which no young man who desired to practise the 'Architecture of Fortune' could afford to neglect. There is a letter *To Sir Henry Wooton*, of which the date is given in two manuscripts as July 20, 1598, where Donne affects to despise the Court and to see through it, and where, although he is only about twenty-five, he refers, as to some distant period, to 'my youths giddiest days'. There is a touch of that same perversity and love of self-torture which often strikes us in the *Elegies* and the *Songs and Sonnets*.

> Here's no more newes, then vertue, 'I may as well
> Tell you *Cales*, or St. *Michaels* tale[2] for newes, as tell
> That vice doth here habitually dwell.
>
> Yet, as to'get stomachs, we walke up and downe,
> And toyle to sweeten rest, so, may God frowne,
> If, but to loth both, I haunt Court, or Towne. . . .

---

[1] p. 212.
[2] 'Tell you the story of the Cadiz and Islands Expeditions.' Cales = Cadiz, and the Islands of St. Michael = the Azores.

Beleeve mee Sir, in my youths giddiest dayes,
When to be like the Court, was a playes praise,
Playes were not so like Courts, as Courts'are like playes.[1]

A glimpse of Donne about this time is given by Sir Richard
Baker, in his *Chronicle of the Kings of England*,[2] where, speaking
of the 'Men of Note' during the reign of James I, he asks the
reader's leave to mention 'two of my own old acquaintance', of
whom 'the one was *Mr. John Donne*, who leaving *Oxford*, lived
at the *Inns of Court*, not dissolute, but very neat, a great Visiter
of Ladies, a great frequenter of Playes, a great Writer of con-
ceited Verses'.

Two other letters, *To Mr. C.B.*, almost certainly that '*Mr.
Christopher Brook*, sometimes Mr. *Donnes* Chamber-fellow in
Lincolns-Inn' mentioned by Walton, and *To Mr. I.L.*, refer to
his unsuccessful efforts to win the favour of a lady whom he
calls 'the Saint of his affection' and his 'Sun'; but they are
written in a style of conventional hyperbole very different from
that of the *Songs and Sonnets*, and probably record a very early
experience.

Indeed, we cannot add much to Walton's narrative, which
proceeds as follows:

> Not long after his return into *England*, that exemplary Pattern
> of Gravity and Wisdom, the Lord *Elsemore*, then Keeper of the
> Great Seal, and *Lord Chancellour of England*, taking notice of his
> Learning, Languages, and other Abilities, and much affecting
> his Person and Behaviour, took him to be his chief Secretary;
> supposing and intending it to be an Introduction to some more
> weighty Employment in the State;[3] for which, his Lordship did
> often protest, he thought him very fit.
>
> Nor did his Lordship in this time of Master *Donne's* attendance
> upon him, account him to be so much his Servant, as to forget
> he was his Friend; and to testifie it, did alwayes use him with
> much courtesie, appointing him a place at his own Table, to
> which he esteemed his Company and Discourse to be a great
> Ornament.
>
> He continued that employment for the space of five years,
> being daily useful, and not mercenary to his Friends. During
> which time he (I dare not say unhappily) fell into such a liking,
> as (with her approbation) increased into a love with a young

---

[1] p. 187.   [2] Edition of 1684, pp. 426–7.
[3] As a matter of fact, as Mr. I. A. Shapiro has shown in a letter to *The
Times Literary Supplement*, March 10, 1932, a beginning was actually made with
this 'more weighty Employment in the State', for on October 1, 1601, Donne
was elected one of the members for Brackley, a constituency in the control of
Lord Ellesmere, then Sir Thomas Egerton.

Gentlewoman that lived in that Family, who was Niece to the Lady *Elsemore*, and Daughter to Sir *George Moor*, then Chancellor of the Garter and Lieutenant of the Tower.

Sir *George* had some intimation of it, and knowing prevention to be a great part of wisdom, did therefore remove her with much haste from that to his own house at *Lothesley*, in the County of *Surry*; but too late, by reason of some faithful promises which were so interchangeably passed, as never to be violated by either party.

These promises were only known to themselves, and the friends of both parties used much diligence, and many arguments to kill or cool their affections to each other: but in vain; for love is a flattering mischief, that hath denied aged and wise men a foresight of those evils that too often prove to be the children of that blind father, a passion! that carries us to commit *Errors* with as much ease as whirlwinds remove feathers, and begets in us an unwearied industry to the attainment of what we desire. And such an Industry did, notwithstanding much watchfulness against it, bring them secretly together (I forbear to tell the manner how) and at last to a marriage too, without the allowance of those friends, whose approbation always was, and ever will be necessary, to make even a vertuous love become lawful.

Sir George More was furious when he heard of the marriage; through the influence of his sister he persuaded or compelled Elsemore, then Sir Thomas Egerton, to dismiss Donne from his service, and did not feel himself sufficiently revenged until Donne and two friends who had, respectively, married him and given away the bride 'were all committed to three several prisons'. As soon as he was free Donne exerted himself to obtain the release of his friends, and he then had to begin a long and expensive lawsuit in order to obtain possession of his wife; 'which proved troublesome and sadly-chargeable to him, whose youth, and travel, and needless bounty, had brought his estate into a narrow compass'. After a time, moved partly by Donne's winning behaviour 'which when it would entice, had a strange kind of elegant irresistible art', and by the fact that most people approved of his daughter's choice, Sir George repented of his harshness and tried to persuade Egerton to readmit Donne into his service: however, he received the reply that although Egerton 'was unfeignedly sorry for what he had done, yet it was inconsistent with his place and credit, to discharge and readmit servants at the request of passionate petitioners'. In order, apparently, to keep up some show of con-

sistency, Sir George had asked that this request should be kept
secret, and he still refused 'to contribute any means that might
conduce to their livelyhood'.[1]

It was perhaps towards the beginning of his love for Anne
More that Donne wrote *The undertaking*, a poem in which he
declares that he has discovered the nature of true love.

> I have done one braver thing
>   Then all the *Worthies* did,
> And yet a braver thence doth spring,
>   Which is, to keepe that hid.
>
> It were but madnes now t'impart
>   The skill of specular stone,
> When he which can have learn'd the art
>   To cut it, can finde none.
>
> So, if I now should utter this,
>   Others (because no more
> Such stuffe to worke upon, there is,)
>   Would love but as before.
>
> But he who lovelinesse within
>   Hath found, all outward loathes,
> For he who colour loves, and skinne,
>   Loves but their oldest clothes.
>
> If, as I have, you also doe
>   Vertue'attir'd in woman see,
> And dare love that, and say so too,
>   And forget the Hee and Shee;
>
> And if this love, though placed so,
>   From prophane men you hide,
> Which will no faith on this bestow,
>   Or, if they doe, deride:
>
> Then you have done a braver thing
>   Then all the *Worthies* did;
> And a braver thence will spring,
>   Which is, to keepe that hid.[2]

And in *The good-morrow* he says to her:

> I wonder by my troth, what thou, and I
> Did, till we lov'd? were we not wean'd till then?
> But suck'd on countrey pleasures, childishly?
> Or snorted we in the seaven sleepers den?
> T'was so; But this, all pleasures fancies bee.
> If ever any beauty I did see,
> Which I desir'd, and got, t'was but a dreame of thee.

[1] World's Classics ed., pp. 26–30.   [2] *Poems*, i. 10.

And now good morrow to our waking soules,
Which watch not one another out of feare;
For love, all love of other sights controules,
And makes one little roome, an every where.
Let sea-discoverers to new worlds have gone,
Let Maps to other, worlds on worlds have showne,
Let us possesse one world, each hath one, and is one.

My face in thine eye, thine in mine appeares,
And true plaine hearts doe in the faces rest,
Where can we finde two better hemispheares
Without sharpe North, without declining West?
What ever dyes, was not mixt equally;
If our two loves be one, or, thou and I
Love so alike, that none doe slacken, none can die.[1]

Notice, in the second stanza, the reference to sea-discoverers and maps. Donne himself had travelled, and the imagery of his poetry is full of references to the new discoveries by sea and land. Later, we shall see him comparing the last journey he will ever undertake to a voyage of discovery—

this is my South-west discoverie
Per fretum febris, by these streights to die.

In the last stanza we find him, in Dryden's words, 'affecting the metaphysics' and

perplexing the minds of the fair sex with nice speculations of philosophy, when he should engage their hearts, and entertain them with the softness of love.[2]

But first, in order that we may appreciate the change which has come over English poetry, let us consider a typical Elizabethan poem (by Sir Philip Sidney) in which a similar idea is expressed:

My true love hath my hart, and I have his,
By just exchange, one for the other giv'ne.
I hold his deare, and myne he cannot misse:
There never was a better bargaine driv'ne.

His hart in me, keepes me and him in one,
My hart in him, his thoughtes and senses guides:
He loves my hart, for once it was his owne:
I cherish his, because in me it bides.[3]

[1] p. 7.
[2] *Essays*, ed. W. P. Ker, ii, 19.
[3] *Works*, ed. Feuillerat, ii, 17.

Sidney's poem requires neither note nor comment, but Professor
Grierson has found it necessary to devote several lines, includ-
ing a quotation from Aquinas, to the elucidation of Donne's
last stanza. Sidney is almost content to ring the changes on
the thought expressed in his first line, but Donne goes farther,
and tries to pack into his poem all the meaning it will hold.
The fact that he and she are completely sufficient for one
another suggests the image of two hemispheres, and this again
suggests the thought that their ideal world is more complete
and perfect than the real one—

> Without sharpe North, without declining West.

But even yet he is not satisfied, and he goes on to illustrate
their ideal unity in terms of the philosophical notion of simple
substance: their souls are so united that they form one simple
substance, and simple substances, God, and the soul which
originates from the breath of God, cannot perish.

This is the chief characteristic of what Dryden and Johnson
called 'metaphysical' poetry, of which Donne's is the first
example in English. In Johnson's words, he

> draws his conceits from recesses of learning not very much fre-
> quented by common readers of poetry.

That is to say, when Donne uses images and comparisons—
and, as we have seen, he often dispenses with them altogether
—they are very often intellectual rather than sensuous or
pictorial. Instead of drawing them from the sights and sounds
of the world around him, he draws them from philosophy,
theology, or science. Other poets, when they wish to communicate a certain mood or feeling, often refer to some sight
or sound with which, in the mind of the reader, the mood or
feeling they desire to communicate may be supposed to be
connected—at any rate, they generally describe or illustrate
what is more complex in terms of what is more simple. Donne,
on the other hand, often illustrates a complex mood or feeling
by reference to what is for most readers still more complex—
to some philosophical or theological conception. A man of
great learning—even in his youth he spent many hours of each
day in study—he applies his learning to the interpretation of
his experience. These abstruse speculations are to his imagination what the classic poets and the books of travel and discovery
and semi-fabulous oriental history were to Marlowe's; they
supply it with a background and a store of imagery. For,

paradoxical as it may seem, Donne's poetry proves that there
is such a thing as intellectual imagery. The earlier Elizabethans, although not perhaps so completely as Donne, had
also contrived to put the whole of themselves into their poetry,
their reading no less than their observation of life; but their
reading was less than Donne's, and had been chiefly in the
poets, especially Ovid, whereas Donne's was chiefly in Aquinas
and the Schoolmen. I can remember hardly any references to
classical mythology in Donne's poetry, from which we may
conclude that to him it had become stale and commonplace,
and that it had no longer what it seems to have had for many
of the earlier Elizabethans, the freshness of a new discovery.[1]
Moreover, although perhaps the distinction is not a very
philosophical one, he was more interested in truth than in
beauty. Milton has often been called a philosophic poet, and
he certainly had a strong *intellectual* interest in philosophy and
theology; but his imagination was fired rather by beauty than
by truth, and many of the most famous passages in *Paradise
Lost*, that, for example, where he declares that Eden was more
beautiful than

> that fair vale
> Of Enna, where Proserpin gathering flowers,
> Herself a fairer flower, by gloomy Dis
> Was gathered, which cost Ceres all that pain
> To seek her through the world

are there simply because Milton's imagination had been from
his youth intoxicated by the echoes of ancient beauty. And
it is the same with most poets: what they chiefly give us are
visions of a reality more beautiful and more splendid than that
we know. But Donne, as I have said, was more interested in
truth than in beauty: we see him eagerly and passionately
searching for the truth about love, the truth about religion. He
is a poet, and therefore he expresses this truth imaginatively;
but, if I may so put it, his imagination always seems to take
fire from his intellect. He does not idealize his experiences
or transform them by association into splendid visions; he
grapples with them, carefully analyses them, and often tries
to interpret them by means of intellectual conceptions. But
although a philosophic or metaphysical poet, he is still a poet,
because he always tries to communicate the concrete experi-

[1] To be precise, there are only two references in the many poems I have
quoted—in *The Indifferent* and in *Loves Usury*—where 'Venus' and the 'God of
Love' appear: however, they are hardly more than convenient abstractions.

ence itself, and not merely the results of his reflection upon it. And not all his poetry is equally metaphysical—in much of his love poetry references to the schoolmen are as infrequent as references to the classics. He nearly always analyses, but he does not always comment. Sometimes, too, he writes a poem that might almost have come from one of the Elizabethan song-books, such as the beautiful song *Sweetest love, I do not goe.*

> Sweetest love, I do not goe,
> For wearinesse of thee,
> Nor in hope the world can show
> A fitter Love for mee;
>   But since that I
> Must dye at last, 'tis best,
> To use my selfe in jest
> Thus by fain'd deaths to dye;
>
> Yesternight the Sunne went hence,
> And yet is here to day,
> He hath no desire nor sense,
> Nor halfe so short a way:
>   Then feare not mee,
> But beleeve that I shall make
> Speedier journeyes, since I take
> More wings and spurres then hee.
>
> O how feeble is mans power,
> That if good fortune fall,
> Cannot adde another houre,
> Nor a lost houre recall!
>   But come bad chance,
> And wee joyne to'it our strength,
> And wee teach it art and length,
> It selfe o'r us to'advance.
>
> When thou sigh'st, thou sigh'st not winde,
> But sigh'st my soule away,
> When thou weep'st, unkindly kinde,
> My lifes blood doth decay.
>   It cannot bee
> That thou lov'st mee, as thou say'st,
> If in thine my life thou waste,
> Thou art the best of mee.
>
> Let not thy divining heart
> Fore thinke me any ill,
> Destiny may take thy part,
> And may thy feares fulfill;

F

> But thinke that wee
> Are but turn'd aside to sleepe;
> They who one another keepe
> Alive, ne'r parted bee.[1]

Ben Jonson declared to Drummond of Hawthornden that 'Done for not keeping of accent deserved hanging', and the charge of 'harshness' was repeated by Dryden and by Johnson, who in his life of Cowley says of the metaphysical poets in general that

> Instead of writing poetry they only wrote verses, and very often such verses as stood the test of the finger better than of the ear; for the modulation was so imperfect, that they were only found to be verses by counting the syllables.

The charge is in the main ill-founded, and due to the prejudices and preconceptions of those who made it. In the first place, Donne was, as Grierson has remarked, a conscious innovator in prosody, who saw that new effects of beauty and passion were to be won by breaking the regular fall of the verse stresses with the intrusion of rhetorical stress on syllables which the metrical pattern leaves unstressed, and that poetry might thus be made to approximate to direct, unconventional, colloquial speech. For example, if in reading the following lines you insist on putting the stresses in the conventional places they will certainly sound harsh:

> If yét I háve not áll thy lóve,
> Deare, Í shall néver háve it áll.

But why not read them like this—

> If *yet* I have not *all* thy love,
> *Deare*, I shall *never* have it all.

And in the second place, poetry so intellectual as much of Donne's will not read itself; it does not even *sound* right until it is understood. On this point Coleridge has a very illuminating observation, in a manuscript note on that song we have just read, *Sweetest love, I do not goe.* He says:

> This beautiful and perfect poem proves by its title 'song' that all Donne's Poems are equally *metrical* (misprints allowed for), tho' *smoothness*, that is to say, the metre necessitating the proper reading, be deemed appropriate to Songs; but, in Poems where the Author *thinks*, and expects the Reader to do so, the sense must be understood in order to ascertain the metre.[2]

[1] p. 18.   [2] Quoted by Gosse, i. 282.

Let us now recapitulate briefly the conclusions we have
reached so far about the style of Donne's poems. (1) Most of
them are intensely realistic; they try to convey as directly as
possible, and without idealization or adornment, a particular
experience in all its complexity and concreteness. (2) Some
of them try to do more than this, to interpret the experience
by means of intellectual as distinct from pictorial symbols.
These are the distinctively 'metaphysical' poems. (3) Some
of them are of slighter texture, and are at once felt to be as
smooth and musical as anything in the Elizabethan song
books; although Coleridge is mainly right in his insistence
that nearly all Donne's poems will be found to have their
proper music if once they are thoroughly understood. Finally,
of these qualities of style it is the realism, the freedom from
conventional imagery and association, the absolute fidelity to
personal experience, that is most striking and most original.

Let us now continue our study of those poems which we
may suppose Donne to have addressed to Anne More after
he had discovered true love.

The Sunne Rising

Busie old foole, unruly Sunne,
  Why dost thou thus,
Through windowes, and through curtaines call on us?
Must to thy motions lovers seasons run?
  Sawcy pedantique wretch, goe chide
  Late schoole boyes, and sowre prentices,
Goe tell Court-huntsmen, that the King will ride,
  Call countrey ants to harvest offices;
Love, all alike, no season knowes, nor clyme,
Nor houres, dayes, moneths, which are the rags of time.

Thy beames, so reverend, and strong
  Why shouldst thou thinke?
I could eclipse and cloud them with a winke,
But that I would not lose her sight so long:
  If her eyes have not blinded thine,
  Looke, and to morrow late, tell mee,
Whether both the'India's of spice and Myne
Be where thou leftst them, or lie here with mee.
Aske for those Kings whom thou saw'st yesterday,
And thou shalt heare, All here in one bed lay.

She'is all States, and all Princes, I,
  Nothing else is.
Princes doe but play us; compar'd to this,
All honor's mimique; All wealth alchimie.

                Thou sunne art halfe as happy'as wee,
            In that the world's contracted thus;
          Thine age askes ease, and since thy duties bee
            To warme the world, that's done in warming us.
          Shine here to us, and thou art every where;
          This bed thy center is, these walls, thy spheare.[1]

Donne's poetry is very various. We may distinguish some of
the most remarkable qualities of his poems, but we cannot
classify them. Here we have, not subtle and learned imagery,
but a series of magnificent hyperboles; and yet these hyperboles, unlike those of the other Elizabethans, are penetrated
with a peculiar wit and humour. Donne combines the splendid
and the familiar, and this familiarity gives an entirely novel
kind of freshness to the poem. People had been accustomed
to hearing the sun addressed as Hyperion, but to hear him
called 'Busie old foole' and 'Sawcy pedantique wretch' was
quite new and rather fascinating. This application of familiar
epithets and comparisons to things which had usually received
dignified ones was one of Donne's innovations, and was imitated, often successfully, by his followers. As we have seen, in
The good-morrow Donne had declared that the ideal world, the
perfect unity, formed by himself and his love, was superior to
the real one. Here he employs the same 'conceit', or conception, and declares that the sun only travels farther to fare worse:

          Shine here to us, and thou art every where.

In *The Anniversarie* he has another variation on this favourite
theme of the completeness and self-sufficiency of their love.
All other things fade and pass away, but their love remains;
and in a sense they may even be said to be happier here on
earth than they will be in heaven, for although they will then
have attained perfect felicity, they will be no happier than the
other spirits, but here on earth they possess a world of their
own of which they are absolute Kings.

          All Kings, and all their favorites,
            All glory of honors, beauties, wits,
          The Sun it selfe, which makes times, as they passe,
          Is elder by a yeare, now, then it was
          When thou and I first one another saw:
          All other things, to their destruction draw,
            Only our love hath no decay;
          This, no to morrow hath, nor yesterday,
          Running it never runs from us away,
          But truly keepes his first, last, everlasting day.
                          [1] *Poems*, i. 11.

Two graves must hide thine and my coarse,
  If one might, death were no divorce.
Alas, as well as other Princes, wee,
(Who Prince enough in one another bee,)
Must leave at last in death, these eyes, and eares,
Oft fed with true oathes, and with sweet salt teares;
  But soules where nothing dwells but love
(All other thoughts being inmates) then shall prove
This, or a love increased there above,
When bodies to their graves, soules from their graves remove.

  And then wee shall be throughly blest,
  But wee no more, then all the rest;
Here upon earth, we'are Kings, and none but wee
Can be such Kings, nor of such subjects bee.
Who is so safe as wee? where none can doe
Treason to us, except one of us two.
  True and false feares let us refraine,
Let us love nobly, and live, and adde againe
Yeares and yeares unto yeares, till we attaine
To write threescore: this is the second of our raigne.[1]

No doubt in his later years Dr. Donne would have regretted the conceit in the last stanza as being almost blasphemous, for Walton tells us that

in his penitential years, viewing some of those pieces that had been loosely (God knows too loosely) scattered in his youth, he wished they had been abortive, or so short-lived that his own eyes had witnessed their funerals.

And in the beautiful poem *The Dreame* he makes a still more audacious application of theological conceptions. He declares that his Mistress is essentially true, a touchstone of reality:

Thou art so truth, that thoughts of thee suffice,
To make dreames truths; and fables histories.

That is to say, he almost attributes to her the quality which Aquinas had attributed to God, in whom not only does truth exist, but who is himself the supreme and original truth. He also attributes to her the power to read thoughts directly:

But when I saw thou sawest my heart,
And knew'st my thoughts, beyond an Angels art—

a power which Aquinas had denied to angels and attributed to God alone:

Cognoscunt Angeli cordium cogitationes in suis effectibus: ut autem in se ipsis sunt, Deo tantum sunt naturaliter cognitae.

[1] p. 24.

Deare love, for nothing lesse then thee
Would I have broke this happy dreame,
    It was a theame
For reason, much too strong for phantasie,
Therefore thou wakd'st me wisely; yet
My Dreame thou brok'st not, but continued'st it,
Thou art so truth, that thoughts of thee suffice,
To make dreames truths; and fables histories;
Enter these armes, for since thou thoughtst it best,
Not to dreame all my dreame, let's act the rest.

As lightning, or a Tapers light,
Thine eyes, and not thy noise wak'd mee;
    Yet I thought thee
(For thou lovest truth) an Angell, at first sight,
But when I saw thou sawest my heart,
And knew'st my thoughts, beyond an Angels art,
When thou knew'st what I dreamt, when thou knew'st when
Excesse of joy would wake me, and cam'st then,
I must confesse, it could not chuse but bee
Prophane, to thinke thee any thing but thee.

Comming and staying show'd thee, thee,
But rising makes me doubt, that now,
    Thou art not thou.
That love is weake, where feare's as strong as hee;
'Tis not all spirit, pure, and brave,
If mixture it of *Feare, Shame, Honor,* have.
Perchance as torches which must ready bee,[1]
Men light and put out, so thou deal'st with mee,
Thou cam'st to kindle, goest to come; Then I
Will dreame that hope againe, but else would die.[2]

It seems possible that while in Egerton's service, either before his marriage to Anne More or before that marriage had been made public, Donne had to make some journey abroad, and that it was on this occasion that he composed the XVIth elegy, *On his Mistris,* which in the Bridgewater Manuscript bears the title *His wife would have gone as his page.* Grierson has a most interesting note:

In connexion with the general theme of this poem it may be noted that in 1605 Sir Robert Dudley, the illegitimate son of the Earl of Leicester, who like Donne served in the Cadiz and

[1] 'If it [a torch] have never been lighted, it does not easily take light, but it must be bruised and beaten first; if it have been lighted and put out . . . it does easily conceive fire.' *Fifty Sermons,* 36, p. 332, quoted by Grierson.
[2] *Poems,* i. 37.

Islands expeditions, left England accompanied by the beautiful
Elizabeth Southwell disguised as a page. At this period the
most fantastic poetry was never more fantastic than life itself.[1]

Lamb admired the poem, as we learn from one of Hazlitt's
most delightful essays, *On Persons one would wish to have seen.*

Dr. Donne was mentioned as a writer of the same period,
with a very interesting countenance, whose history was singular,
and whose meaning was often quite as *uncomeatable* [as that of
Fulke Greville, the friend of Sir Philip Sidney, whom Lamb had
just mentioned], without a personal citation from the dead, as
that of any of his contemporaries. The volume was produced;
and while some one was expatiating on the exquisite simplicity
and beauty of the portrait prefaced to the old editions, Ayrton
got hold of the poetry, and exclaiming, 'What have we here?'
read the following:

> Here lies a She-Sun and a He-Moon there—
> She gives the best light to his sphear
> Or each is both, and all, and so
> They unto one another nothing owe.

There was no resisting this, till Lamb, seizing the volume,
turned to the beautiful *Lines to his Mistress,* dissuading her from
accompanying him abroad, and read them with suffused
features and a faltering tongue.

> By our first strange and fatall interview,
> By all desires which thereof did ensue,
> By our long starving hopes, by that remorse
> Which my words masculine perswasive force
> Begot in thee, and by the memory
> Of hurts, which spies and rivals threatned me,
> I calmly beg: But by thy fathers wrath,
> By all paines, which want and divorcement hath,
> I conjure thee, and all the oathes which I
> And thou have sworne to seale joynt constancy,
> Here I unsweare, and oversweare them thus,
> Thou shalt not love by wayes so dangerous.
> Temper, ô faire Love, loves impetuous rage,
> Be my true Mistris still, not my faign'd Page;
> I'll goe, and, by thy kinde leave, leave behinde
> Thee, onely worthy to nurse in my minde,
> Thirst to come backe; ô if thou die before,
> My soule from other lands to thee shall soare.
> Thy (else Almighty) beautie cannot move
> Rage from the Seas, nor thy love teach them love,

[1] ii. 88.

Nor tame wilde Boreas harshnesse; Thou hast reade
How roughly hee in peeces shivered
Faire Orithea, whom he swore he lov'd.
Fall ill or good, 'tis madnesse to have prov'd
Dangers unurg'd; Feed on this flattery,
That absent Lovers one in th'other be.
Dissemble nothing, not a boy, nor change
Thy bodies habite, nor mindes; bee not strange
To thy selfe onely; All will spie in thy face
A blushing womanly discovering grace;
Richly cloath'd Apes, are call'd Apes, and as soone
Ecclips'd as bright we call the Moone the Moone.
Men of France, changeable Camelions,
Spittles of diseases, shops of fashions,
Loves fuellers, and the rightest company
Of Players, which upon the worlds stage be,
Will quickly know thee, and no lesse, alas!
Th'indifferent Italian, as we passe
His warme land, well content to thinke thee Page,
Will hunt thee with such lust, and hideous rage,
As *Lots* faire guests were vext. But none of these
Nor spungy hydroptique Dutch shall thee displease,
If thou stay here. O stay here, for, for thee
England is onely a worthy Gallerie,
To walke in expectation, till from thence
Our greatest King call thee to his presence.
When I am gone, dreame me some happinesse,
Nor let thy lookes our long hid love confesse,
Nor praise, nor dispraise me, nor blesse nor curse
Openly loves force, nor in bed fright thy Nurse
With midnights startings, crying out, oh, oh
Nurse, ô my love is slaine, I saw him goe
O'r the white Alpes alone; I saw him I,
Assail'd, fight, taken, stabb'd, bleed, fall, and die.
Augure me better chance, except dread *Iove*
Thinke it enough for me to'have had thy love.[1]

Then there is *The Canonization*, which was perhaps written after
his marriage, during those exasperating weeks when, as Walton has told us, his wife was detained from him. Here are the
first two stanzas:

For Godsake hold your tongue, and let me love,
  Or chide my palsie, or my gout,
My five gray haires, or ruin'd fortune flout,
  With wealth your state, your minde with Arts improve,

[1] i. III.

Take you a course, get you a place,
　　Observe his honour, or his grace,
Or the Kings reall, or his stamped face
　　Contemplate, what you will, approve,
　　So you will let me love.

Alas, alas, who's injur'd by my love?
　　What merchants ships have my sighs drown'd?
Who saies my teares have overflow'd his ground?
　　When did my colds a forward spring remove?
　　　When did the heats which my veines fill
　　　Adde one more to the plaguie Bill?
Soldiers finde warres, and Lawyers finde out still
　　Litigious men, which quarrels move,
　　Though she and I do love.[1]

Let us now consider a group of what we may call philosophical love poems, in which Donne, having at last discovered
true love, tries to analyse it and to say what it is, and to distinguish the parts played in it by the body and by the mind.
The most complete and the most famous expression of this
philosophy of love is *The Exstasie*.

Where, like a pillow on a bed,
　　A Pregnant banke swel'd up, to rest
The violets reclining head,
　　Sat we two, one anothers best.
Our hands were firmely cimented
　　With a fast balme, which thence did spring,
Our eye-beames twisted, and did thred
　　Our eyes, upon one double string;
So to'entergraft our hands, as yet
　　Was all the meanes to make us one,
And pictures in our eyes to get
　　Was all our propagation.
As 'twixt two equall Armies, Fate
　　Suspends uncertaine victorie,
Our soules, (which to advance their state,
　　Were gone out,) hung 'twixt her, and mee.
And whil'st our soules negotiate there,
　　Wee like sepulchrall statues lay;
All day, the same our postures were,
　　And wee said nothing, all the day.
If any, so by love refin'd,
　　That he soules language understood,
And by good love were growen all minde,
　　Within convenient distance stood,

[1] p. 14.

He (though he knew not which soule spake,
   Because both meant, both spake the same)
Might thence a new concoction take,
   And part farre purer then he came.
This Extasie doth unperplex
   (We said) and tell us what we love,
Wee see by this, it was not sexe,
   Wee see, we saw not what did move:

[Once, when reading this poem, it occurred to me that the word
'sex', as an abstract term denoting the complex physical relations
between man and woman, had not been used again in this way
until quite modern times; and on consulting the *Oxford Dictionary*
I found that my supposition was correct. Could we desire a
stronger proof of the extraordinary modernity of Donne in his
attitude to this question?]

But as all severall soules containe
   Mixture of things, they know not what,
Love, these mixt soules, doth mixe againe,
   And makes both one, each this and that.
A single violet transplant,
   The strength, the colour, and the size,
(All which before was poore, and scant,)
   Redoubles still, and multiplies.
When love, with one another so
   Interinanimates two soules,
That abler soule, which thence doth flow,
   Defects of lonelinesse controules.
Wee then, who are this new soule, know,
   Of what we are compos'd, and made,
For, th'Atomies of which we grow,
   Are soules, whom no change can invade,
But O alas, so long, so farre
   Our bodies why doe wee forbeare?
They are ours, though they are not wee, Wee are
   The intelligences, they the spheare.
We owe them thankes, because they thus,
   Did us, to us, at first convay,
Yeelded their forces, sense, to us,
   Nor are drosse to us, but allay.
On man heavens influence workes not so,
   But that it first imprints the ayre,
Soe soule into the soule may flow,
   Though it to body first repaire.
As our blood labours to beget
   Spirits, as like soules as it can,

Because such fingers need to knit
   That subtile knot, which makes us man:
So must pure lovers soules descend
   T'affections, and to faculties,
Which sense may reach and apprehend,
   Else a great Prince in prison lies.

[Here Donne borrows an illustration from that medieval physiology, which even in his own day was still regarded as scientific.
The problem was to explain how the soul, being immaterial, could
act upon the body; and the solution was that the soul did not act
upon the body directly, but used as its instrument what were called
'spirits', a kind of vapour produced by the brain. Burton (quoted
by Grierson) describes it as a 'common tye or medium betwixt the
body and the soule'.]

To'our bodies turne wee then, that so
   Weake men on love reveal'd may looke;
Loves mysteries in soules doe grow,
   But yet the body is his booke.
And if some lover, such as wee,
   Have heard this dialogue of one,
Let him still marke us, he shall see
   Small change, when we'are to bodies gone.[1]

Donne holds, then, that although love has its root in sex,
it rises to a point where sex is forgotten. As he had declared
in *The undertaking*, one can only understand the nature of true
love if one is able to rise above its physical basis:

If, as I have, you also doe
   Vertue'attir'd in woman see,
And dare love that, and say so too,
   And forget the Hee and Shee.

Nevertheless, 'the body is his booke'. In *The Primrose*, where
he is trying to express his idea of a perfect woman, he says:

      should she
Be more then woman, shee would get above
All thought of sexe, and thinke to move
My heart to study her, and not to love.[2]

And in *Aire and Angels*, a very subtle poem, he regretfully admits that absolutely perfect love between men and women is
not possible. Love, like its parent the soul, must take

limmes of flesh, and else could nothing doe;

[1] p. 51.   [2] p. 61.

but when love assumes the body of Donne's mistress his appearance is too dazzling and disturbing:

> For, nor in nothing, nor in things
> Extreme, and scatt'ring bright, can love inhere.

Love, to be perfect, would require to assume a body of air, like that assumed by angels when they appear to men. And yet even then he would not be perfect; for just as the body of air is less pure than the angels who assume it, so even the purest kind of love between man and woman must always be dependent on some kind of sexual feeling, and therefore less pure than the ideal which each is able to form.

> Twice or thrice had I loved thee,
> Before I knew thy face or name;
> So in a voice, so in a shapelesse flame,
> *Angells* affect us oft, and worship'd bee;
>   Still when, to where thou wert, I came,
> Some lovely glorious nothing I did see.
>   But since my soule, whose child love is,
> Takes limmes of flesh, and else could nothing doe,
>   More subtile then the parent is,
> Love must not be, but take a body too,
>   And therefore what thou wert, and who,
>   I bid Love aske, and now
> That it assume thy body, I allow,
> And fixe it selfe in thy lip, eye, and brow.
>
> Whilst thus to ballast love, I thought,
> And so more steddily to have gone,
> With wares which would sinke admiration,
> I saw, I had loves pinnace overfraught,
>   Ev'ry thy haire for love to worke upon
> Is much too much, some fitter must be sought;
>   For, nor in nothing, nor in things
> Extreme, and scatt'ring bright, can love inhere;
>   Then as an Angell, face, and wings
> Of aire, not pure as it, yet pure doth weare,
>   So thy love may be my loves spheare;
>   Just such disparitie
> As is twixt Aire and Angells puritie,
> 'Twixt womens love, and mens will ever bee.[1]

Here Donne seems to regret the existence of that physical basis of love which elsewhere, as we have seen, he accepts as a necessary condition; and in the poem *Loves growth* the fact that love

[1] p. 22.

alters with the seasons suggests to him that it is not an essence,
a simple substance, a pure, immaterial thing like the soul, but
a mixture, a thing partly material and therefore liable to corruption. Nevertheless, in the last stanza he tries to accept this
limitation and to transcend it.

> I scarce beleeve my love to be so pure
>   As I had thought it was,
>   Because it doth endure
> Vicissitude, and season, as the grasse;
> Me thinkes I lyed all winter, when I swore,
> My love was infinite, if spring make'it more.
>
> But if this medicine, love, which cures all sorrow
> With more, not onely bee no quintessence,
> But mixt of all stuffes, paining soule, or sense,
> And of the Sunne his working vigour borrow,
> Love's not so pure, and abstract, as they use
> To say, which have no Mistresse but their Muse,
> But as all else, being elemental too,
> Love sometimes would contemplate, sometimes do.
>
> And yet no greater, but more eminent,
>   Love by the spring is growne;
>   As, in the firmament,
> Starres by the Sunne are not inlarg'd, but showne.
> Gentle love deeds, as blossomes on a bough,
> From loves awakened root do bud out now.
> If, as in water stir'd more circles bee
> Produc'd by one, love such additions take,
> Those like so many spheares, but one heaven make,
> For, they are all concentrique unto thee.
> And though each spring doe adde to love new heate,
> As princes doe in times of action get
> New taxes, and remit them not in peace,
> No winter shall abate the springs encrease.[1]

For, despite some occasional regrets, Donne's habitual mood
is that of *The Exstasie*; he insists on the mutual interdependence
of body and soul, and on the necessity of fully recognizing the
claims of both. There is an interesting passage in one of his
verse-letters to the Countess of Bedford, written probably some
years later than the poems we have been discussing, where,
although his main theme is the degradation of the soul by the
body, he pauses, in a kind of parenthesis, to reflect on the degradation which the body thus inflicts upon itself, depriving

[1] p. 33.

itself of its true dignity, which is to be the casket of the
soul:

> What hate could hurt our bodies like our love?[1]
>   Wee (but no forraine tyrants could) remove
>   These not ingrav'd, but inborne dignities,
>   Caskets of soules; Temples, and Palaces:
>   For, bodies shall from death redeemed bee,
>   Soules but preserv'd, not naturally free.[2]

Let us conclude this discussion of Donne's love-poetry with
three stanzas from the poem *A Valediction: of the booke.*

> Study our manuscripts, those Myriades
>   Of letters, which have past twixt thee and mee,
>   Thence write our Annals, and in them will bee
> To all whom loves subliming fire invades,
>   Rule and example found;
>   There, the faith of any ground
>   No schismatique will dare to wound,
>   That sees, how Love this grace to us affords,
> To make, to keep, to use, to be these his Records.

> This Booke, as long-liv'd as the elements,
>   Or as the worlds forme, this all-graved tome
>   In cypher writ, or new made Idiome,
> Wee for loves clergie only'are instruments:
>   When this booke is made thus,
>   Should againe the ravenous
>   Vandals and Goths inundate us,
>   Learning were safe; in this our Universe
> Schooles might learne Sciences, Spheares Musick, Angels Verse.

> Here Loves Divines, (since all Divinity
>   Is love or wonder) may finde all they seeke,
>   Whether abstract spirituall love they like,
> Their Soules exhal'd with what they do not see,
>   Or, loth so to amuze
>   Faiths infirmitie, they chuse
>   Something which they may see and use;
>   For, though minde be the heaven, where love doth sit,
> Beauty a convenient type may be to figure it.[3]

III

After describing how Sir George More was finally persuaded
to acquiesce in the marriage, 'but yet refused to contribute any

---

[1] i.e. 'of them'.   [2] p. 197.   [3] pp. 30–1.

means that might conduce to their livelyhood', Walton continues:

> Mr. *Donnes* estate was the greatest part spent in many and chargeable Travels, Books and dear-bought Experience: he out of all employment that might yield a support for himself and wife, who had been curiously and plentifully educated; both their natures generous, and accustomed to confer, and not to receive Courtesies: These and other considerations, but chiefly that his wife was to bear a part in his sufferings, surrounded him with many sad thoughts, and some apparent apprehensions of want.[1]

For a time Anne More's cousin, Sir Francis Wolly, of Pirford in Surrey, received them into his house. Then, in order to be near London, they moved first to Camberwell and in 1605 to Mitcham, where Donne left his wife and family and took lodgings in the Strand, his purpose being not only to enjoy the conversation of his friends, but to be near the court and to those who could use their influence to get him some desirable appointment. For years Donne used every effort to obtain such a position as his great abilities and accomplishments deserved, but chance, or, as it seemed to Walton, Providence, was against him.

'It hath been observed by wise and considering men', says this faithful biographer and friend,

> that Wealth hath seldom been the Portion, and never the Mark to discover good People; but, that Almighty God, who disposeth all things wisely, hath of his abundant goodness denied it (he only knows why) to many, whose minds he hath enriched with the greater Blessings of *Knowledge* and *Vertue*, as the fairer Testimonies of his love to Mankind; and this was the present condition of this man of so excellent Erudition and Endowments; whose necessary and daily expenses were hardly reconcileable with his uncertain and narrow estate. Which I mention, for that at this time there was a most generous offer made him for the moderating of his worldly cares; the declaration of which shall be the next employment of my Pen.

Walton then relates how Dr. Morton, who later became Bishop of Durham and who, at the age of ninety-four, was still living when Walton wrote, sent for Donne and expressed himself as follows:

> 'Mr. *Donne*, I know your Education and Abilities; I know your expectation of a State-employment; and I know your

[1] World's Classics ed., pp. 30–1.

fitness for it; and I know too, the many delays and contingencies
that attend Court-promises; and let me tell you that, my love
begot by our long friendship, and your merits, hath prompted
me to such an inquisition after your present temporal estate,
as makes me no stranger to your necessities; which I know
to be such as your generous spirit could not bear, if it were
not supported with a pious Patience: you know I have
formerly perswaded you to wave your Court-hopes, and enter
into holy Orders; which I now again perswade you to embrace,
with this reason added to my former request: The King hath
yesterday made me Dean of *Gloucester*, and I am also possessed
of a Benefice, the profits of which are equal to those of my
Deanry; I will think my Deanry enough for my maintenance
(who am and resolve to dye a single man) and will quit my
Benefice, and estate you in it, (which the Patron is willing I
shall do) if God shall incline your heart to embrace this motion.
Remember, Mr. *Donne*, no mans Education or Parts make him
too good for this employment, *which is to be an Ambassadour for
the God of glory, that God who by a vile death opened the gates of life
to mankind*. Make me no present answer; but remember your
promise, and return to me the third day with your Resolution.'

At the hearing of this, Mr. *Donne's* faint breath and perplext
countenance gave a visible testimony of an inward conflict; but
he performed his promise and departed without returning an
answer till the third day, and then his answer was to this effect:

'My most worthy and most dear friend, since I saw you, I
have been faithful to my promise, and have also meditated
much of your great kindness, which hath been such as would
exceed even my gratitude; but that it cannot do; and more I
cannot return you, and I do that with an heart full of Humility
and Thanks, though I may not accept of your offer; but, Sir,
my refusal is not for that I think my self too good for that calling,
for which Kings, if they think so, are not good enough: nor for
that my Education and Learning, though not eminent, may
not, being assisted with Gods Grace and Humility, render me
in some measure fit for it: but, I dare make so dear a friend as
you are my Confessor; some irregularities of my life have been
so visible to some men, that though I have, I thank God, made
my peace with him by penitential resolutions against them, and
by the assistance of his Grace banish'd them my affections; yet
this, which God knows to be so, is not so visible to man, as to
free me from their censures, and it may be that sacred calling
from a dishonour. And besides, whereas it is determined by the
best of *Casuists*, that *Gods Glory should be the first end, and a maintenance the second motive to embrace that calling*; and though each
man may propose to himself both together; yet the first may
not be put last without a violation of Conscience, which he that

searches the heart will judge. And truly my present condition is such, that if I ask my own Conscience, whether it be reconcileable to that rule, it is at this time so perplexed about it, that I can neither give my self nor you an answer. You know, Sir, who sayes, *Happy is that man whose Conscience doth not accuse him for that thing which he does.* To these I might add other reasons that disswade me; but I crave your favour that I may forbear to express them, and, thankfully decline your offer.'

This was his present resolution; but, the heart of man is not in his own keeping; and he was destined to this sacred service by an higher hand; a hand so powerful, as at last forced him to a compliance: of which I shall give the Reader an account before I shall give a rest to my Pen.[1]

Not only does Morton speak of 'my love begot by our long friendship and your merits'; there is also evidence that Donne had been Morton's assistant in that great theological controversy of which I cannot do better than abridge Gosse's account.

Bishop Bancroft's preoccupation with the Puritans had given the English Catholics a chance to reassert themselves, and on the 17th of May 1604 James consulted Parliament on the propriety of passing new laws to 'hem them in'. Three weeks later a Bill against Jesuits, seminary priests, and recusants was introduced into the Lords, and passed in July after its severity had been increased by the Commons. James, however, repented of his harshness and refused to take advantage of it. In a decree issued from his manor of Oatlands on the 16th of July 1604 he expressed his desire for moderation in the treatment of recusants, in order that

> that uniformity which we desire may be wrought by clemency and by weight of reason, and not by rigour of law.

There followed an increased output of theological and argumentative literature; and things might have remained like this but for the impudent demand of Spain that Prince Charles should be educated as a Catholic; this angered James, and since he was also alarmed by the increase in the number of recusants, he resolved to take more strenuous measures for the banishment of priests and the conversion of the laity. And the chief instrument for the conversion of the laity was Thomas Morton. He had made the recusant arguments his peculiar study, and he now undertook to champion the Church of England against them. He was intimately connected with the Huntingdon family, and since the fifth earl had married one

[1] pp. 31–5.

of the daughters of Lady Egerton, the third wife of Donne's old patron, it has been suggested that it was the Countess of Huntingdon who recommended Donne as an assistant. Evidence of Donne's activity in working for Morton still exists in the form of various controversial pamphlets in which are found his signature or slight observations in his handwriting; and Dr. Jessopp, one of the greatest authorities on this subject, declared that

> even if we had not been told that [Donne] gave Morton constant and valuable help, a comparison of the authorities quoted and referred to in Morton's *Catholic Appeal* with those set down in Donne's *Pseudo-Martyr*, would convince a careful reader of the fact. The curious and out-of-the-way books cited in both works are very numerous and not to be found elsewhere.[1]

Thus, when in 1607 Morton became Dean of Gloucester and made Donne the offer which Walton describes, he had probably enjoyed his assistance for some time, and had been able to form a just estimate of his abilities. Gosse finds it difficult to believe that the account which Morton gave Walton of Donne's reasons for refusing to enter the Church at this time was correct, and insists that there is no evidence that Donne's conduct since his marriage had been other than exemplary; he suggests that the real reasons were intellectual, that Donne had not yet been able to convince himself that the truth lay with the Church of England. However, it is significant that in a letter which Gosse himself assigns to the summer of this year Donne speaks for the first time of the Church of England as 'ours';[2] and although right up to the moment of his final decision we see Donne hesitating between ecclesiastical and secular preferment, there is no reason to suppose that at this time he was not deterred in part, at any rate, by conscientious scruples, as Morton reports. Nevertheless, it is difficult to suppose that this was his *only* motive in refusing. Leslie Stephen suggests that he was 'morbidly sensitive to the opinions of his fellows, and aware that if he had taken orders, all the courtiers, and most of his friends, would have given the obvious reason—Here is a man in difficulties, taking orders in order to escape them'; but Donne was in still greater difficulties and with still less hope of escaping from them when he finally allowed himself to be persuaded by King James; and we must also remember that while the acceptance of Morton's offer would have sent him to remote York-

---

[1] Goss, i. 147–50, 245.   [2] i. 170–1.

shire, far from his court friends, the King's offer was accompanied by liberal offers of preferment—a fact which certainly encourages the possibly unjust suspicion that had Morton's offer been more attractive Donne's scruples might have been less; for common experience suggests that inclination, perhaps unconscious, towards or against something proposed often determines whether or no perfectly honest scruples shall influence our will.

'He was much importuned by many friends', says Walton,

> to make his constant residence in *London*, but he still denied it, having setled his dear wife and children at *Micham*, and near some friends that were bountiful to them and him: for they, God knows, needed it: and that you may the better now judge of the then present Condition of his mind and fortune, I shall present you with an extract collected out of some few of his many Letters.
> ——*And the reason why I did not send an answer to your last weeks letter, was, because it then found me under too great a sadness; and at present 'tis thus with me: There is not one person, but my self, well of my family: I have already lost half a Child, and with that mischance of hers, my wife is fallen into such a discomposure, as would afflict her too extreamly, but that the sickness of all her other children stupifies her: of one of which, in good faith, I have not much hope: and these meet with a fortune so ill provided for Physick, and such relief, that if God should ease us with burials, I know not how to perform even that: but I flatter my self with this hope, that I am dying too: for I cannot waste faster then by such griefs. As for,——*
>
> *Aug.* 10.   From my hospital
>   at *Micham*,
>   JOHN DONNE.[1]

Although it is rarely possible to date Donne's letters precisely, it would seem that very shortly after his marriage, which wrecked his ambitions and condemned him to a long period of enforced inactivity, there occurred in the relationship of those various 'humours' which—to employ the language of contemporary physiology—composed his 'temperament' a considerable and decisive alteration. The habitual tone of his mind became more and more coloured by that 'melancholy' to which he had always been subject, and although still a young man he began to look back upon the days of love-songs

---

[1] World's Classics ed., p. 36. This letter as quoted by Walton differs in some particulars from the 1651 version (pp. 151–3), which is addressed to 'The Honourable Sir R. D.' and which can be approximately dated by its reference, in a postscript, to the Somerset *Epithalamium*. Somerset's marriage with the Countess of Essex took place on December 26, 1613.

and satires as (to borrow a phrase of Shelley's) 'a part of me that is already dead'. That 'other port' of his mind (to recur to Raleigh's great image) becomes less 'desolate and over-grown with grass'; although from time to time, even during his latest years, the former is still frequented, to a degree not a little surprising, sometimes perhaps disconcerting, to modern readers, 'by the entrance of manifold vanities'. His letters reveal a deep and tender affection for his wife and children and a desire to hide from them, so far as possible, his frequent fits of depression; but so long as he remained a layman he was never able to conceal from himself that his marriage had been a grave imprudence and had ruined what might have been a brilliant career. Writing to Sir Henry Wotton in 1612 from Paris, whither he had accompanied Sir Robert Drury, he says:

> You know I have been no coward, nor unindustrious in at-tempting that [sc. 'my fortune']; nor will I give it over yet. If at last, I must confesse, that I dyed ten years ago, yet as the Primitive Church admitted some of the *Jews* Ceremonies, not for perpetuall use, but because they would bury the Synagogue honourably, though I dyed at a blow then when my courses were diverted, yet it wil please me a little to have had a long funerall, and to have kept my self so long above ground without putrefaction.[1]

Partly from conscientious scruples, partly because he cher-ishes a different ideal of life, he cannot reconcile himself to the priesthood, cannot abandon his hopes of state preferment, of an ambassadorship or secretaryship; yet at the same time he feels that there is an immense distance between the man he now is and the youthful lover and satirist—a distance which he never suggests it is either possible or desirable to decrease. Perhaps he feared his temperament, feared to expose himself to temptations which might lead him to neglect the respon-sibilities he had incurred. Perhaps a kind of artistic conscience, a recognition that for everything there is a season and a time, that 'decorum' must be observed in life no less than in art, that the actor must conform to his role, led him to accept melancholy and 'retirednesse', in spite of all complainings and depressions, with a kind of gusto, as experiences which he was called upon to realize, and while continually hoping and striving for the possibility of progress, for the opportunity of congenial activity, to reject utterly the anodyne of mere distractions or of retreats into a life that had been already

---

[1] *Letters*, 1651, pp. 121–2; Gosse, i. 291.

lived. He refused to repeat himself, and in the letters and
poems written during these years we may observe the progress
from Jack Donne to Dr. Donne.

Interesting in this connexion is the verse-letter *To Mr. Row-
land Woodward*, which, since Woodward appears to have gone
to Venice with Sir Henry Wotton in 1604, Grierson thinks was
probably written before that date, when Donne would be
living in 'a retirednesse' at Pirford or Camberwell. One
manuscript states that the poem was written 'to one that
desired some of his papers'; this would explain the first two
stanzas, in which, if Grierson's date is correct, Donne reveals,
not more than two years after his marriage, that attitude of
distance and detachment towards his former life and interests
which recurs so often in his letters.

> Like one who'in her third widdowhood doth professe
> Her selfe a Nunne, tyed to retirednesse,
> So'affects my muse now, a chaste fallownesse;
>
> Since shee to few, yet to too many'hath showne
> How love-song weeds, and Satyrique thornes are growne
> Where seeds of better Arts, were early sown.[1]

And several years later, in a letter to his friend Sir Henry
Goodyer, written probably in 1609 or 1610, there seems to be
a reference to one of his songs, about which Goodyer had expressed some opinion: 'I doe not condemn in my self', says
Donne, 'that I have given my wit such evaporations, as those,
if they be free from prophaneness, or obscene provocations.'[2]

The other letter that Walton quotes is rather garbled, so we
will read it in its original form. Donne speaks of the slightness
of his hold on life, the mistakes of his youth, the uncertainty
of his prospects, the misery of being without any definite occupation and of feeling that he is taking no vital part in the life
of his time. For with his restless and feverish intellect Donne
was one of those who to find happiness must identify themselves
with some great cause or purpose—one of those to whom
Goethe's famous lines are peculiarly applicable:

> Und so lang du das nicht hast,
> Dieses: Stirb und werde!
> Bist du nur ein trüber Gast
> Auf der dunklen Erde.

But he had not yet found that cause for which he could die to
live.

Two of the most precious things which God hath afforded us

[1] *Poems*, i. 185.   [2] *Letters*, 1651, p. 36; Gosse, i. 197.

here, for the agony and exercise of our sense and spirit, which are a thirst and inhiation after the next life, and a frequency of prayer and meditation in this, are often envenomed, and putrified, and stray into a corrupt disease. . . . With the first of these I have often suspected my self to be overtaken; which is, with a desire of the next life: which though I know it is not meerly out of a wearinesse of this, because I had the same desires when I went with the tyde, and enjoyed fairer hopes then now: yet I doubt worldly encombrances have encreased it. I would not that death should take me asleep. I would not have him meerly seise me, and onely declare me to be dead, but win me, and overcome me.[1]

Notice this passage. Donne confesses that even from the days of his wild youth he has been preoccupied not only with a desire for immortality, but with a desire to experience death, to experience the dissolution of the union between body and soul. Throughout most of his life he seems to have enjoyed poor health; and this, together with his many anxieties and his disappointed hopes, seems to have made him feel that his hold on life was very slight, and to have increased his introspective tendency and his habit of reflecting on the relations between the soul, or mind, and the body. In the preface to that youthful *tour de force*, *Biathanatos*, where he defends the legitimacy, under certain circumstances, of suicide, he very candidly declares:

I have often such a sickely inclination. And, whether it be, because I had my first breeding and conversation with men of a suppressed and afflicted Religion, accustomed to the despite of death, and hungry of an imagin'd Martyrdome; Or that the common Enemie find that doore worst locked against him in mee; Or that there bee a perplexitie and flexibility in the doctrine it selfe; Or because my Conscience ever assures me, that no rebellious grudging at Gods gifts, nor other sinfull concurrence accompanies these thoughts in me, or that a brave scorn, or that a faint cowardlinesse beget it, whensoever any affliction assailes me, mee thinks I have the keyes of my prison in mine owne hand, and no remedy presents it selfe so soone to my heart, as mine own sword. Often Meditation of this hath wonne me to a charitable interpretation of their action, who dy so: and provoked me a little to watch and exagitate their reasons, which pronounce so peremptory judgements upon them.[2]

The letter that we were reading continues:

When I must shipwrack, I would do it in a Sea, where mine

[1] *Letters*, 1651, pp. 49–50; Gosse, i. 190–1.   [2] pp. 17–18.

impotencie might have some excuse; not in a sullen weedy lake,
where I could not have so much as exercise for my swimming.
Therefore I would fain do something; but that I cannot tell
what, is no wonder. For to chuse, is to do: but to be no part
of any body, is to be nothing. At most, the greatest persons, are
but great wens, and excrescences; men of wit and delightfull
conversation, but as moales for ornament, except they be so
incorporated into the body of the world, that they contribute
something to the sustentation of the whole. This I made
account that I begun early, when I undertook[1] the study of our
laws: but was diverted by the worst voluptuousnes, which is an
Hydroptique immoderate desire of humane learning and languages: beautifull ornaments to great fortunes; but mine needed
an occupation, and a course which I thought I entred well into,
when I submitted my self to such a service, as I thought might
[have] imployed those poor advantages, which I had. [He is
probably referring to his service with Egerton.] And there I
stumbled too, yet I would try again: for to this hour I am
nothing, or so little, that I am scarce subject and argument good
enough for one of mine own letters: yet I fear, that doth not
ever proceed from a good root, that I am so well content to be
lesse, that is dead.[2]

And in another letter to the same friend, Sir Henry Goodyer,
he says:

Because I am in a place and season where I see every thing
bud forth, I must do so too, and vent some of my meditations
to you; the rather because all other buds being yet without taste
or virtue, my Letters may be like them. The pleasantnesse of
the season displeases me. Every thing refreshes, and I wither,
and I grow older and not better, my strength diminishes, and
my load growes.[3]

Observe how Donne speaks of what he calls his 'nothingness', his feeling of isolation and of unrelatedness to the general
scheme of things. It was probably in some such mood as this
that he composed those two very subtle and difficult poems,
A nocturnall upon S. Lucies day, Being the shortest day, and *Twicknam garden*, although they were written somewhat later, after he
had become the friend and ardent admirer of Lucy, Countess
of Bedford. In the *Nocturnall* he imagines that she is dead, and
declares that without her his life is vanity; in *Twicknam garden*
he declares that his unrequited love for her is able to 'convert
manna to gall'. These are the ostensible themes, but of both
the real theme, I fancy, is that mood of dejection which we

[1] 1651, 'understood'.   [2] *Letters*, 1651, pp. 50–2; Gosse, i. 191.
[3] *Letters*, 1651, p. 78; Gosse, i. 185.

have seen expressed in the letters just quoted. Their intense, brooding atmosphere, their perfect communication of a complex and very personal *mood* is in some ways much more akin to the work of Baudelaire, Verlaine, and other modern poets, than to anything else in English poetry before the twentieth century.

> Tis the yeares midnight, and it is the dayes,
> *Lucies*, who scarce seaven houres herself unmaskes,
>   The Sunne is spent, and now his flasks
>   Send forth light squibs, no constant rayes;
>   The worlds whole sap is sunke:
> The generall balme th'hydroptique earth hath drunk,
> Whither, as to the beds-feet, life is shrunke,
> Dead and enterr'd; yet all these seeme to laugh,
> Compar'd with mee, who am their Epitaph.
>
> Study me then, you who shall lovers bee
> At the next world, that is, at the next spring:
>   For I am every dead thing,
>   In whom love wrought new Alchimie.
>   For his art did expresse
> A quintessence even from nothingnesse,
> From dull privations, and leane emptinesse:
> He ruin'd mee, and I am re-begot
> Of absence, darknesse, death; things which are not.
>
> All others, from all things, draw all that's good,
> Life, soule, forme, spirit, whence they beeing have;
>   I, by loves limbecke, am the grave
>   Of all, that's nothing. Oft a flood
>   Have wee two wept, and so
> Drownd the whole world, us two; oft did we grow
> To be two Chaosses, when we did show
> Care to ought else; and often absences
> Withdrew our soules, and made us carcasses.
>
> But I am by her death, (which word wrongs her)
> Of the first nothing, the Elixer grown;
>   Were I a man, that I were one,
>   I needs must know; I should preferre,
>   If I were any beast,
> Some ends, some means; Yea plants, yea stones detest,
> And love; All, all some properties invest;
> If I an ordinary nothing were,
> As shadow, a light, and body must be here.

But I am None; nor will my Sunne renew.
You lovers, for whose sake, the lesser Sunne
  At this time to the Goat is runne
  To fetch new lust, and give it you,
    Enjoy your summer all;
Since shee enjoyes her long nights festivall,
Let mee prepare towards her, and let mee call
This houre her Vigill, and her Eve, since this
Both the yeares, and the dayes deep midnight is.[1]

In this poem we have Donne in his most metaphysical mood, and with the aid of Grierson's excellent commentary I will try to make its meaning more comprehensible.

    For I am every dead thing,
    In whom love wrought new Alchimie.
      For his art did expresse
    A quintessence even from nothingnesse,
    From dull privations, and leane emptinesse:
    He ruin'd mee, and I am re-begot
    Of absence, darknesse, death; things which are not.

'From me, who was nothing', says Donne, 'Love extracted the very quintessence of nothingness—made me more nothing than I already was. My state was already one of "dull privations, and leane emptinesse", but Love reduced it still further, making me once more the non-entity I was before I was created.'

    But I am by her death, (which word wrongs her)
    Of the first nothing, the Elixer grown.

Here Donne pushes the annihilation farther. Made nothing by Love, by the death of her he loves he is made the elixir (i.e. the quintessence), not now of ordinary nothing, but of 'the first nothing', the nothing which preceded God's first act of creation. The poem turns upon the thought of degrees in nothingness.

    Were I a man, that I *were* one,
    I needs must *know*; I should preferre,
      If I were any *beast*,
    Some ends, some means; Yea plants, yea stones detest,
    And love.

Here Donne is referring to the Aristotelian doctrine of the soul. The soul of man is rational and self-conscious: hence, says

------

[1] *Poems*, i. 44.

Donne, if I *were* a man I should *know* that I were a man. The soul of beasts is perceptive and moving, and therefore able to 'prefer', i.e. to choose, select ends and means; but to Donne everything is indifferent and he is unable to choose one thing rather than another. Even the vegetative soul of plants selects what it can feed on and rejects what it cannot, and so far detests and loves; but Donne now feels too exhausted for either love or hatred. And stones, which have no soul, attract and repel.

> If I an *ordinary* nothing were,
> As shadow, a *light*, and *body* must be here.

Here a passage in Donne's sermons will help us:

> A shadow is nothing, yet, if the rising or falling sun shines out and there be no shadow, I will pronounce there is no body in that place neither.

He is not even an *ordinary* nothing, like a shadow, for a shadow must be the shadow of something and must be caused by a light from somewhere; but his love, who was *his* light, has gone—

> nor will my Sunne renew.

On *Twicknam garden* the best commentary is some words in one of the letters we have just read:

> 'The pleasantnesse of the season displeases me. Every thing refreshes, and I wither.'

> Blasted with sighs, and surrounded with teares,
>   Hither I come to seeke the spring,
>   And at mine eyes, and at mine eares,
> Receive such balmes, as else cure every thing;
>   But O, selfe traytor, I do bring
> The spider love, which transubstantiates all,
>   And can convert Manna to gall,
> And that this place may thoroughly be thought
>   True Paradise, I have the serpent brought.

> 'Twere wholsomer for mee, that winter did
>   Benight the glory of this place,
>   And that a grave frost did forbid
> These trees to laugh, and mocke mee to my face;
>   But that I may not this disgrace
> Indure, nor yet leave loving, Love let mee
>   Some senslesse peece of this place bee;
> Make me a mandrake, so I may groane here,
>   Or a stone fountaine weeping out my yeare.

Hither with christall vyals, lovers come,
  And take my teares, which are loves wine,
  And try your mistresse Teares at home,
For all are false, that tast not just like mine;
  Alas, hearts do not in eyes shine,
Nor can you more judge womans thoughts by teares,
  Then by her shadow, what she weares.
O perverse sexe, where none is true but shee,
  Who's therefore true, because her truth kills mee.[1]

But the most complete and universal expression of Donne's melancholy, that melancholy which, as I have already re-marked, is so characteristic of seventeenth-century literature, and which we too easily overlook in the literature of the pre-ceding age, is to be found in the two *Anniversaries* which he dedicated to the memory of the daughter of his friend and patron Sir Robert Drury. After quoting the letters on which we have been commenting, Walton continues:

> By this you have seen, a part of the picture of his narrow fortune, and the perplexities of his generous mind; and thus it continued with him for about two years; all which time his family remained constantly at *Micham*; and to which place he often retir'd himself, and destined some days to a constant study of some points of Controversie betwixt the *English* and *Roman Church*; and especially those of *Supremacy* and *Allegiance*: and, to that place and such studies he could willingly have wedded himself during his life: but the earnest perswasion of friends became at last to be so powerful, as to cause the removal of himself and family to *London*, where Sir *Robert Drewry*, a Gentle-man of a very noble estate, and a more liberal mind, assigned him and his wife an useful apartment in his own large house in *Drewry lane*, and not only rent-free, but was also a cherisher of his studies, and such a friend as sympathized with him and his in all their joy and sorrows.[2]

Sir Robert Drury of Hawstead, in Suffolk, was one of the wealthiest men in England. He had formed great hopes for his only daughter Elizabeth, having even conceived the ambi-tion of marrying her to Prince Henry; and when she died in 1610 at the age of fifteen he was overwhelmed with grief. His extraordinary generosity towards Donne may well have been due to the fact that the poet commemorated the death of his child in *An Anatomy of the World. Wherein, by occasion of the untimely death of Mistris Elizabeth Drury the frailty and the decay*

---

[1] p. 28.   [2] World's Classics ed., pp. 38–9.

of this whole world is represented. This poem, which contains some of the most splendid verse he ever wrote, was published in'1611; and in 1612 it was republished with the additional title *The First Anniversarie*, together with a second poem on the same subject entitled *The Progres of the Soule. Wherein: By Occasion Of The Religious Death of Mistris Elizabeth Drury, the incommodies of the Soule in this life, and her exaltation in the next, are Contemplated.* This poem also bore the sub-title *The Second Anniversarie.* At the beginning of the second poem Donne declares that it is his intention to compose one of these Anniversaries every year, and he expresses the hope that his example will be followed by succeeding poets, and that in this way

> These Hymnes thy issue, may encrease so long,
> As till Gods great *Venite* change the song.

However, Donne wrote no more Anniversaries, perhaps because, as his letters reveal, the poems gave considerable offence to the Countess of Bedford and his other noble friends. Ben Jonson declared to Drummond

> that Dones Anniversarie was profane and full of Blasphemies that he told Mr. Donne, if it had been written of ye Virgin Marie it had been something to which he answered that he described the Idea of a Woman, and not as she was.[1]

This, as Grierson remarks, is a better defence than any in Donne's letters, but it is not a complete description.

> The burden of the whole is an impassioned and exalted *meditatio mortis* based on two themes common enough in mediaeval devotional literature—a *De Contemptu Mundi*, and a contemplation of the Glories of Paradise.[2]

These two poems contain the finest expression of some of Donne's most characteristic ideas. Let us consider some of them—but first let me refer once again to something on which I touched lightly in my introductory remarks: that there is in Elizabethan literature, and still more in the literature of the seventeenth century, a strain of meditation which is more characteristic of what we usually mean by the Middle Ages than of what we usually mean by the Renaissance. Indeed, we are too apt to forget that the phrases 'Middle Ages' and 'Renaissance' are after all only rough generalizations. They are very valuable generalizations; they were reached only after a long process of study and reflection and of attempts to realize and

---

[1] *Works*, ed. Herford and Simpson, i. 133.   [2] *Poems*, ii. 188.

define certain characteristic differences between two great
epochs of human history; they enable us to introduce a certain
order and unity into a multitude of particular facts, and to
interpret them in the light of general ideas; but nevertheless,
like all generalizations, they are rough and ready, and are no
substitutes for independent thought and observation. There
is no hard line between what we call the Middle Ages and what
we call the Renaissance. In England, for example, the Middle
Ages did not suddenly come to an end somewhere about the
accession of Henry VIII. The two epochs run into one another.
We often find in what we have been taught to call the Middle
Ages things that once seemed especially characteristic of what
we have been taught to call the Renaissance, and in what we
have been taught to call the Renaissance things that once
seemed especially characteristic of what we have been taught
to call the Middle Ages. And in Donne, whose restless curiosity
and bold speculation seem especially characteristic of the Renaissance, the elements of what we may roughly call medieval-
ism are exceptionally strong—much stronger than in Marlowe,
for example. Moreover, as I also suggested in my introductory remarks, certain characteristic medieval conceptions were
even intensified by certain of the characteristic movements and
ideas of the Renaissance. When the world was shown to be a
more wonderful and fascinating place than had formerly been
supposed, fuller of opportunities for power and enjoyment, the
old medieval antithesis between the world and the spirit, the
immortal spirit deflected from its proper object by the specious
attractions of the world, was strengthened. Again, the Middle
Ages loved to dwell on the limitations of man, on the depth
of his ignorance, the smallness of his knowledge, the slightness of his capacity to increase that knowledge. One remembers Dürer's engraving where Melancholy, surrounded
by mathematical instruments and insoluble problems, sadly reflects on her ignorance. Well! one of the characteristics of the
Renaissance was that to many men the boundaries of possible
knowledge seemed to have been almost indefinitely extended.
There was a 'renovation and new spring of knowledge', as
Bacon said. Men applied themselves to learning of every kind
with tremendous enthusiasm and persistence, cherishing great
hopes. In the seventeenth century we can perceive two distinct attitudes to knowledge. The experimental scientists remain cheerful and confident; but many of the great amateur
scholars, the great polymaths, who had been assimilating every

possible kind of knowledge in the hope that somehow it would find its place in a great synthesis, began to perceive that of the things which seemed to them really important they knew little more than when they had begun. They became sceptical about the possible attainments of human knowledge, and the new discoveries in astronomy and other sciences merely increased their scepticism. Much of what they had laboriously learnt had been proved to be false: was it not likely that in a short time the new discoveries would in their turn be superseded? Were things that were hailed as new discoveries really anything more than new kinds of error? Where was it all tending? What was the object of it all? Thus another characteristic medieval conception, the insignificance of human knowledge, was intensified by the Renaissance.

Again, another characteristic medieval conception, extending far back into classical antiquity, was that the world was decaying, that it was running down like a clock; that the seasons were becoming more and more unfavourable, that men were becoming smaller in stature, weaker in health, more wicked in their ways. Well! especially during the seventeenth century, this characteristic medieval conception was intensified by certain consequences of the Renaissance and of what in many countries was but another aspect of the Renaissance, the Protestant Reformation. All over Europe Protestants were fighting against the established faith, peoples were arming against their rulers, the divine right of kings was being questioned. In England the nation was being divided by religious and economic controversies. The times were out of joint, and to many it seemed obvious that the world was rapidly accelerating in its process of degeneration and decomposition as it approached the end of its course.

Let us now see how Donne expresses some of these characteristic medieval conceptions in his *Anniversaries*. 'The world decays'—that is almost the whole subject of the *First Anniversarie*.

> Then, as mankinde, so is the worlds whole frame
> Quite out of joynt, almost created lame:
> For, before God had made up all the rest,
> Corruption entred, and deprav'd the best:
> It seis'd the Angels, and then first of all
> The world did in her cradle take a fall,
> And turn'd her braines, and tooke a generall maime,
> Wronging each joynt of th'universall frame.

The noblest part, man, felt it first; and than
Both beasts and plants, curst in the curse of man.
So did the world from the first houre decay,
That evening was beginning of the day,
And now the Springs and Sommers which we see,
Like sonnes of women after fiftie bee.
And new Philosophy calls all in doubt,
The Element of fire is quite put out;
The Sun is lost, and th'earth, and no mans wit
Can well direct him where to looke for it.
And freely men confesse that this world's spent,
When in the Planets, and the Firmament
They seeke so many new; they see that this
Is crumbled out againe to his Atomies.
'Tis all in peeces, all cohaerence gone;
All just supply, and all Relation:
Prince, Subject, Father, Sonne, are things forgot,
For every man alone thinkes he hath got
To be a Phoenix, and that then can bee
None of that kinde, of which he is, but hee.[1]

Heaven seems farther away now that astrology has been discredited:

What Artist now dares boast that he can bring
Heaven hither, or constellate any thing,
So as the influence of those starres may bee
Imprison'd in an Hearbe, or Charme, or Tree,
And doe by touch, all which those stars could doe?
The art is lost, and correspondence too.[2]

And Donne concludes:

Shee, shee is dead; shee's dead; when thou knowst this,
Thou knowst how drie a Cinder this world is.
And learn'st thus much by our Anatomy,
That 'tis in vaine to dew, or mollifie
It with thy teares, or sweat, or blood: nothing
Is worth our travaile, griefe, or perishing,
But those rich joyes, which did possesse her heart,
Of which she's now partaker, and a part.[3]

Later Donne expressed the same idea in his sermons:

As the world is the whole frame of the world, God hath put into it a reproofe, a rebuke, lest it should seem eternall, which is, a sensible decay and age in the whole frame of the world, and every piece thereof. The seasons of the yeare irregular and

[1] ll. 191–218.   [2] ll. 391–6.   [3] ll. 427–34.

distempered; the Sun fainter, and languishing; men lesse in stature, and shorter-lived. No addition, but only every yeare, new sorts, new species of wormes, and flies, and sicknesses, which argue more and more putrefaction of which they are engendred. And the Angels of heaven, which did so familiarly converse with men in the beginning of the world, though they may not be doubted to perform to us still their ministeriall assistances, yet they seem so far to have deserted this world, as that they do not appeare to us, as they did to those our Fathers. . . . Lest the world (as the world signifies the whole frame of the world) should glorifie it selfe, or flatter, and abuse us with an opinion of eternity, we may admit usefully (though we do not conclude peremptorily) this observation to be true, that there is a reproofe, a rebuke born in it, a sensible decay and mortality of the whole world.[1]

And we find the same conviction expressed by Henry Reynolds, the friend of Michael Drayton, in his *Mythomystes*, a little book published about 1633 and very valuable for an understanding of many of the characteristic ideas of the metaphysical poets. He says:

I haue thought vpon the times wee liue in, and am forced to affirme the world is decrepit, and, out of its age & doting estate, subiect to all the imperfections that are inseparable from that wracke and maime of Nature, that the young behold with horror, and the sufferers thereof lye vnder with murmur and languishment. Euen the generall Soule of this great Creature, whereof euery one of ours is a seuerall peece, seemes bedrid, as vpon her deathbed and neere the time of her dissolution to a second better estate and being; the yeares of her strength are past, and she is now nothing but disease, for the Soules health is no other then meerely the knowledge of the Truth of things: Which health the worlds youth inioyed, and hath now exchanged for it all the diseases of all errors, heresies, and different sects and schismes of opinions and vnderstandings in all matter of Arts, Sciences, and Learnings whatsoeuer.[2]

Observe how Reynolds, like Donne, sees in that experimental philosophy, 'new philosophy', which was one of the most characteristic products of Bacon's 'renovation and new spring of knowledge', nothing but further evidence that the world is decaying. To many men it seemed that to confusion in politics, the social system, and divinity had been superadded confusion in the whole realm of knowledge.

[1] *LXXX Sermons*, 1640, p. 357.
[2] *Critical Essays of the Seventeenth Century*, ed. Spingarn, i. 144.

In the *Second Anniversarie* Donne thus meditates on the limitations of human knowledge:

> What hope have wee to know our selves, when wee
> Know not the least things, which for our use be?
> Wee see in Authors, too stiffe to recant,
> A hundred controversies of an Ant;
> And yet one watches, starves, freeses, and sweats,
> To know but Catechismes and Alphabets
> Of unconcerning things, matters of fact;
> How others on our stage their parts did Act;
> What *Caesar* did, yea, and what *Cicero* said.
> Why grasse is greene, or why our blood is red,
> Are mysteries which none have reach'd unto.
> In this low forme, poore soule, what wilt thou doe?
> When wilt thou shake off this Pedantery,
> Of being taught by sense, and Fantasie?
> Thou look'st through spectacles; small things seeme great
> Below; But up unto the watch-towre get,
> And see all things despoyl'd of fallacies:
> Thou shalt not peepe through lattices of eyes,
> Nor heare through Labyrinths of eares, nor learne
> By circuit, or collections to discerne.
> In heaven thou straight know'st all, concerning it,
> And what concernes it not, shalt straight forget.[1]

And in his sermons Donne expresses the same pessimism with regard to the possibilities of human knowledge:

> In entring upon the first branch of our first part, That in spiritual things nothing is perfect, we may well afford a kinde of spirituall nature to knowledge; And how imperfect is all our knowledge? What one thing doe we know perfectly? Whether wee consider Arts, or Sciences, the servant knows but according to the proportion of his Masters knowledge in that Art, and the Scholar knows but according to the proportion of his Masters knowledge in that Science; Young men mend not their sight by using old mens Spectacles; and yet we looke upon Nature, but with *Aristotles* Spectacles, and upon the body of man, but with *Galens*, and upon the frame of the world, but with *Ptolomies* Spectacles. . . . And if there be any addition to knowledge, it is rather a new knowledge, then a greater knowledge; rather a singularity in a desire of proposing something that was not knowne at all before, then an emproving, an advancing, a multiplying of former inceptions; and by that meanes, no knowledge comes to be perfect.[2]

---

[1] ll. 279–300.   [2] *LXXX Sermons*, 1640, p. 818.

It is worth noticing that the attitude to knowledge which Donne here expresses was regarded by Bacon as one of the greatest hindrances to the Advancement of Learning. Never mind what Aristotle said, exclaims Bacon; look at the thing for yourself, practise experiment and the method of induction; and those who followed his advice really did, in certain matters, come to be wiser than Aristotle. But Donne seems to have regarded 'new philosophy' chiefly as a disturbing influence and as an argument for scepticism as to the possibilities of human knowledge. Like Bacon, he admits that we cannot become wiser than Aristotle if we merely follow Aristotle; but, unlike Bacon, he suggests no alternative. He and many other seventeenth-century scholars and thinkers seem to have reached the conviction that everything worth knowing had already been discovered. Hence in their attitude to knowledge they are either pessimistic and sceptical or humorous and fantastic. The imperfection of human knowledge is either an argument for the necessity of revelation or a reason for refusing to take human knowledge too seriously—for suggesting that of merely human knowledge one kind is hardly more important than another, and that accordingly the imagination may be allowed to wander among its provinces at will. To Burton and Sir Thomas Browne learning is a game which they pretend to take seriously. In his early poems we have seen Donne playing with the counters of knowledge; his later works suggest that as a result of his intense and laborious studies he had found that much knowledge increaseth sorrow. We have already heard him, in one of his letters to Goodyer, speak of his early 'hydroptique immoderate desire of humane learning and languages'; and in one of his sermons there is a passage which has a distinctly autobiographical flavour. He is declaring that it is impossible for a man, by any kind of diversion, to escape from the hand of God.

If he take up another Comfort, that though health and wealth decay, though he be poore and weake, yet he hath learning, and philosophy, and morall constancy, and he can content himselfe with himselfe, he can make his study a Court, and a few Books shall supply to him the society and the conversation of many friends, there is another worme to devoure this too, the hand of divine Justice shall grow heavy upon him, in a sense of an unprofitable retirednesse, in a disconsolate melancholy, and at last, in a stupidity, tending to desperation.[1]

[1] *LXXX Sermons*, p. 579.

But the great theme of the *Second Anniversarie* is the antithesis between the world and the spirit, the transitoriness and unsatisfactoriness of all earthly enjoyments, the incommodities suffered by the soul in the body, the insignificance of man when considered *sub specie temporis*.

> And what essential joy can'st thou expect
> Here upon earth? what permanent effect
> Of transitory causes? Dost thou love
> Beauty? (And beauty worthy'st is to move)
> Poore cousened cousenor, *that* she, and *that* thou,
> Which did begin to love, are neither now;
> You are both fluid, chang'd since yesterday;
> Next day repaires, (but ill) last dayes decay.
> Nor are, (although the river keepe the name)
> Yesterdaies waters, and to daies the same.
> So flowes her face, and thine eyes, neither now
> That Saint [i.e. your Mistress], nor Pilgrime [i.e. yourself],
>   which your loving vow
> Concern'd, remaines; but whil'st you thinke you bee
> Constant, you'are hourely in inconstancie.
> Honour may have pretence unto our love,
> Because that God did live so long above
> Without this Honour, and then lov'd it so,
> That he at last made Creatures to bestow
> Honour on him; not that he needed it,
> But that, to his hands, man might grow more fit.
> But since all Honours from inferiours flow,
> (For they doe give it; Princes doe but shew
> Whom they would have so honor'd) and that this
> On such opinions, and capacities
> Is built, as rise and fall, to more and lesse:
> Alas, 'tis but a casuall happinesse.[1]
>
> Thinke further on thy selfe, my Soule, and thinke
> How thou at first wast made but in a sinke;
> Thinke that it argued some infirmitie,
> That those two soules, which then thou foundst in me,
> Thou fedst upon, and drewst into thee, both
> My second soule of sense, and first of growth.
> Thinke but how poore thou wast, how obnoxious;
> Whom a small lumpe of flesh could poyson thus.
> This curded milke, this poore unlittered whelpe
> My body, could, beyond escape or helpe,
> Infect thee with Originall sinne, and thou
> Couldst neither then refuse, nor leave it now.

[1] ll. 387–412.

Thinke that no stubborne sullen Anchorit,
Which fixt to a pillar, or a grave, doth sit
Bedded, and bath'd in all his ordures, dwels
So fowly as our Soules in their first-built Cels.
Thinke in how poore a prison thou didst lie
After, enabled but to suck, and crie.
Thinke, when 'twas growne to most, 'twas a poore Inne,
A Province pack'd up in two yards of skinne,
And that usurp'd or threatned with the rage
Of sicknesses, or their true mother, Age.
But thinke that Death hath now enfranchis'd thee,
Thou hast thy'expansion now, and libertie;
Thinke that a rustie Peece, discharg'd, is flowne
In peeces, and the bullet is his owne,
And freely flies: This to thy Soule allow,
Thinke thy shell broke, thinke thy Soule hatch'd but now.[1]

Some of the most impressive passages in Donne's sermons
are on this theme, the Insignificance of Man.

Man is, sayes the Prophet *Esay, Quasi stilla situlae, As a drop
upon the bucket.* Man is not all that, not so much as that, as a
drop upon the bucket, but *quasi,* something, some little thing
towards it; and what is a drop upon the bucket, to a river, to
a sea, to the waters above the firmament? Man to God? *Man
is,* sayes the same Prophet in the same place, *Quasi momentum
staterae;* we translate it, *As small dust upon the balance*: Man is not
all that, not that small graine of dust; but *quasi,* some little
thing towards it: And what can a graine of dust work in govern-
ing the balance? What is man that God should be mindfull
of him? Vanity seemes to be the lightest thing, that the Holy
Ghost could name; and when he had named that, he sayes, and
sayes, and sayes, often, very, very often, *All is vanity.* But when
he comes to waigh man with vanity it selfe, he findes man
lighter then vanity: *Take,* sayes he, *great men, and meane men
altogether, and altogether they are lighter then vanity.* When that great
Apostle sayes of himselfe, that he was in *nothing behinde the very
chiefest of the Apostles,* and yet, for all that, sayes he was nothing;
who can thinke himselfe any thing, for being a Giant in pro-
portion, a Magistrate in power, a Rabbi in learning, an Oracle
in Counsell? Let man be something; how poore, and incon-
siderable a ragge of this world, is man? Man, whom *Paracelsus*
would have undertaken to have made, in a Limbeck, in a
Furnace: Man, who, if they were altogether, all the men, that
ever were, and are, and shall be, would not have the power of
one Angel in them all, whereas all the Angels, (who, in the
Schoole are conceived to be more in number, then, not onely

<hr>

[1] ll. 157–84.

all the Species, but all the individualls of this lower world) have not in them all, the power of one finger of Gods hand: Man, of whom when *David* had said, (as the lowest diminution that he could put upon him) *I am a worme and no man*, He might have gone lower, I am a man and no worm; for man is so much lesse then a worm, as that wormes of his own production, shall feed upon his dead body in the grave, and an immortall worm gnaw his conscience in the torments of hell.[1]

And now, with these passages fresh in our minds, let us recall one written by Donne's greatest contemporary—thàt speech of the Duke in *Measure for Measure*, when, disguised as a friar, he visits Claudio in prison—Claudio whose life can only be saved at the cost of his sister's dishonour—and persuades him to be 'absolute for death'. It is one of those many speeches which contain far more than the dramatic purpose required and where, as in Hamlet's great soliloquy and in the sonnet beginning 'Tyr'd with all these for restfull death I cry', Shakespeare himself seems to speak and to express a not unfamiliar mood.

> Be absolute for death: either death or life
> Shall thereby be the sweeter. Reason thus with life:
> If I do loose thee, I do loose a thing
> That none but fooles would keepe: a breath thou art,
> Seruile to all the skyie influences,
> That dost this habitation where thou keepst
> Hourely afflict: Meerely, thou art deaths foole,
> For him thou labourst by thy flight to shun,
> And yet runst toward him still. Thou art not noble,
> For all th'accomodations that thou bearst,
> Are nurst by basenesse: Thou'rt by no meanes valiant,
> For thou dost feare the soft and tender forke
> Of a poore worme: thy best of rest is sleepe,
> And that thou oft prouoakst, yet grosselie fearst
> Thy death, which is no more. Thou art not thy selfe,
> For thou exists on manie a thousand graines
> That issue out of dust. Happie thou art not,
> For what thou hast not, still thou striu'st to get,
> And what thou hast forgetst. Thou art not certaine,
> For thy complexion shifts to strange effects,
> After the Moone: If thou art rich, thou'rt poore,
> For like an Asse, whose backe with Ingots bowes,
> Thou bearst thy heauie riches but a iournie,
> And death vnloads thee; Friend hast thou none.
> For thine owne bowels which do call thee, sire
> The meere effusion of thy proper loines

[1] *LXXX Sermons*, pp. 64–5.

Do curse the Gowt, Sapego, and the Rheume
For ending thee no sooner. Thou hast nor youth, nor age
But as it were an after-dinners sleepe
Dreaming on both, for all thy blessed youth
Becomes as aged, and doth begge the almes
Of palsied-Eld: and when thou art old, and rich
Thou hast neither heate, affection, limbe, nor beautie
To make thy riches pleasant: what's yet in this
That beares the name of life? Yet in this life
Lie hid moe thousand deaths; yet death we feare
That makes these oddes, all euen.[1]

Shakespeare's mind also had 'two ports'. 'What a piece of worke is a man!' exclaims Hamlet,

> how Noble in Reason? how infinite in faculty? in forme and mouing how expresse and admirable? in Action, how like an Angel? in apprehension, how like a God? the beauty of the world, the Parragon of Animals.

And yet, as he handles Yorick's skull, he asks:

> Dost thou thinke *Alexander* lookt o'this fashion i'th'earth? . . . To what base vses we may returne *Horatio*.

Indeed, to a careful reader it soon becomes apparent that Shakespeare owed as much to what we commonly understand by the Middle Ages as to what we commonly understand by the Renaissance.

To conclude this study of the *Anniversaries* let us consider the great passage in which Donne contemplates in imagination the moment of his own death. One of the most remarkable differences between the literature, not only of the Middle Ages, but also of a great part of that of the sixteenth and seventeenth centuries, and our own, is the frequency of references to, and meditations upon, death. The modern mind tries not to think of death until it is at hand, but to what we may call the medieval mind it was continually present, as may be seen perhaps most clearly in that great series of woodcuts by Hans Holbein entitled *The Dance of Death*. In a number of pictures representing men and women of all classes of society appears death the skeleton, not as a mere symbol, but as an actor in the drama, full of energy and power, and more alive than those creatures of flesh and blood whom he destroys. He is represented as taking an active part in the affairs of men, and as a friend or an enemy according to their dispositions. The

[1] III. i. 5–41.

knight he strikes down from behind on the battle-field, but
he entices the child-like old man with music to the edge of the
grave. He waits upon the king at table as his true servant, but
he helps Adam to till the ground. He plucks the sleeve of a
duke who is chatting with his courtiers and taking no notice of
a poor woman who is trying to attract his attention. He taps
the shoulder of a judge who is turning away from a poor man
and holding out his hand to a rich one who is fumbling in his
purse. He thrusts himself in between an advocate and a rich
client, while a poor client stands by in despair. We see a
proud empress, magnificently dressed, walking with her atten-
dants; but death has taken her arm and she is standing on the
brink of the grave. In fact, we have a set of variations on the
old song:

> Mitten wir im Leben
> Sind vom Tod umgeben—

'in the midst of life we are surrounded by death'.

A certain preoccupation with death, with its inevitability,
with the terror of its summons, with the horrors of the grave,
is one of the characteristics of much of our older literature, and
one of those in respect of which it seems most remote from our
present ways of thinking and feeling. Are we braver and more
philosophic than our ancestors, or are we simply more in-
sensible and indifferent? Fully to explain this difference of
feeling would be a very difficult task. Something, no doubt,
is due to the teaching of the Church, and to the theological
ideas then generally accepted; and here perhaps we may
observe that with their continual repetition of *respice finem*
our ancestors were wiser than ourselves, although with what
was essentially true in their view of life there was mingled a
material and superstitious element akin to that *religio* which
Lucretius attacked as the source of the greatest evils, filling
men's minds with vain terrors and inclining their hearts to
cruelty:

> Tantum religio potuit suadere malorum.

Something again is no doubt due to the fact that the conditions
of life made it harder to forget about death; men lived in the
midst of

> plague, pestilence, and famine; battle, murder and sudden
> death,

as our noble Litany reminds us. We must remember that in
the autumn of nearly every year the terrible plague descended

upon London, often with such severity that all places of public amusement were closed to prevent the spread of infection. Every one who has read any poetry at all is familiar with the beautiful song

Spring, the sweete Spring, is the yeres pleasant King

written by that cheerful Elizabethan, Thomas Nashe, and placed by Palgrave at the very beginning of the *Golden Treasury*, with the result that to many, no doubt, it has seemed to strike the keynote of Elizabethan poetry. It occurs in *A Pleasant Comedie, called Summers last Will and Testament*, in which Summer, whose death is approaching, calls upon the other seasons to give an account of their stewardship. Before Spring enters and sings that song we all know there is a lament for the passing of Summer and the dread approach of Autumn and the plague:

Fayre Summer droops, droope men and beasts therefore:
So fayre a summer looke for neuer more.
All good things vanish, lesse then in a day,
Peace, plenty, pleasure, sodainely decay.
  Goe not yet away, bright soule of the sad yeare;
  The earth is hell when thou leau'st to appeare.[1]

And later we have one of the most beautiful and poignant of all Elizabethan songs:

Adieu, farewell earths blisse,
This world vncertaine is,
Fond are lifes lustfull ioyes,
Death proues them all but toyes,
None from his darts can flye;
I am sick, I must dye:
  Lord, haue mercy on vs.

Rich men, trust not in wealth,
Gold cannot buy you health;
Physick himselfe must fade.
All things to end are made,
The plague full swift goes bye;
I am sick, I must dye:
  Lord, haue mercy on vs.

Beauty is but a flowre,
Which wrinckles will devoure,
Brightnesse falls from the ayre,
Queenes haue died yong and faire,
Dust hath closde *Helens* eye.
I am sick, I must dye:
  Lord, haue mercy on vs.

  [1] *Works*, ed. McKerrow, iii, p. 236.

Strength stoopes vnto the graue,
Wormes feed on *Hector* braue,
Swords may not fight with fate,
Earth still holds ope her gate.
Come, come, the bells do crye.
I am sick, I must dye:
  Lord, haue mercy on vs.

Wit with his wantonnesse
Tasteth deaths bitternesse:
Hels executioner
Hath no eares for to heare
What vaine art can reply.
I am sick, I must dye:
  Lord, haue mercy on vs.

Haste therefore eche degree,
To welcome destiny:
Heauen is our heritage,
Earth but a players stage,
Mount wee vnto the sky.
I am sick, I must dye:
  Lord, haue mercy on vs.[1]

In order to understand the Elizabethan age we must put this, and also Summer's last song, beside that of Spring:

Autumne hath all the Summers fruitefull treasure;
Gone is our sport, fled is poore *Croydens* pleasure:
Short dayes, sharpe dayes, long nights come on a pace,
Ah, who shall hide vs from the Winters face?
Colde doth increase, the sicknesse will not cease,
And here we lye, God knowes, with little ease:
  From winter, plague, & pestilence, good Lord, deliuer vs.

London dooth mourne, Lambith is quite forlorne,
Trades cry, Woe worth that ever they were borne:
The want of Terme is towne and Cities harme;
Close chambers we do want, to keepe vs warme,
Long banished must we liue from our friends:
This lowe built house will bring vs to our ends.
  From winter, plague, & pestilence, good Lord, deliuer vs.[2]

During the plague of 1625 Donne sought refuge at Chelsea, then a country village, in the house of Sir John Danvers, the second husband of his friend Mrs. Herbert, and in a remarkable letter he describes some of the horrors he saw:

But by reason that these infections are not so frequent with us, the horror, I presume, was greater here; for the citizens

[1] p. 282.   [2] p. 292.

fled away, as out of a house on fire, and stuffed their pockets with their best ware, and threw themselves into the highways, and were not received so much as into barns, and perished so, some of them with more money about them than would have bought the village where they died.[1]

Death was a familiar and terrible thing, and Donne's sermons are full of impressive meditations thereon. For example:

Adam might have liv'd, if he would, but *I cannot.* God hath placed an *Ecce*, a marke of my death, upon every thing living, that I can set mine eye upon; every thing is a remembrancer, every thing is a Judge upon me, and pronounces, I *must* dye. The whole frame of the world is mortall, *Heaven and Earth passe away*: and upon us all, there is an irrecoverable Decree past, *statutum est,* It *is appointed to all men, that they shall once dye.* But when? quickly; If thou looke up into the aire, *remember that thy life is but a winde,* If thou see a cloud in the aire, aske St. *James* his question, what is your life? and give St. *James* his answer, *It is a vapour* that *appeareth and vanisheth away.* If thou behold a *Tree,* then *Job* gives thee a comparison of thy selfe; A *Tree* is an *embleme* of thy selfe; nay a Tree is the *originall,* thou art but the *copy,* thou art not so good as it: for, *There is hope of a tree* (as you reade there) *if the roote wax old,* if *the stock* be dead, if it be cut down, yet by *the sent of the waters,* it will *bud,* but *man is sick,* and *dyeth, and where is he?* he shall not wake againe, till heaven be no more. Looke upon the *water,* and we are as that, and as that spilt upon the ground: Looke to the *earth,* and we are not like that, but we are earth it self: At our Tables we feed upon the dead and in the Temple we tread upon the dead: and when we meet in a Church, God hath made many *echoes,* many testimonies of our death, in the walls, and in the windowes, and he onely knowes, whether he will not make another testimony of our mortality, of the youngest amongst us, before we part, and make the very *place of our buriall,* our *deathbed.*[2]

I think we find no difficulty in sympathizing with the profound feeling of such a passage as this; but there are others, where Donne dwells on the physical horrors of death and of the grave, which seem strange and repugnant to modern taste. Shakespeare recognized the dramatic value of an appeal to this fear of death, as to other terrors lurking in the background of the mind, and he often made use of it—in Juliet's frantic exclamation about the bones of her dead ancestors, and in that tremendous passage in *Measure for Measure* where, for the

---

[1] Gosse, ii. 222.   [2] *Fifty Sermons,* 1649, p. 270.

moment, both Claudio's resolution and his sense of honour
are shattered by the prospect of escape.

> *Cla.* If it were damnable, he being so wise,
> Why would he for the momentarie tricke
> Be perdurablie fin'de? Oh *Isabell.*
>   *Isa.* What saies my brother?
>   *Cla.* Death is a fearefull thing.
>   *Isa.* And shamed life, a hatefull.
>   *Cla.* I, but to die, and go we know not where,
> To lie in cold obstruction, and to rot,
> This sensible warme motion, to become
> A kneaded clod; And the delighted spirit
> To bath in fierie floods, or to recide
> In thrilling Region of thicke-ribbed Ice,
> To be imprison'd in the viewlesse windes
> And blowne with restlesse violence round about
> The pendant world: or to be worse then worst
> Of those, that lawlesse and incertaine thought,
> Imagine howling, 'tis too horrible.
> The weariest, and most loathed worldly life
> That Age, Ache, penury, and imprisonment
> Can lay on nature, is a Paradise
> To what we feare of death.[1]

Over and over again in his sermons we find Donne imagining
to himself all the horrors of death and of the grave and of what
lost souls may have to endure after death; resolutely facing
them and grappling with them, and trying to rid himself of that

> Sinne of feare, that when I have spunne
> My last thred, I shall perish on the shore.

To triumph over the fear of death, or, rather, over the fear
of what may come after death, was for him the supreme test
of faith, and it is a battle which he is continually re-fighting,
both with himself and with his congregation.

   Here, then, is that great passage in the *Second Anniversarie* to
which I referred, the passage where Donne contemplates in
imagination the moment of his own death:

> Shee to whose person Paradise adher'd,
> As Courts to Princes, shee whose eyes ensphear'd
> Star-light enough, t'have made the South controule,
> (Had shee beene there) the Star-full Northerne Pole,
> Shee, shee is gone; she is gone; when thou knowst this,
> What fragmentary rubbidge this world is

[1] III. i. 113–32.

Thou knowest, and that it is not worth a thought;
He honors it too much that thinkes it nought.
Thinke then, my soule, that death is but a Groome,
Which brings a Taper to the outward roome,
Whence thou spiest first a little glimmering light,
And after brings it nearer to thy sight:
For such approaches doth heaven make in death.
Thinke thy selfe labouring now with broken breath,
And thinke those broken and soft Notes to bee
Division, and thy happyest Harmonie.
Thinke thee laid on thy death-bed, loose and slacke;
And thinke that, but unbinding of a packe,
To take one precious thing, thy soule from thence.
Thinke thy selfe parch'd with fevers violence,
Anger thine ague more, by calling it
Thy Physicke; chide the slacknesse of the fit.
Thinke that thou hear'st thy knell, and think no more,
But that, as Bels cal'd thee to Church before,
So this, to the Triumphant Church, calls thee.
Thinke Satans Sergeants round about thee bee,
And thinke that but for Legacies they thrust;
Give one thy Pride, to'another give thy Lust:
Give them those sinnes which they gave thee before,
And trust th'immaculate blood to wash thy score.
Thinke thy friends weeping round, and thinke that they
Weepe but because they goe not yet thy way.
Thinke that they close thine eyes, and thinke in this,
That they confesse much in the world amisse,
Who dare not trust a dead mans eye with that,
Which they from God, and Angels cover not.
Thinke that they shroud thee up, and think from thence
They reinvest thee in white innocence.
Thinke that thy body rots, and (if so low,
Thy soule exalted so, thy thoughts can goe,)
Think thee a Prince, who of themselves create
Wormes which insensibly devoure their State.
Thinke that they bury thee, and thinke that right
Laies thee to sleepe but a Saint Lucies night.[1]

IV

And now, after so many defeated efforts and disappointed
hopes, another attempt was made to persuade Donne to enter
into holy orders, this time by a greater authority than Morton.
Walton records that, probably during the winter of 1609,
Donne had an audience with James on the subject of the dis-

[1] ll. 77–120.

putes about the Oaths of Supremacy and Allegiance, as the result of which Donne wrote his *Pseudo-Martyr*, which appeared in 1610; and that

> When the King had read and considered that Book, he perswaded Mr. Donne to enter into the Ministery; to which at that time he was, and appeared very unwilling, apprehending it (such was his mistaking modesty) to be too weighty for his Abilities.[1]

The King's will ultimately prevailed; but in his account of Donne's final resolve Walton has omitted many interesting and important circumstances which led up to it. In the course of his attempts to gain influence at court Donne had secured an introduction to James's favourite Robert Carr, who in 1611 was created Viscount Rochester and in 1613 Earl of Somerset; and the history of his relationship with this disreputable nobleman forms a curious chapter in his life. Bacon was to declare that 'All Rising to *Great Place*, is by a winding Staire', and owing partly to the evils inherent in the system of patronage, very many of the greatest men of this age seem to have practised at one time or another what Bacon called the 'architecture of fortune', so that mingled with their great qualities there often appears a strain of something very like baseness or sycophancy. During the three years that had elapsed since his interview with James the failure of other hopes seems to have led Donne to reconsider his decision not to enter the Church; for when he first introduced himself to Carr in a letter, written probably in October 1612, under cover of one to his friend Lord Hay, he declared:

> Having obeyed at last, after much debatement within me, the Inspirations (as I hope) of the Spirit of God, and resolved to make my Profession Divinitie: I make account, that I do but tell your Lordship, what God hath told me, which is, That it is in this course, if in any, that my service may be of use to this Church and State.[2]

And in the covering letter to Hay he said:

> I make account, that it is in one instant, that I tell his and your Lordship, that I have brought all my distractions together, and find them in a resolution, of making Divinity my Profession, that I may try, whether my poor Studies, which have

---

[1] World's Classics ed., p. 45.
[2] *A Collection of Letters made by Sᵣ Tobie Mathews, Kᵗ*, 1660, pp. 319–20; Gosse, ii. 20.

profited me nothing, may profit others in that course; in which also a fortune may either be better made, or, at least, better missed, than in anie other.[1]

Carr, however, seems to have dissuaded Donne from this resolution, for a year later we find him asking the Earl of Somerset, as he then was, to use his influence to get him the ambassadorship at Venice. The first letter is a definite request, the second a humble reminder:

> It is now somewhat more than a year, since I took the boldnesse, to make my purpose of professing Divinitie known to your Lordship, as to a person, whom God had made so great an instrument of his providence in this Kingdome, as that nothing in it should be done without your knowledge, your Lordship exercised upon me then many of your vertues, for besides, that by your bounty I have lived ever since, it hath been through your Lordships advice, and inspiration of new hopes into me, that I have lived cheerfullie.[2]

This man whom Donne addresses as 'a great instrument of God's providence in this Kingdom' had already begun to play his part in one of the darkest scandals of the age, and there is evidence that he had promised Donne his patronage if Donne would use his legal knowledge to help him procure a divorce between Frances Howard and the Earl of Essex, and also that he had proposed that Donne should write an epithalamium to celebrate his approaching marriage with the woman who was still Essex's wife. One letter begins:

> After I was grown to be your Lordships, by all the titles that I could thinke upon, it hath pleased your Lordship to make another title to me, by buying me.[3]

And in another 'To my worthy friend G. K.', written on January 19 (?1613), he says:

> Sir, I can only say in generall, that some appearances have been here, of some treatise concerning this Nullity, which are said to proceed from *Geneva*, but are beleeved to have been done within doors, by encouragements of some whose names I will not commit to this letter. My poor study having lyen that way, it may prove possible, that my weak assistance may be of use in the matter, in a more serious fashion, then an Epithalamion.[4]

---

[1] *Sir T. M.*, p. 322; Gosse, ii. 22.   [2] *Sir T. M.*, p. 314; Gosse, ii. 41.
[3] 1651, p. 290; Gosse, ii. 23.   [4] 1651, p. 180; Gosse, ii. 25.

A year later Donne made his last attempt to secure secular preferment, for in 1614 he was elected a Member of Parliament for Taunton, and sat from April 5 until the dissolution on June 7. Mr. Shapiro, to whom we owe this information, remarks:

> Donne's membership of Parliament in 1614 reinforces other evidence that he was at this time making energetic efforts to obtain political preferment, and supports the conclusion that his final decision to enter the Church, made a few months after the 'Addled' Parliament was dissolved, was taken with extreme reluctance and only because, all hope of civil preferment having failed and his fortunes being now desperate, Donne saw in the Church the only means of providing for his family.[1]

Now at last Somerset seems to have made some attempt to redeem his promises, for he invited Donne to join him at Theobalds, where he was staying with the King, and promised to obtain for him a vacant clerkship to the council. James, however, as Walton tells us, had decided that Donne was to enter the Church:

> *I know Mr.* Donne *is a learned man, has the abilities of a learned Divine; and will prove a powerful Preacher, and my desire is to prefer him that way, and in that way, I will deny you nothing for him.*[2]

While at Theobalds Donne seems to have discovered for the first time that Somerset and Archbishop Abbot were bitter enemies, and accordingly, on December 3, 1614, he wrote to his father-in-law Sir George More, asking him to try to discover whether the Archbishop knew anything of his relations with Somerset—a fact which suggests that although he had now at last consented to enter the Church he was unwilling to proceed if it should turn out that his chances of preferment had been impaired. However, the result of his inquiries seems to have been reassuring, for in January 1615 he was ordained, and preferment followed rapidly.

Nevertheless, although Donne seems to have been led rather by circumstances than by choice to enter the Church, and although Walton's repeated assertion that it was only conscientious scruples that deterred him hardly seems to fit the facts, having made his final decision he devoted all his energies to his new calling. He often referred with gratitude to the King's refusal to prefer him in any other way, and declared

---

[1] *T.L.S.*, March 16, 1932.   [2] World's Classics ed., pp. 45–6.

that he saw in it the hand of Providence. And no doubt it was his continual battle with what he considered to be his worldliness and lack of faith, together with his consciousness of the irregularities of his early life, and his conviction, forced upon him by many bitter disappointments, of the vanity of all attempts to escape, as he would put it, from the hand of God, that helped to make him the most powerful and popular preacher of his age. He who described with such vividness and analysed with such subtlety all the varieties of sin and temptation had been himself, in his own estimation, a great sinner; he whose great text was *vanitas vanitatum* had himself experienced more deeply than most men the vanity of all human hopes and ambitions; and he who spoke of the necessity of faith was himself continually battling for faith—in a word, he was preaching to himself as well as to his congregation.

'And now', says Walton,

all his studies which had been occasionally diffused, were all concentred in Divinity. Now he had a new calling, new thoughts, and a new imployment for his wit and eloquence: Now all his earthly affections were changed into divine love; and all the faculties of his own soul, were ingaged in the Conversion of others: In preaching the glad tidings of Remission to repenting Sinners, and peace to each troubled soul. To these he applied himself with all care and diligence: and now, such a change was wrought in him, that he could say with David, *Oh how amiable are thy Tabernacles, O Lord God of Hosts!* Now he declared openly, *that when he required a temporal, God gave him a spiritual blessing.* And that, *he was now gladder to be a door-keeper in the house of God, then he could be to injoy the noblest of all temporal imployments.*

Presently after he entred into his holy profession, the King sent for him, and made him his Chaplain in Ordinary; and promised to take a particular care for his preferment.

And though his long familiarity with Scholars, and persons of greatest quality, was such as might have given some men boldness enough to have preached to any eminent Auditory; yet his modesty in this imployment was such, that he could not be perswaded to it, but went usually accompanied with some one friend, to preach privately in some village, not far from *London*: his first Sermon being preached at *Paddington*. This he did, till His Majesty sent and appointed him a day to preach to him at *White-hall*, and, though much were expected from him, both by His Majesty and others, yet he was so happy (which few are) as to satisfie and exceed their expectations: preaching the Word so, as shewed his own heart was possest with those very thoughts and joys that he laboured to distill into others: A Preacher in earnest; weeping sometimes for his Auditory, sometimes with them: alwayes preaching to himself, like an Angel from a cloud, but in none; carrying some, as St. *Paul* was, to Heaven in holy raptures, and inticing others by a sacred Art and Courtship to amend their lives; here picturing a vice so as to make it ugly to those that practised it; and a vertue so, as to make it be beloved even by those that lov'd it not; and all this with a most particular grace and an unexpressible addition of comeliness.[1]

In August 1617 his wife died, and during the long period of solitary grief that followed Donne became, as Walton tells us, finally 'crucified to the world'. It was characteristic of the man that he did not try to suppress his grief or turn to things that might distract him from it, but chose rather to regard it as an opportunity for the exercise of repentance and renunciation. As he declared in one of his sermons:

David knew he could not retyre himselfe from God in his bedchamber; Guards and Ushers could not keepe him out. He knew he could not defend himselfe from God in his Army; for *the Lord of Hosts is Lord of his Hosts*. If he *fled to Sea, to Heaven, to Hell*, he was sure to meet *God there*; and there thou shalt meet him too, if thou fly from God, to the reliefe of outward comforts, of musicke, of mirth, of drinke, of cordialls, of Comedies, of conversation. Not that such recreations are unlawfull; the minde hath her physick as well as the body; but when thy sadnesse proceeds from a sense of thy sinnes, (which is Gods key to the doore of his mercy, put into thy hand) it is a new, and a greater sin, to goe about to overcome that holy sadnesse, with these prophane diversions. . . . There is no recourse but to God, no reliefe but in God; and therefore *David* applied himselfe to the right method, to make his first accesse to God.[2]

'In this retiredness', says Walton,

which was often from the sight of his dearest friends, he became *crucified to the world*, and all those vanities, those imaginary pleasures that are daily acted on that restless stage; and they were as perfectly crucified to him. Nor is it hard to think (being passions may be both changed, and heightned by accidents) but that that abundant affection which once was betwixt him and her, who had long been the delight of his eyes, and the Companion of his youth; her, with whom he had divided so many pleasant sorrows, and contented fears, as Common-people are not capable of; not hard to think but that

[1] pp. 48–9.   [2] *LXXX Sermons*, pp. 500–1.

she, being now removed by death, a commeasurable grief took as full a possession of him as joy had done; and so indeed it did: for now his very soul was elemented of nothing but sadness; now, grief took so full a possession of his heart, as to leave no place for joy: If it did? It was a joy to be alone, where like a *Pelican in the wilderness*, he might bemoan himself without witness or restraint, and pour forth his passions like *Job* in the days of his affliction, *Oh that I might have the desire of my heart! Oh that God would grant the thing that I long for!* For then, *as the grave is become her house*, so I would hasten to make it mine also; *that we two might there make our beds together in the dark*. Thus as the *Israelites* sate mourning by the rivers of *Babylon*, when they remembred *Sion*; so he gave some ease to his oppressed heart by thus venting his sorrows: Thus he began the day, and ended the night; ended the restless night and began the weary day in *Lamentations*. And, thus he continued till a consideration of his new ingagements to God, and St. *Pauls Wo is me, if I preach not the Gospel*: disper'st those sad clouds that had then benighted his hopes, and now forc'd him to behold the light.[1]

About this time he was made Divinity Reader to the Benchers of Lincoln's Inn,

being most glad to renew his intermitted friendship with those whom he so much loved; and where he had been a *Saul*, though not to persecute Christianity, or to deride it, yet in his irregular youth to neglect the visible practice of it: there to become a *Paul*, and preach salvation to his beloved brethren.[2]

In 1619 he accompanied his friend the Earl of Doncaster, formerly Lord Hay, on an embassy to Frederic and Elizabeth of Bohemia, and the sermon in which he bade farewell to his congregation at Lincoln's Inn contains some of the most tender and beautiful things in English prose. After having asked them to remember him during his long absence,

as I shall do you in the eares of that God, to whom the farthest East, and the farthest West are but as the right and left ear in one of us,

he proceeds, as is usual with him, to 'enlarge this meditation', and speaks of another journey and a longer absence:

That if I never meet you again till we have all passed the gate of death, yet in the gates of heaven, I may meet you all, and there say to my Saviour and your Saviour, that which he said to his Father and our Father, *Of those whom thou hast given me, have I not lost one.*[3]

And for himself also he considered the journey as symbolic

[1] World's Classics ed., pp. 51–2.   [2] pp. 52–3.   [3] *XXVI Sermons*, 1660, p. 280.

—symbolic of the journey he was continually striving to accomplish, from the pleasures and ambitions of the world to the complete and single-hearted service of God; and he has expressed this meditation in one of the most characteristic of his poems:

A Hymne to Christ, at the Authors last going into Germany

In what torne ship soever I embarke,
That ship shall be my embleme of thy Arke;
What sea soever swallow mee, that flood
Shall be to mee an embleme of thy blood;
Though thou with clouds of anger do disguise
Thy face; yet through that maske I know those eyes,
   Which, though they turne away sometimes,
     They never will despise.

I sacrifice this Iland unto thee,
And all whom I lov'd there, and who lov'd mee;
When I have put our seas twixt them and mee,
Put thou thy sea betwixt my sinnes and thee.
As the trees sap doth seeke the root below
In winter, in my winter now I goe,
   Where none but thee, th'Eternall root
     Of true Love I may know.

Nor thou nor thy religion dost controule,
The amorousnesse of an harmonious Soule,
But thou would'st have that love thy selfe: As thou
Art jealous, Lord, so I am jealous now,
Thou lov'st not, till from loving more, thou free
My soule: Who ever gives, takes libertie:
   O, if thou car'st not whom I love
     Alas, thou lov'st not mee.

Seale then this bill of my Divorce to All,
On whom those fainter beames of love did fall;
Marry those loves, which in youth scattered bee
On Fame, Wit, Hopes (false mistresses) to thee.
Churches are best for Prayer, that have least light:
To see God only, I goe out of sight:
   And to scape stormy dayes, I chuse
     An Everlasting night.[1]

The story of the last years of Donne's life has been so beautifully told by Walton that I will ask the reader to turn to his pages, and merely content myself with reminding him that in 1621 Donne was made Dean of St. Paul's and that he died ten years later. Nevertheless, before turning to his religious poetry,

[1] *Poems*, i. 352.

I will just mention the little book of *Devotions upon Emergent Occasions*, which he composed during a serious illness in 1623, and which throws a vivid light on his character and ways of thinking. Prefixed to it are some Latin verses describing the various stages of his sickness and of his recovery, and sometimes a line, sometimes a phrase from these verses furnishes the text for each section of the book, these sections, twenty-three in all, consisting of a Meditation followed by what he calls an Expostulation and a Prayer. The text of the thirteenth Meditation does not at first sight seem very promising.

> Ingeniumque malum, numeroso stigmate, fassus
> Pellitur ad pectus, Morbique Suburbia, Morbus,

'The Sicknes declares the infection and malignity thereof by spots.' We can't expect much from this, you might say. Nevertheless, Donne ingeniously extracts from it one of his finest and most characteristic meditations. The physicians try to comfort him by saying that although it is now clear that he is dangerously ill, they have at last discovered the nature of his disease, and know how to proceed. Small comfort, this! thinks Donne; I may die before they are able to help me. They give me a gleam of hope, but at the same time they increase my anxiety—an apt symbol of the relations between human happiness and human misery!

> Wee say, that the world is made of *sea*, & *land*, as though they were equal; but we know that ther is more *sea* in the *Western*, then in the *Eastern Hemisphere*: we say that the *Firmament* is full of *starres*; as though it were equally full; but we know, that there are more *stars* vnder the *Northerne*, then vnder the *Southern Pole*. Wee say, the *Elements* of man are *misery*, and *happinesse*, as though he had an equal proportion of both, and the dayes of man vicissitudinary, as though he had as many *good* days, as *ill*, and that he lived vnder a perpetuall *Equinoctial*, *night*, and *day* equall, good and ill fortune in the same measure. But it is far from that; hee *drinkes misery*, & he *tastes happinesse*; he *mowes misery*, and hee *gleanes happinesse*; hee *iournies in misery*, he does but *walke in happinesse*; and which is worst, his misery is *positiue*, and *dogmaticall*, his happinesse is but *disputable*, and *problematicall*; All men call *Misery*, *Misery*, but *Happinesse* changes the name, by the taste of man.[1]

'The Recreations of his youth', says Walton,

> were *Poetry*, in which he was so happy, as if nature and all her varieties had been made only to exercise his sharp wit, and

[1] 1624, pp. 312–14.

high fancy; and in those pieces which were facetiously Composed
and carelessly scattered (most of them being written before the
twentieth year of his age) it may appear by his choice Metaphors,
that both *Nature* and all the *Arts* joyned to assist him with their
utmost skill.

It is a truth, that in his penitential years, viewing some of
those pieces that had been loosely (God knows too loosely)
scattered in his youth, he wish't they had been abortive, or so
short liv'd that his own eyes had witnessed their funerals: But
though he was no friend to them, he was not so fallen out with
heavenly Poetry as to forsake that: no not in his declining age;
witnessed then by many Divine Sonnets, and other high, holy,
and harmonious Composures. Yea, even on his former sick-bed
he wrote this heavenly *Hymn*, expressing the great joy that then
possest his soul in the Assurance of Gods favour to him when he
Composed it.[1]

A Hymne to God the Father
I
Wilt thou forgive that sinne where I begunne,
   Which was my sin, though it were done before?
Wilt thou forgive that sinne; through which I runne,
   And do run still: though still I do deplore?
     When thou hast done, thou hast not done,
      For, I have more.

II
Wilt thou forgive that sinne which I have wonne
   Others to sinne? and, made my sinne their doore?
Wilt thou forgive that sinne which I did shunne
   A yeare, or two: but wallowed in, a score?
     When thou hast done, thou hast not done,
      For I have more.

III
I have a sinne of feare, that when I have spunne
   My last thred, I shall perish on the shore;
But sweare by thy selfe, that at my death thy sonne
   Shall shine as he shines now, and heretofore;
     And, having done that, Thou haste done,
      I feare no more.

I have the rather mentioned this *Hymn*, for that he caus'd it
to be set to a most grave and solemn Tune, and to be often
sung to the *Organ* by the *Choristers* of St. *Pauls* Church, in his
own hearing; especially at the Evening Service, and at his
return from his Customary Devotions in that place, did occasionally say to a friend, *The words of this* Hymn *have restored to me
the same thoughts of joy that possest my Soul in my sickness when I*

[1] The poem is here given in Grierson's text (i. 369).

86 METAPHYSICAL POETS

*composed it. And, O the power of Church-musick! that Harmony added
to this Hymn has raised the Affections of my heart, and quickned my
graces of zeal and gratitude; and I observe, that I always return from
paying this publick duty of Prayer and Praise to God, with an
unexpressible tranquillity of mind, and a willingness to leave the
world.*[1]

Donne's religious poetry is extraordinarily personal and sincere; its range of experience is not perhaps very varied, but its
appeal is universal—as significant to the Catholic and the non-
conformist as to the Anglican.

'I have a sinne of feare'—this note continually recurs, in the
poems as in the sermons, where some of the most impressive
passages are on the terrible contemplation of being deserted
by God.

Let me wither and weare out mine age in a discomfortable,
in an unwholesome, in a penurious prison, and so pay my debts
with my bones, and recompence the wastfulnesse of my youth,
with the beggery of mine age; Let me wither in a spittle under
sharpe, and foule, and infamous diseases, and so recompence
the wantonnesse of my youth, with that loathsomnesse in mine
age; yet, if God with-draw not his spirituall blessings, his Grace,
his Patience, If I can call my suffering his Doing, my passion
his Action, All this that is temporall, is but a caterpiller got
into one corner of my garden, but a mill-dew fallen upon one
acre of my Corne; The body of all, the substance of all is safe,
as long as the soule is safe. But when I shall trust to that, which
wee call a good spirit, and God shall deject, and empoverish,
and evacuate that spirit, when I shall rely upon a morall
constancy, and God shall shake, and enfeeble, and enervate,
destroy and demolish that constancy; when I shall think to
refresh my selfe in the serenity and sweet ayre of a good conscience, and God shall call up the damps and vapours of hell
itselfe, and spread a cloud of diffidence, and an impenetrable
crust of desperation upon my conscience; when health shall
flie from me, and I shall lay hold upon riches to succour me,
and comfort me in my sicknesse, and riches shall flie from me,
and I shall snatch after favour, and good opinion, to comfort
me in my poverty; when even this good opinion shall leave me,
and calumnies and misinformations shall prevaile against me;
when I shall need peace, because there is none but thou, O
Lord, that should stand for me, and then shall finde, that all
the wounds that I have, come from thy hand, all the arrowes
that stick in me, from thy quiver; when I shall see, that because
I have given my selfe to my corrupt nature, thou hast changed

[1] World's Classics ed., pp. 61–2.

thine; and because I am all evill towards thee, therefore thou hast given over being good towards me; When it comes to this height, that the fever is not in the humors, but in the spirits, that mine enemy is not an imaginary enemy, fortune, nor a transitory enemy, malice in great persons, but a reall, and an irresistible, and an inexorable, and an everlasting enemy, The Lord of Hosts himselfe, The Almighty God himselfe, the Almighty God himselfe onely knowes the waight of this affliction, and except hee put in that *pondus gloriae*, that exceeding waight of an eternall glory, with his owne hand, into the other scale, we are waighed downe, we are swallowed up, irreparably, irrevocably, irrecoverably, irremediably.[1]

Donne's sombre and somewhat hectic genius, together with the fact that in all his sermons he is more especially wrestling with himself, with his own sins, with his own inability to live up to his conception of righteousness, leads him to dwell very often on the awfulness of God, on the terrible prospect of being deserted by him; and yet he often pauses and tries to calm his fears by remembering *pondus gloriae*. Thus, in the same sermon, after he has been dwelling on the miseries and afflictions of man, he concludes:

But then there is *Pondus Gloriae, An exceeding waight of eternall glory*, and that turnes the scale; for as it makes all worldly prosperity as dung, so it makes all worldly adversity as feathers.[2]

He does this in one of the greatest of his sonnets, where after a terrible and sublime vision of the Last Judgement, expressed in verse whose movement has something of the long, sustained blast of those trumpets he invokes, he calms himself and quietly remembers that pardon and a confidence which no terrors can shake are to be had here and now for sincere repentance.

At the round earths imagin'd corners, blow
Your trumpets, Angells, and arise, arise
From death, you numberlesse infinities
Of soules, and to your scattred bodies goe,
All whom the flood did, and fire shall o'erthrow,
All whom warre, dearth, age, agues, tyrannies,
Despaire, law, chance, hath slaine, and you whose eyes,
Shall behold God, and never tast deaths woe.
But let them sleepe, Lord, and mee mourne a space,
For, if above all these, my sinnes abound,
'Tis late to aske abundance of thy grace,
When wee are there; here on this lowly ground,
Teach mee how to repent; for that's as good
As if thou'hadst seal'd my pardon, with thy blood.[3]

---

[1] *LXXX Sermons*, pp. 665–6.   [2] Ibid., p. 665.   [3] *Poems*, i. 325.

But that mood of perfect joy and security which seems to have become almost habitual with certain practitioners of the religious life is rarely attained by Donne, and then only for brief moments. Almost every one of these sonnets is the record of a spiritual conflict against that 'sinne of feare'.

> Thou hast made me, And shall thy worke decay?
> Repaire me now, for now mine end doth haste,
> I runne to death, and death meets me as fast,
> And all my pleasures are like yesterday;
> I dare not move my dimme eyes any way,
> Despaire behind, and death before doth cast
> Such terrour, and my feeble flesh doth waste
> By sinne in it, which it t'wards hell doth weigh;
> Onely thou art above, and when towards thee
> By thy leave I can looke, I rise againe;
> But our old subtle foe so tempteth me,
> That not one houre my selfe I can sustaine;
> Thy Grace may wing me to prevent his art,
> And thou like Adamant draw mine iron heart.[1]

> This is my playes last scene, here heavens appoint
> My pilgrimages last mile; and my race
> Idly, yet quickly runne, hath this last pace,
> My spans last inch, my minutes latest point,
> And gluttonous death, will instantly unjoynt
> My body, and soule, and I shall sleepe a space,
> But my'ever-waking part shall see that face,
> Whose feare already shakes my every joynt:
> Then, as my soule, to'heaven her first seate, takes flight,
> And earth-borne body, in the earth shall dwell,
> So, fall my sinnes, that all may have their right,
> To where they'are bred, and would presse me, to hell.
> Impute me righteous, thus purg'd of evill,
> For thus I leave the world, the flesh, the devill.[2]

His restless intellect, forever re-examining and leading him to doubt the premises which his faith has accepted, hinders that complete self-surrender and perfect union with Christ for which he longs.

> Batter my heart, three person'd God; for, you
> As yet but knocke, breathe, shine, and seeke to mend;
> That I may rise, and stand, o'erthrow mee,'and bend
> Your force, to breake, blowe, burn and make me new.
> I, like an usurpt towne, to'another due,
> Labour to'admit you, but Oh, to no end,
> Reason your viceroy in mee, mee should defend,

But is captiv'd, and proves weake or untrue.
Yet dearely'I love you,'and would be loved faine,
But am betroth'd unto your enemie:
Divorce mee,'untie, or breake that knot againe,
Take mee to you, imprison mee, for I
Except you'enthrall mee, never shall be free,
Nor ever chast, except you ravish mee.[1]

Donne's religious poetry is, as I have said, intensely personal.
His 'sinne of feare' was partly due to his perpetual consciousness of the errors of younger days; and sometimes with a kind
of sad humour that is both like and unlike Herbert's he recognizes the continuity between Jack Donne and Dr. Donne, declaring that he is as 'humorous' in his repentance as formerly
in his profane love, and that because he once suffered the pains
of love he must now suffer those of remorse.

Oh, to vex me, contraryes meet in one:
Inconstancy unnaturally hath begott
A constant habit; that when I would not
I change in vowes, and in devotione.
As humorous is my contritione
As my prophane Love, and as soone forgott:
As ridlingly distemper'd, cold and hott,
As praying, as mute; as infinite, as none.
I durst not view heaven yesterday; and to day
In prayers, and flattering speaches I court God:
To morrow I quake with true feare of his rod.
So my devout fitts came and go away
Like a fantastique Ague: save that here
Those are my best dayes, when I shake with feare.[2]

O might those sighes and teares returne againe
Into my breast and eyes, which I have spent,
That I might in this holy discontent
Mourne with some fruit, as I have mourn'd in vaine;
In mine Idolatry what showres of raine
Mine eyes did waste? what griefs my heart did rent?
That sufferance was my sinne; now I repent;
'Cause I did suffer I must suffer paine.
Th'hydroptique drunkard, and night-scouting thiefe,
The itchy Lecher, and selfe tackling proud
Have the remembrance of past joyes, for reliefe
Of comming ills. To (poore) me is allow'd
No ease; for, long, yet vehement griefe hath beene
Th'effect and cause, the punishment and sinne.[3]

[1] p. 328.   [2] p. 331.   [3] p. 323.

But he remembers too that he believed, or pretended to believe, that beauty was a sign of pity.

> What if this present were the worlds last night?
> Marke in my heart, O Soule, where thou dost dwell,
> The picture of Christ crucified, and tell
> Whether that countenance can thee affright,
> Teares in his eyes quench the amasing light,
> Blood fills his frownes, which from his pierc'd head fell.
> And can that tongue adjudge thee unto hell,
> Which pray'd forgivenesse for his foes fierce spight?
> No, no; but as in my idolatrie
> I said to all my profane mistresses,
> Beauty, of pitty, foulnesse onely is
> A signe of rigour: so I say to thee,
> To wicked spirits are horrid shapes assign'd,
> This beauteous forme assures a pitious minde.[1]

Nevertheless, in spite of these doubts and fears, Walton tells us that Donne said to his physician that he was

> so far from fearing death, which to others is the King of Terrors, that he long'd for the day of his dissolution;

and in what is perhaps the finest of his sonnets he faces the great enemy

> *Atque metus omnes et inexorabile fatum*
> *Subiecit pedibus.*

> Death be not proud, though some have called thee
> Mighty and dreadfull, for, thou art not soe,
> For, those, whom thou think'st, thou dost overthrow,
> Die not, poore death, nor yet canst thou kill mee.
> From rest and sleepe, which but thy pictures bee,
> Much pleasure, then from thee, much more must flow,
> And soonest our best men with thee doe goe,
> Rest of their bones, and soules deliverie.
> Thou art slave to Fate, Chance, kings, and desperate men,
> And dost with poyson, warre, and sicknesse dwell,
> And poppie, or charmes can make us sleepe as well,
> And better then thy stroake; why swell'st thou then?
> One short sleepe past, wee wake eternally,
> And death shall be no more; death, thou shalt die.[2]

[1] p. 328.   [2] p. 326.

In the following sonnet is expressed another important aspect of Donne's religion:

> Show me deare Christ, thy spouse, so bright and clear.
> What! is it She, which on the other shore
> Goes richly painted? or which rob'd and tore
> Laments and mournes in Germany and here?
> Sleepes she a thousand, then peepes up one yeare?
> Is she selfe truth and errs? now new, now outwore?
> Doth she, and did she, and shall she evermore
> On one, on seaven, or on no hill appeare?
> Dwells she with us, or like adventuring knights
> First travaile we to seeke and then make Love?
> Betray kind husband thy spouse to our sights,
> And let myne amorous soule court thy mild Dove,
> Who is most trew, and pleasing to thee, then
> When she'is embrac'd and open to most men.[1]

This sonnet was first published in Gosse's *Life*—why it had remained in manuscript Grierson has suggested to us in an illuminating note:

> It is clear enough why this sonnet was not published. It would have revealed Donne, already three years in orders, as still conscious of all the difficulties involved in a choice between the three divisions of Christianity—Rome, Geneva (made to include Germany), and England. This is the theme of his earliest serious poem, the *Satyre III*, and the subject recurs in the letters and sermons. Donne entered the Church of England not from a conviction that it, and it alone, was the true Church, but because he had first reached the position that there is salvation in each: 'You know I never fettered nor imprisoned the word Religion; not straitening it Frierly, *ad Religiones factitias*, (as the *Romans* call well their orders of Religion) nor immuring it in a *Rome*, or a *Wittemberg*, or a *Geneva*; they are all virtuall beams of one Sun, and wheresoever they find clay hearts, they harden them, and moulder them into dust; and they entender and mollifie waxen. They are not so contrary as the North and South Poles; and that they are connaturale pieces of one circle.' *Letters*, p. 29.[2]

Indeed, in his ability to recognize the characteristic merits both of the Roman and of the Reformed Churches, and in his desire, expressed many times in his letters both before and after he had entered holy orders, for a conception of Christianity which should transcend particular forms of worship, Donne is almost unique in his age. Thus, in a letter to his friend Sir

---

[1] p. 330.   [2] ii. 235–6.

Henry Goodyer, written probably in 1609 or 1610, and promising to send a copy of a poem to which I shall refer later, he
mentions a rumour that the celebrated Hugh Broughton had
been induced to go over to Rome

> onely to serve the Christian Churches in controversies with the
> Jews, without indangering himself to change of his perswasion
> in particular deductions between these Christian Churches, or
> being enquired of, or tempted thereunto. . . . You shall see in
> that course of opposing the Jews, he will produce worthy things:
> and our Church will perchance blush to have lost a Souldier
> fit for that great battell; and to cherish onely those single
> Duellisms, between *Rome* and *England*, or that more single,
> and almost self-homicide, between the unconformed Ministers,
> and Bishops.[1]

And in another letter to Goodyer, referring to *An Answer to a
Catholic Englishman* by William Barlow, bishop of Lincoln, published in 1609, he says:

> It hath refreshed, and given new justice to my ordinary
> complaint, That the Divines of these times, are become meer
> Advocates, as though Religion were a temporall inheritance;
> they plead for it with all sophistications, and illusions, and
> forgeries: And herein are they likest Advocates, that though
> they be feed by the way, with Dignities, and other recompenses,
> yet that for which they plead is none of theirs. They write for
> Religion, without it.

And after criticizing the book, Donne continues:

> I know (as I begun) I speak to you who cannot be scandal-
> ized, and that neither measure Religion (as it is now called)
> by Unitie, nor suspect Unity, for these interruptions . . . for,
> whether the Maior and Aldermen fall out, (as with us and the
> Puritans; Bishops against Priests) or the Commoners voyces
> differ who is Maior, and who Aldermen, or what their Juris-
> diction, (as with the Bishop of *Rome*, or whosoever) yet it is
> still one Corporation.[2]

Again, writing to Sir Tobie Matthew from Cologne during
his visit to Germany in 1619 he says:

> That which I add, I am farre from applying to you, but it
> is true, That we are fallen into so slack and negligent times,
> that I have been sometimes glad to hear, that some of my

[1] 1651, pp. 35–6; Gosse, i. 196–7.   [2] 1651, pp. 160–4; Gosse, i. 221–3.

friends have differed from me in Religion. It is some degree
of an union to be united in a serious meditation of God, and
to make any Religion the rule of our actions.[1]

Nevertheless, although he was able to see good on both
sides, Donne seems to have been of the opinion that as a general
rule it is best for men to keep to the religion they were born in.
Writing to his friend Sir Henry Goodyer, probably in 1615,
Donne warns him that his

> true opinion, that in all Christian professions there is way to
> salvation,

may, unless carefully expressed, lead to misconstruction.

> This I have feared, because hertofore the inobedient Puritans,
> and now the over-obedient Papists attempt you. It hath hurt
> very many, not in their conscience, nor ends, but in their reputa-
> tion, and ways, that others have thought them fit to be wrought
> upon. As some bodies are as wholesomly nourished as ours,
> with Akornes, and endure nakednesse, both which would be
> dangerous to us, if we for them should leave our former habits,
> though theirs were the Primitive diet and custome: so are many
> souls well fed with such formes and dressings of Religion, as
> would distemper and misbecome us, and make us corrupt to-
> wards God, if any humane circumstance moved it, and in the
> opinion of men, though none. You shall seldome see a Coyne,
> upon which the stamp were removed, though to imprint it
> better, but it looks awry and squint. And so, for the most part,
> do mindes which have received divers impressions.[2]

It has been said that Donne made no original contribution
to theology: of theology in the technical sense this may well be
true, and I cannot pretend to say how much the value of
Donne's writings is thereby diminished. Nevertheless, I will
venture to say that to religious experience in general his contribution was very valuable indeed, and that some of the things
he has said on the subject of toleration are far in advance of
the general thought of his age.

> Beloved, there are some things in which all Religions agree;
> The worship of God, The holinesse of life; And therefore, if
> when I study this holinesse of life, and fast, and pray, and sub-
> mit my selfe to discreet, and medicinall mortifications, for the
> subduing of my body, any man will say, this is Papisticall,
> Papists doe this, it is a blessed Protestation, and no man is the
> lesse a Protestant, nor the worse a Protestant for making it,

[1] *Sir T. M.*, p. 337; Gosse, ii. 137.   [2] 1651, pp. 101–2; Gosse, ii. 78.

Men and brethren, I am a Papist, that is, I will fast and pray
as much as any Papist, and enable my selfe for the service of
my God, as seriously, as sedulously, as laboriously as any Papist.
So, if when I startle and am affected at a blasphemous oath, as
at a wound upon my Saviour, if when I avoyd the conversation
of those men, that prophane the Lords day, any other will say
to me, This is Puritanicall, Puritans do this, It is a blessed
Protestation, and no man is the lesse a Protestant, nor the worse
a Protestant for making it, Men and Brethren, I am a Puritan,
that is, I wil endeavour to be pure, as my Father in heaven is
pure, as far as any Puritan.[1]

I have already mentioned that the letter to Goodyer written
about 1609 or 1610 promised his friend a copy of a new
poem.

Since my imprisonment in my bed, I have made a meditation
in verse, which I call a Litany. . . . That by which it will
deserve best acceptation, is, That neither the Roman Church
need call it defective, because it abhors not the particular
mention of the blessed Triumphers in heaven; nor the Reformed
can discreetly accuse it, of attributing more then a rectified
devotion ought to doe.[2]

It is a long poem, and, as in most of Donne's long poems, the
inspiration is not equally sustained throughout; but there are
several stanzas which have always seemed to me among the
noblest in the whole range of our religious poetry. In these
utterances of a perplexed and tormented soul, turning for comfort to him with whom there is no variableness neither shadow
of turning, the differences between Roman, Anglican, and
Puritan wither and vanish like a burnt scroll. As Mr. Birrell
said of Newman's famous hymn, 'the believer often cannot
say more, the unbeliever will never willingly say less'.

Father of Heaven, and him, by whom
It, and us for it, and all else, for us
Thou madest, and govern'st ever, come
And re-create mee, now growne ruinous:
My heart is by dejection, clay,
And by selfe-murder, red.
From this red earth, O Father, purge away
All vicious tinctures, that new fashioned
I may rise up from death, before I'am dead. . . .

---

[1] *LXXX Sermons*, p. 493.   [2] 1651, pp. 32–4; Gosse, i. 195–6.

O Holy Ghost, whose temple I
Am, but of mudde walls, and condensed dust,
   And being sacrilegiously
Halfe wasted with youths fires, of pride and lust,
     Must with new stormes be weatherbeat;
     Double in my heart thy flame,
Which let devout sad teares intend; and let
(Though this glasse lanthorne, flesh, do suffer maime)
Fire, Sacrifice, Priest, Altar be the same. . . .

   And whil'st this universall Quire,
That Church in triumph, this in warfare here,
   Warm'd with one all-partaking fire
Of love, that none be lost, which cost thee deare,
     Prayes ceaslesly,'and thou hearken too,
     (Since to be gratious
Our taske is treble, to pray, beare, and doe)
Heare this prayer Lord: O Lord deliver us
From trusting in those prayers, though powr'd out thus.

   From being anxious, or secure,
Dead clods of sadnesse, or light squibs of mirth,
   From thinking, that great courts immure
All, or no happinesse, or that this earth
     Is only for our prison fram'd,
     Or that thou art covetous
To them whom thou lovest, or that they are maim'd
From reaching this worlds sweet, who seek thee thus,
With all their might, Good Lord deliver us.

   From needing danger, to bee good,
From owing thee yesterdaies teares to day,
   From trusting so much to thy blood,
That in that hope, wee wound our soule away,
     From bribing thee with Almes, to excuse
     Some sinne more burdenous,
From light affecting, in religion, newes,
From thinking us all soule, neglecting thus
Our mutuall duties, Lord deliver us. . . .

   Through thy submitting all, to blowes
Thy face, thy clothes to spoile; thy fame to scorne,
   All waies, which rage, or Justice knowes,
And by which thou could'st shew, that thou wast **born;**
     And through thy gallant humblenesse
     Which thou in death did'st shew,
Dying before thy soule they could expresse,
Deliver us from death, by dying so,
To this world, ere this world doe bid us goe.

When senses, which thy souldiers are,
Wee arme against thee, and they fight for sinne,
　When want, sent but to tame, doth warre
And worke despaire a breach to enter in,
　　When plenty, Gods image, and seale
　　Makes us Idolatrous,
And love it, not him, whom it should reveale,
When wee are mov'd to seeme religious
Only to vent wit, Lord deliver us.

　In Churches, when the'infirmitie
Of him which speakes, diminishes the Word,
　When Magistrates doe mis-apply
To us, as we judge, lay or ghostly sword,
　　When plague, which is thine Angell, raignes,
　　Or wars, thy Champions, swaie,
When Heresie, thy second deluge, gaines;
In th'houre of death, the'Eve of last judgement day,
Deliver us from the sinister way.

　Heare us, O heare us Lord; to thee
A sinner is more musique, when he prayes,
　Then spheares, or Angels praises bee,
In Panegyrique Allelujaes;
　　Heare us, for till thou heare us, Lord
　　We know not what to say;
Thine eare to'our sighes, teares, thoughts gives voice and word.
O Thou who Satan heard'st in Jobs sicke day,
Heare thy selfe now, for thou in us dost pray. . . .

　That learning, thine Ambassador,
From thine allegiance wee never tempt,
　That beauty, paradises flower
For physicke made, from poyson be exempt,
　　That wit, borne apt high good to doe,
　　By dwelling lazily
On Natures nothing, be not nothing too,
That our affections kill us not, nor dye,
Heare us, weake ecchoes, O thou eare, and cry.[1]

Although, as I have said, this poem is universal in its transcen-
dence of ecclesiastical differences, yet in the subtlety of the
temptations from which it asks deliverance it is, once again,
intensely personal, and could only have been written by
Donne.

　And now let us turn to the last poem Donne ever wrote, the
Hymne to God my God, in my sicknesse. Perhaps in no single poem
has he expressed so much of himself: his whole life seems to

　　　　　　　[1] *Poems,* i. 338.

pass before us—the lover of music, who wrote songs and sonnets
both in the days of his 'Idolatry' and in his 'penitential years';
the lover of curious analogies and resemblances; the traveller,
who more than most men had been affected by the implica-
tions of the new discoveries of his age, and who found a world
of poetry in maps, '*Anyan*, and *Magellan*, and *Gibraltare*'; the
preacher, whose sermon had always been directed as much to
himself as to his congregation—they are all here. And here
too is that mood of joy and peace and perfect security which
seems only rarely to have been granted him, and which he has
expressed in one perfect passage in the sermons:

. . . but I will finde out another death, *mortem raptus*, a death of
rapture, and of extasie, that death which S. *Paul* died more
then once, The death which S. *Gregory* speaks of, *Divina contem-
platio quoddam sepulchrum animae*, The contemplation of God, and
heaven, is a kinde of buriall, and Sepulchre, and rest of the
soule; and in this death of rapture, and extasie, in this death
of the Contemplation of my interest in my Saviour, I shall
finde my self, and all my sins enterred, and entombed in his
wounds, and like a Lily in Paradise, out of red earth, I shall
see my soule rise out of his blade, in a candor, and in an
innocence, contracted there, acceptable in the sight of his
Father.[1]

Since I am comming to that Holy roome,
    Where, with thy Quire of Saints for evermore,
I shall be made thy Musique; As I come
    I tune the Instrument here at the dore,
    And what I must doe then, thinke here before.

Whilst my Physitians by their love are growne
    Cosmographers, and I their Mapp, who lie
Flat on this bed, that by them may be showne
    That this is my South-west discoverie
    Per fretum febris, by these streights to die,

I joy, that in these straits, I see my West;
    For, though theire currants yeeld returne to none,
What shall my West hurt me? As West and East
    In all flatt Maps (and I am one) are one,
    So death doth touch the Resurrection.

Is the Pacifique Sea my home? Or are
    The Easterne riches? Is *Ierusalem*?
Anyan, and *Magellan*, and *Gibraltare*,
    All streights, and none but streights, are wayes to them,
    Whether where *Iaphet* dwelt, or *Cham*, or *Sem*.

[1] *LXXX Sermons*, pp. 273-4.

3886   O

We thinke that *Paradise* and *Calvarie*,
  Christs Crosse, and *Adams* tree, stood in one place;
Looke Lord, and finde both *Adams* met in me;
  As the first *Adams* sweat surrounds my face,
  May the last *Adams* blood my soule embrace.

So, in his purple wrapp'd receive mee Lord,
  By these his thornes give me his other Crowne;
And as to others soules I preach'd thy word,
  Be this my Text, my Sermon to mine owne,
  Therfore that he may raise the Lord throws down.[1]

Old St. Paul's, like its greatest preacher, has long since mouldered into dust, but his beautiful monument still survives, with the epitaph, composed by himself, which fittingly preserves for us his favourite conceit of the continuity of east and west:

Hic licet in Occiduo Cinere Aspicit Eum
Cujus nomen est Oriens.

[1] *Poems*, i. 368.

GEORGE HERBERT

I

GEORGE HERBERT was born at Montgomery Castle
on April 3, 1593. On his father's side he was descended
from a long line of soldiers, and his mother, Magdalen New-
port, was one of the most celebrated women of her time, and
enjoyed for many years the devoted friendship and admiration
of John Donne.

In one of his poems Herbert says to God:

> Whereas my birth and spirit rather took
> The way that takes the town;
> Thou didst betray me to a lingring book,
> And wrap me in a gown.

He was aware that the life he seemed compelled to lead was
not in accordance with the traditions of his family. His eldest
brother, Edward, Lord Herbert of Cherbury, had a varied
and adventurous career as soldier, diplomat, poet, and philosopher; Richard and William died in the Flemish wars;
Thomas entered the navy; Henry pushed his fortunes at
court, and became Master of the Revels, an office in which
he was reconfirmed after the Restoration. It is important to
remember these facts; for although the picture of Herbert as
a mild and retiring gentleman with a taste for flowers will
square neither with his poetry as a whole nor with an attentive
reading of Walton's *Life*, it is a picture that has been so often
painted that memories of it tend to thrust themselves between
the reader and Herbert's poetry. It is therefore worth while
to insist that the blood in Herbert's veins was that of his
soldier ancestors and of his active and ambitious brothers,
one of whom, Lord Herbert of Cherbury, after remarking
that his brother's life 'was most holy and exemplary, in so
much that about Salisbury, where he lived beneficed for many
years, he was little less than sainted', adds that 'he was not
exempt from passion and choler, being infirmities to which
all our race is subject'.

In 1609, at the age of sixteen, Herbert entered Trinity
College, Cambridge, where he was to spend the next eighteen
years of his life.

> And in *Cambridge*, [says Walton[1]] we may find our *George
> Herberts* behaviour to be such, that we may conclude he con-

[1] Walton's *Life of Herbert* was first published in 1670.

secrated the first-fruits of his early age to vertue, and a serious study of learning. And that he did so, this following Letter and Sonnet which were in the first year of his going to *Cambridge* sent his dear Mother for a New-years gift, may appear to be some testimony.

'But I fear the heat of my late *Ague* hath dried up those springs, by which Scholars say, the Muses use to take up their habitations. However, I need not their help, to reprove the vanity of those many Love-poems, that are daily writ and consecrated to *Venus*; nor to bewail that so few are writ, that look towards *God* and *Heaven*. For my own part, my meaning (*dear Mother*) is in these Sonnets, to declare my resolution to be, that my poor Abilities in *Poetry* shall be all, and ever consecrated to Gods glory; and I beg you to receive this as one testimony.

> *My God, where is that ancient heat towards thee,*
>   *Wherewith whole showls of* Martyrs *once did burn,*
> *Besides their other flames? Doth Poetry*
>   *Wear* Venus *Livery? only serve her turn?*
> *Why are not* Sonnets *made of thee? and layes*
>   *Vpon thine Altar burnt? Cannot thy love*
> *Heighten a spirit to sound out thy praise*
> *As well as any she? Cannot thy* Dove
> *Out-strip their* Cupid *easily in flight?*
>   *Or, since thy ways are deep, and still the same*
>   *Will not a verse run smooth that bears thy name!*
> *Why doth that fire, which by thy power and might*
>   *Each breast does feel, no braver fuel choose*
>   *Than that, which one day,* Worms *may chance refuse.*
> *Sure Lord, there is enough in thee to dry*
>   *Oceans of* Ink; *for, as the Deluge did*
>   *Cover the Earth, so doth thy Majesty:*
> *Each cloud distils thy praise, and doth forbid*
> *Poets to turn it to another use.*
>   *Roses and* Lillies *speak thee; and to make*
>   *A pair of Cheeks of them, is thy abuse.*
> *Why should I* Womens *eyes for Chrystal take?*
> *Such poor invention burns in their low mind*
>   *Whose fire is wild, and doth not upward go*
>   *To praise, and, on thee Lord, some* Ink *bestow.*
> *Open the bones, and you shall nothing find*
>   *In the best* face *but* filth; *when Lord, in thee*
>   *The* beauty *lies, in the* discovery.   G. H.'

This was his resolution at the sending this Letter to his dear Mother; about which time, he was in the Seventeenth year of his Age.[1]

       [1] World's Classics ed., pp. 267–9.

This resolve to dedicate to the service of religion those talents with which most of his contemporaries were decorating other themes is more finely and maturely expressed in the poem *Jordan*:

> Who sayes that fictions onely and false hair
> Become a verse? Is there in truth no beautie?
> Is all good structure in a winding stair?
> May no lines passe, except they do their dutie
>   Not to a true, but painted chair?
>
> Is it no verse, except enchanted groves
> And sudden arbours shadow course-spunne lines?
> Must purling streams refresh a lovers loves?
> Must all be vail'd, while he that reades, divines,
>   Catching the sense at two removes?
>
> Shepherds are honest people; let them sing:
> Riddle who list, for me, and pull for Prime.
> I envie no mans nightingale or spring;
> Nor let them punish me with losse of ryme,
>   Who plainly say, *My God, My King.*[1]

Herbert quickly distinguished himself as a scholar, and in due course was elected a fellow of his college. From the beginning of his career it was his mother's wish that he should enter the priesthood, a wish in which her son, at first at any rate, seems to have cheerfully acquiesced; but as the years passed, more worldly interests and ambitions seem to have increased their claims on his attention, to have flourished for a time alongside of his original resolution, and then gradually to have suppressed it. The turning-point, no doubt, was his election, on January 21, 1619/20, to the Public Oratorship, a position generally recognized as a stepping-stone to court or state preferment, and which his predecessor, Sir Francis Nethersole, left to become Secretary of State. Of the stages in this conversion from religious to secular ambitions Walton tells us nothing, and our only other records of these years at Cambridge are a few letters which Walton printed as an appendix to his *Life*. The earliest of these, written in 1618, is to Herbert's father-in-law Sir John Danvers, requesting more money to buy books. Its tone is sober and studious, but Walton's remark that 'if during this time he exprest any Error, it was, that he kept himself too much retir'd, and at too great a distance with all his inferiours: and his cloaths seem'd to

[1] *The Temple*, 1633, p. 48.

prove, that he put too great a value on his parts and Parent-
age'[1] may perhaps justify a suspicion that if the money re-
quested was supplied it did not all go to the booksellers. The
letter gives an interesting picture of Herbert, and is worth
quoting in full.

Sir,
    I Dare no longer be silent, least while I think I am modest,
I wrong both my self, and also the confidence my Friends have
in me, wherefore I will open my case unto you, which I think
deserves the reading at the least; and it is this, I want Books
extreamly; You know Sir, how I am now setting foot into
Divinity, to lay the platform of my future life, and shall I then
be fain always to borrow Books, and build on anothers foundation? What Tradesman is there who will set up without his Tools?
Pardon my boldness Sir, it is a most serious Case, nor can I
write coldly in that, wherein consisteth the making good of my
former education, of obeying that Spirit which hath guided me
hitherto, and of atchieving my (I dare say) holy ends. This
also is aggravated, in that I apprehend what my Friends would
have been forward to say, if I had taken ill courses, *Follow your
Book, and you shall want nothing*: You know Sir, it is their
ordinary speech, and now let them make it good; for, since,
I hope, I have not deceived their expectation, let not them
deceive mine: But perhaps they will say, you are sickly, you
must not study too hard; it is true (God knows) I am weak, yet
not so, but that every day, I may step one step towards my
journies end; and I love my friends so well, as that if all things
proved not well, I had rather the fault should lie on me, than
on them; but they will object again, What becomes of your
Annuity? Sir, if there be any truth in me, I find it little enough
to keep me in health. You know I was sick last Vacation,
neither am I yet recovered, so that I am fain ever and anon,
to buy somewhat tending towards my health, for infirmities are
both painful and costly. Now this *Lent* I am forbid utterly to
eat any Fish, so that I am fain to dyet in my Chamber at mine
own cost; for in our publick Halls, you know, is nothing but
Fish and Whit-meats: Out of *Lent* also, twice a Week, on
Fridays and *Saturdays*, I must do so, which yet sometimes I fast.
Sometimes also I ride to *New-Market*, and there lie a day or
two for fresh Air; all which tend to avoiding of costlier matters,
if I should fall absolutely sick: I protest and vow, I even study
Thrift, and yet I am scarce able with much ado to make one
half years allowance, shake hands with the other: And yet if
a Book of four or five Shillings, come in my way, I buy it,
though I fast for it; yea, sometimes of Ten Shillings: But, alas

    [1] World's Classics ed., p. 270.

Sir, what is that to those infinite Volumes of Divinity, which yet every day swell, and grow bigger. Noble Sir, pardon my boldness, and consider but these three things. First, the Bulk of Divinity. Secondly, the time when I desire this (which is now, when I must lay the foundation of my whole life). Thirdly, what I desire, and to what end, not vain pleasures, nor to a vain end. If then, Sir, there be any course, either by engaging my future Annuity, or any other way, I desire you, Sir, to be my Mediator to them in my behalf.

Now I write to you, Sir, because to you I have ever opened my heart; and have reason, by the Patents of your perpetual favour to do so still, for I am sure you love

March 18. 1617.   *Your faithfullest Servant,*
Trin. Coll.   GEORGE HERBERT.[1]

No doubt Herbert caught eagerly at what seemed an opportunity of escaping from this difficult and rather humiliating position into an ampler and more exciting way of life. In the next letter, written evidently in 1619, he requests Sir John Danvers to convey to Sir Francis Nethersole, now Secretary of State, a letter from the Master of Trinity recommending Herbert as a candidate for the Oratorship. The enthusiasm with which he speaks of the position suggests that Walton has laid too much emphasis on the studious and saintly aspect of his early years at Cambridge—that indeed, the 'holy Mr. Herbert' of Bemerton has cast a kind of reflected light back upon those years; for up to this point in Walton's biography that little touch about the fine clothes is the only hint of an aspect of the young man's character which is revealed in the following passage:

> The Orators place [he tells Sir John Danvers] (that you may understand what it is) is the finest place in the University, though not the gainfullest; yet that will be about 30 l. *per an.* but the commodiousness is beyond the Revenue; for the Orator writes all the University Letters, makes all the Orations, be it to King, Prince, or whatever comes to the University; to requite these pains, he takes place next the Doctors, is at all their Assemblies and Meetings, and sits above the Proctors, is Regent or Non-regent at his pleasure, and such like Gaynesses, which will please a young man well.[2]

Nevertheless Herbert seems still to have retained, though perhaps rather more vaguely and faintly, his resolution of entering the Church; for when he learns that Sir Francis

[1] World's Classics ed., pp. 328–9.   [2] World's Classics ed., p. 330.

Nethersole fears that the Oratorship may distract him from this purpose, he takes pains, in a letter to Sir John Danvers, to allay the suspicion:

Sir,

    I understand by Sir *Francis Nethersols* Letter that he fears I have not fully resolved of the matter, since this place being civil may divert me too much from Divinity, at which, not without cause, he thinks, I aim; but I have wrote him back, that this dignity, hath no such earthiness in it, but it may very well be joined with Heaven; or if it had to others, yet to me it should not, for ought I yet knew; and therefore I desire him to send me a direct answer in his next Letter.[1]

However, after he had been elected to the Oratorship, and, in contrast to his former retired and often embarrassing position, had enjoyed public admiration and court favour, Sir Francis Nethersole's fears were justified, and the office being civil, Herbert's ambitions became civil too. Walton, as I have said, does not record the stages of this conversion, but resumes his narrative after it had taken place.

    At this time of being *Orator*, he had learnt to understand the *Italian, Spanish*, and *French* Tongues very perfectly; hoping that as his Predecessors, so he might in time attain the place of a *Secretary of State*, he being at that time very high in the Kings favour; and not meanly valued and lov'd by the most eminent and most powerful of the Court-Nobility: This, and the love of a Court-conversation mixt with a laudible ambition to be something more than he then was, drew him often from *Cambridge* to attend the *King* wheresoever the Court was, who then gave him a *Sine Cure*, which fell into his Majesties disposal, I think, by the death of the Bishop of St. *Asaph*. It was the same, that Queen *Elizabeth* had formerly given to her Favourite Sir *Philip Sidney*; and valued to be worth an hundred and twenty pound *per Annum*. With this, and his Annuity, and the advantage of his Colledge, and of his Oratorship, he enjoyed his gentile humor for cloaths, and Court-like company, and seldom look'd towards *Cambridge*, unless the King were there, but then he never fail'd; and, at other times, left the manage of his Orators place, to his learned friend Mr. *Herbert Thorndike*, who is now Prebend of *Westminster*.

    I may not omit to tell, that he had often design'd to leave the University, and decline all Study, which he thought did impair his health; for he had a body apt to a *Consumption*, and to *Fevers*, and other infirmities which he judg'd were increas'd by his

[1] World's Classics ed., p. 332.

Studies; for he would often say, 'He had too thoughtful a Wit: a Wit, like a Pen-knife in too narrow a sheath, too sharp for his Body:' But his Mother would by no means allow him to leave the University, or to travel; and, though he inclin'd very much to both, yet he would by no means satisfie his own desires at so dear a rate, as to prove an undutiful Son to so affectionate a Mother; but did always submit to her wisdom. . . .

In this time of Mr. Herberts attendance and expectation of some good occasion to remove from *Cambridge*, to Court; God, in whom there is an unseen Chain of Causes, did in a short time put an end to the lives of two of his most obliging and most powerful friends, *Lodowick* Duke of *Richmond*, and *James* Marquess of Hamilton; and not long after him King *James* died also, and with them, all Mr. *Herbert's* Court-hopes: So that he presently betook himself to a Retreat from *London*, to a Friend in *Kent*, where he liv'd very privately, and was such a lover of solitariness, as was judg'd to impair his health, more then his Study had done. In this time of Retirement, he had many Conflicts with himself, Whether he should return to the painted pleasures of a Court-life, or betake himself to a study of Divinity, and enter into Sacred Orders? (to which his dear Mother had often persuaded him.) These were such Conflicts, as they only can know, that have endur'd them; for ambitious Desires, and the outward Glory of this World, are not easily laid aside; but, at last, God inclin'd him to put on a resolution to serve at his Altar.[1]

In 1626 he was ordained Deacon and made Prebendary of Leighton Ecclesia, near Huntingdon. The first duty he set himself was the collection of funds to rebuild Leighton church, and in the course of this work he seems for the first time to have renewed a slight and early acquaintance with the celebrated Nicholas Ferrar, who with his family and some relatives had established a strict religious community at Little Gidding, only five miles from Leighton, and who may have exercised some considerable influence on Herbert's final decision. For, although Walton does not say so, his narrative seems to imply that the crisis which led Herbert to accept minor orders and the Prebend of Leighton was followed by yet another period of doubt and irresolution. In the same year, 1626,[2] he was threatened with consumption, and to try the effect of a change of air he left Cambridge and resided with his brother,

---

[1] World's Classics ed., pp. 274–7.
[2] Walton (p. 284) says '1629', but its place in the narrative and Walton's statement that the illness occurred in 'the 34th year of his Age' makes it almost certain that the 9 represents a turned 6.

Sir Henry Herbert, in Essex, and with Lord Danvers in Wilt-
shire. His mother, whose influence on him had been great
and whose desire that he should enter the priesthood had been
consistent, died in 1628, in which year Herbert resigned the
Oratorship; and a year later 'he declar'd his resolution both
to marry, and to enter into the Sacred Orders of Priesthood'.
A wife was found for him in the daughter of one of his friends,
and shortly after his marriage his kinsman, Philip, Earl of
Pembroke, obtained the King's permission to present him
with the Rectorship of Bemerton, near Salisbury.

But though Mr. *Herbert* had formerly put on a resolution for
the Clergy: yet, at receiving this presentation, the apprehension
of the last great Account that he was to make for the Cure of
so many Souls, made him fast and pray often, and consider,
for not less than a month: in which time he had some resolutions to decline both the Priesthood, and that Living. And in
this time of considering, *He endur'd* (as he would often say)
*such spiritual Conflicts, as none can think, but only those that have
endur'd them.*[1]

He was instituted to the Rectorship on April 26, 1630, and
five months later was ordained priest.

When at his Induction he was shut into *Bemerton* Church,
being left there alone to Toll the Bell, (as the Law requires
him:) he staid so much longer than an ordinary time, before
he return'd to those Friends that staid expecting him at the
Church-door, that his Friend, Mr. *Woodnot*, look'd in at the
Church-window, and saw him lie prostrate on the ground
before the Altar: at which time and place (as he after told Mr.
Woodnot) he set some Rules to himself, for the future manage of
his life; and then and there made a vow, to labour to keep them.
And the same night that he had his Induction, he said to Mr.
*Woodnot, I now look back upon my aspiring thoughts, and think my
self more happy than if I had attain'd what then I so ambitiously
thirsted for: And, I can now behold the Court with an impartial Eye,
and see plainly, that it is made up of Fraud, and Titles, and Flattery,
and many other such empty, imaginary painted Pleasures: Pleasures,
that are so empty, as not to satisfy when they are enjoy'd; but in God and
his service, is a fulness of all joy and pleasure, and no satiety: And
I will now use all my endeavours to bring my Relations and Dependents
to a love and relyance on him, who never fails those that trust him.
But above all, I will be sure to live well, because the vertuous life of a
Clergyman, is the most powerful eloquence to persuade all that see it, to
reverence and love, and at least, to desire to live like him. And this I will*

[1] World's Classics ed., p. 287.

do, because I know we live in an Age that hath more need of good examples, than precepts. *And I beseech that God, who hath honour'd me so much as to call me to serve him at his Altar: that as by his special grace he hath put into my heart these good desires, and resolutions: so, he will by his assisting grace give me ghostly strength to bring the same to good effect: and I beseech him that my humble and charitable life may so win upon others, as to bring glory to my* JESUS, whom I have this day taken to be my Master and Governour; *and I am so proud of his service, that I will alwaies observe, and obey, and do his Will; and alwaies call him* Jesus my Master, *and I will always contemn my birth, or any title or dignity that can be conferr'd upon me, when I shall compare them with my title of being a* Priest, *and serving at the* Altar *of* Jesus my Master.[1]

From Walton's beautiful account of Herbert's example and influence a few short extracts must suffice.

And for the time of his appearing [in the church], it was strictly at the Canonical hours of 10 and 4; and then and there, he lifted up pure and charitable hands to God in the midst of the Congregation. And he would joy to have spent that time in that place, where the honour of his *Master Jesus* dwelleth; and there, by that inward devotion which he testified constantly by an humble behaviour, and visible adoration, he, like *Josua* brought not only *his own Houshold thus to serve the Lord*; but brought most of his Parishioners, and many Gentlemen in the Neighbourhood, constantly to make a part of his Congregation twice a day; and some of the meaner sort of his Parish, did so love and reverence Mr. *Herbert*, that they would let their Plow rest when Mr. *Herberts Saints-Bell* rung to Prayers, that they might also offer their devotions to God with him: and would then return back to their Plow. And his most holy life was such, that it begot such reverence to God, and to him, that they thought themselves the happier, when they carried Mr. *Herberts* blessing back with them to their labour. . . .

His chiefest recreation was Musick, in which heavenly Art he was a most excellent Master, and did himself compose many *divine Hymns* and *Anthems*, which he set and sung to his *Lute* or *Viol*; and, though he was a lover of retiredness, yet his love to *Musick* was such, that he went usually twice every week on certain appointed days, to the *Cathedral Church* in *Salisbury*; and at his return would say, *That his time spent in Prayer, and Cathedral Musick, elevated his Soul, and was his Heaven upon Earth*: But before his return thence to *Bemerton*, he would usually sing and play his part, at an appointed private Musick-meeting; and, to justifie this practice, he would often say, *Religion does not banish mirth, but only moderates, and sets rules to it.*

[1] World's Classics ed., pp. 289–90.

And as his desire to enjoy *his Heaven upon Earth*, drew him twice every week to *Salisbury*, so his walks thither, were the occasion of many happy accidents to others: of which I will mention some few. . . .

In another walk to *Salisbury*, he saw a poor man, with a poorer horse, that was fall'n under his Load; they were both in distress, and needed present help; which Mr. *Herbert* perceiving, put off his Canonical Coat, and help'd the poor man to unload, and after, to load his horse: The poor man blest him for it: and he blest the poor man; and was so like the *good Samaritan*, that he gave him money to refresh both himself and his horse; and told him, *That if he lov'd himself, he should be merciful to his Beast.* —Thus he left the poor man, and at his coming to his musical friends at *Salisbury*, they began to wonder that Mr. *George Herbert* which us'd to be so trim and clean, came into that company so soyl'd and discompos'd; but he told them the occasion: And when one of the company told him, *He had disparag'd himself by so dirty an employment;* his answer was, *That the thought of what he had done, would prove Musick to him at Midnight; and that the omission of it, would have upbraided and made discord in his Conscience, whensoever he should pass by that place; for, if I be bound to pray for all that be in distress, I am sure that I am bound so far as it is in my power to practise what I pray for. And though I do not wish for the like occasion every day, yet let me tell you, I would not willingly pass one day of my life without comforting a sad soul, or shewing mercy; and I praise God for this occasion:* And now let's tune our Instruments.[1]

He only remained three years in the calling which he entered after so many conflicts and hesitations, for he died in 1633, before he had completed his fortieth year. 'Thus he liv'd, and thus he dy'd like a Saint, unspotted of the World, full of Alms-deeds, full of Humility, and all the examples of a vertuous life.'

II

Before proceeding to a study of Herbert's poetry it is desirable to form the clearest possible conception of his character as a whole; for as I have already hinted, certain important traits in his character are insufficiently emphasized by Walton and are of course completely absent from the conventional portrait, that portrait which has prevented so many readers of Herbert's poetry from seeing what is really there. The demand that poetry should be self-explanatory and capable of producing its full effect independently of biographical or

[1] World's Classics ed., pp. 302–5.

historical comment, is one which, though fundamentally sound, requires considerable qualification. The purpose of a poem, considered as something offered by the author to the public, is to enable the reader to recreate in himself the experience in and out of which it was born—a purpose which, it seems clear, can never be completely realized, since the possibility of its realization depends on what must always be relative, the sensitiveness and sympathy of the reader, and, in some measure, the range and nature of his own experience. It seems foolish therefore to neglect or to reject whatever may increase sensitiveness and sympathy or supply deficiencies in experience. And although in the last analysis all poetry is universal, it is permissible to distinguish between poetry which starts from a basis of very general and widely shared experience, and poetry which starts from an experience that may be very personal and peculiar. The second kind of poetry may often be quite as valuable as the first, the region of reality which it finally illuminates and interprets may be equally extensive and important, but the starting-point may be more difficult to reach, and perhaps many readers can only reach it after a careful study of the poet's life, and after sharing the experience of readers and critics who have already established communication. And with such poetry it is very necessary to begin at the beginning, at the true starting-point; otherwise much that is beautiful and significant will be unperceived and much that seems clear will be only half-understood.

In the first place, then, it must be insisted that Herbert's emotional nature was strong and complex. His brother Lord Herbert says of him that

> He was not exempt from passion and choler, being infirmities to which all our race is subject; but that excepted, without reproach in his actions.

Energy and resolution were spiritual qualities to which he attached great importance, as may be seen in the following stanzas from the *Church-porch*:

> Art thou a Magistrate? then be severe:
> If studious; copie fair, what time hath blurr'd;
> Redeem truth from his jawes: if souldier,
> Chase brave employments with a naked sword
>   Throughout the world. Fool not: for all may have,
>   If they dare try, a glorious life, or grave. . . .

When thou dost purpose ought, (within thy power)
Be sure to doe it, though it be but small:
Constancie knits the bones, and makes us stowre,
When wanton pleasures beckon us to thrall.
    Who breaks his own bond, forfeiteth himself:
    What nature made a ship, he makes a shelf. . . .

Let thy minde still be bent, still plotting where,
And when, and how the businesse may be done.
Slacknesse breeds worms; but the sure traveller,
Though he alight sometimes, still goeth on.
    Active and stirring spirits live alone. [i.e. only]
    Write on the others, Here lies such a one.[1]

Many interesting traits of character are revealed in the
little book *The Country Parson,* first published in 1652, but
which Herbert completed in 1632, and of which he says in a
short preface:

> I have resolved to set down the Form and Character of a
> true Pastour, that I may have a Mark to aim at: which also
> I will set as high as I can, since hee shoots higher that threatens
> the Moon, then hee that aims at a Tree.

It was long before the lower clergy enjoyed the respect and
social position which are accorded to them to-day. Herbert
speaks of 'the generall ignominy which is cast upon the profession'; Donne in his lines *To Mr.* Tilman *after he had taken
orders* exclaims:

> Why doth the foolish world scorne that profession,
> Whose joyes passe speech? Why do they think unfit
> That Gentry should joyne families with it?

In 1670 John Eachard inquired into 'The Grounds and
Occasions of the Contempt of the Clergy and Religion'; and
it must have occurred to readers of Fielding that the slight
consideration accorded to Parson Adams was not uncon-
nected with the prevalence of Parson Trullibers. It was
not unnatural therefore that when a court friend heard of
Herbert's intention of entering the Church he should have
tried to dissuade him from it 'as too mean an employment and
too much below his birth, and the excellent abilities and
endowments of his mind'. Herbert's reply was:

> It hath been formerly judged that the Domestick Servants
> of the King of Heaven, should be of the noblest Families on
> Earth: and, though the iniquity of the late Times have made

[1] *The Temple,* 1633, pp. 4, 5, 12.

Clergy-men meanly valued, and the sacred name of *Priest* contemptible; yet I will labour to make it honourable, by consecrating all my learning, and all my poor abilities, to advance the glory of that God that gave them; knowing, that I can never do too much for him, that hath done so much for me, as to make me a Christian. And I will labour to be like my Saviour, by making Humility lovely in the eyes of all men, and by following the merciful and meek example of my *dear Jesus*.[1]

This humility, mercy, and meekness are apparent on almost every page of the *Country Parson*, but there are hints too of that aristocracy and independence of spirit which were no less characteristic of the author.

Those that live in Noble Houses are called Chaplains, whose duty and obligation being the same to the Houses they live in, as a Parsons to his Parish, in describing the one (which is indeed the bent of my Discourse) the other will be manifest. Let not Chaplains think themselves so free, as *many of them do*, and because they have different Names, think their Office different. Doubtlesse they are Parsons of the families they live in, and are entertained to that end, either by an open, or implicite Covenant. Before they are in Orders, they may be received for Companions, or discoursers; but after a man is once Minister, he cannot agree to come into any house, where he shall not exercise what he is, unlesse he forsake his plough, and look back. Wherfore they are not to be over-submissive, and base, but to keep up with the Lord and Lady of the house, and to preserve a boldness with them and all, even so farre as reproofe to their very face, when occasion cals, but seasonably and discreetly. They who do not thus, while they remember their earthly Lord, do much forget their heavenly; they wrong the Priesthood, neglect their duty, and shall be so farre from that which they seek with their over-submissivenesse, and cringings, that they shall ever be despised. They who for the hope of promotion neglect any necessary admonition, or reproofe, sell (with Judas) their Lord and Master.[2]

If there be any of the gentry or nobility of the Parish, who sometimes make it a piece of state not to come at the beginning of service with their poor neighbours, but at mid-prayers, both to their own loss, and of theirs also who gaze upon them when they come in, and neglect the present service of God, he by no means suffers it, but after divers gentle admonitions, if they persevere, he causes them to be presented [i.e. to be brought before the Bishop or Archdeacon for an offence against the

<hr>

[1] World's Classics ed., p. 277.   [2] Chap. ii, 1652, pp. 4–6.

Canons]: or if the poor Churchwardens be affrighted with their greatness, notwithstanding his instruction that they ought not to be so, but even to let the world sinke, so they do their duty; he presents them himself, only protesting to them, that not any ill will draws him to it, but the debt and obligation of his calling, being to obey God rather then men.[1]

Aristocratic too in the highest sense—perhaps slightly reminiscent of Milton—is the following passage:

The Parsons yea is yea, and nay nay; and his apparrell plaine, but reverend, and clean, without spots, or dust, or smell; the purity of his mind breaking out, and dilating it selfe even to his body, cloaths, and habitation.[2]

Indeed Oley remarked in his Preface to the *Country Parson* that he had not 'offerred to describe that person of his, which afforded so unusuall a contesseration of Elegancies, and set of Rarities to the Beholder'.[3]

In his poem *The British Church* Herbert expresses his loyalty and admiration for the Church of England, contrasting it favourably with those of Rome and Geneva:

> I joy, dear Mother, when I view
> Thy perfect lineaments, and hue
>   Both sweet and bright.
>
> Beautie in thee takes up her place,
> And dates her letters from thy face,
>   When she doth write.
>
> A fine aspect in fit array,
> Neither too mean, nor yet too gay,
>   Shows who is best.
>
> Outlandish looks may not compare:
> For all they either painted are,
>   Or else undrest.
>
> She on the hills which wantonly
> Allureth all, in hope to be
>   By her preferr'd,
>
> Hath kiss'd so long her painted shrines,
> That ev'n her face by kissing shines,
>   For her reward.
>
> She in the valley is so shie
> Of dressing, that her hair doth lie
>   About her eares:

[1] Chap. vi, p. 20.   [2] Chap. iii, p. 9.   [3] C5.

While she avoids her neighbours pride,
She wholly goes on th'other side,
    And nothing wears.

But dearest Mother, (what those misse)
The mean thy praise and glorie is,
    And long may be.

Blessed be God, whose love it was
To double-moat thee with his grace,
    And none but thee.[1]

It is easy to read into this poem the spirit of Tennyson in a complacent and anti-foreign mood, to exhibit it as a specimen of the mild Herbert's simple faith, and perhaps to add a few remarks on the rectory lawn and the *Christian Year*—easy, but not very intelligent. It is true that Herbert had not Donne's curious interest in theological subtleties and that he does not seem to have been assailed by speculative doubts:

> Curiosity in prying into high speculative and unprofitable questions, is another great stumbling block to the holinesse of Scholers,

he says in the *Country Parson*.[2] His attitude to religion is essentially practical, and holiness is the quality he demands in a sermon:

> By these and other means the Parson procures attention; but the character of his Sermon is Holiness; he is not witty, or learned, or eloquent, but Holy. A Character, that *Hermogenes* never dream'd of, and therefore he could give no precepts thereof. But it is gained first, by choosing texts of Devotion, not Controversie, moving and ravishing texts, whereof the Scriptures are full. Secondly, by dipping, and seasoning all our words and sentences in our hearts, before they come into our mouths, truly affecting, and cordially expressing all that we say; so that the auditors may plainly perceive that every word is hart-deep.[3]

> Judged by his devotion to the Church of England [says Palmer], by his hostility to her foes, and by his insistence on elaborate ritual, Herbert is a High Churchman; but there is no indication that he held the tenet distinctive of High Churchmanship, the belief that his ecclesiastical system had been designed and established by Christ. He never defends his position by maintaining for it an injunction of Christ or an Apostolic model. On the contrary, he employs tests much more verifiable.[4]

[1] 1633, p. 102.   [2] 1652, chap. ix, p. 36.   [3] Chap. vii, p. 24.
[4] *Life and Works of George Herbert*, Vol. i, p. 80.

He sees in the Church of England, in fact, an admirable instrument and organization for the promotion of holiness. In the *Country Parson*, after giving some rules for the furnishing of the Church, he concludes:

> And all this he doth, not as out of necessity, or as putting a holiness in the things, but as desiring to keep the middle way between superstition, and slovenliness, and as following the Apostles two great and admirable Rules in things of this nature: The first whereof is, *Let all things be done decently, and in order*: The second, *Let all things be done to edification*, 1 Cor. 14. For these two rules comprize and include the double object of our duty, God, and our neighbour; the first being for the honour of God; the second for the benefit of our neighbour. So that they excellently score out the way, and fully, and exactly contain, even in externall and indifferent things, what course is to be taken; and put them to shame, who deny the Scripture to be perfect.[1]

His defence of uniformity is on the same lines. Speaking of 'The Parson Catechizing', he says:

> He useth, and preferreth the ordinary Church-Catechism, partly for obedience to Authority, partly for uniformity sake, that the same common truths may be every where professed, especially since many remove from Parish to Parish, who like Christian Souldiers are to give the word, and to satisfie the Congregation by their Catholick answers.[2]

The outlines of his faith were simple perhaps—there is no trace of mysticism in his writings; but the service he practised and recommended was emphatically a reasonable one; and indeed in his insistence that religion must be reasonable, no less than in his broad-minded attitude to ceremonies and in his conviction that the final test of a religion must be the life and temper it produces, he is not only in the tradition of Hooker, but bears some resemblance to the Cambridge Platonists. Walton has told us how he tried to give his congregation a rational justification for every part of the Church ritual, and in the chapter 'The Parson Praying' we seem to see Herbert at work:

> Besides his example, he having often instructed his people how to carry themselves in divine service, exacts of them all possible reverence, by no means enduring either talking, or sleeping, or gazing, or leaning, or halfe-kneeling, or any undutifull behaviour in them, but causing them, when they sit,

---

[1] Chap. xiii, pp. 58–9.　　　　　　　　[2] Chap. xxi, p. 82.

or stand, or kneel, to do all in a strait, and steady posture, as attending to what is done in the Church, and every one, man and child, answering aloud both Amen, and all other answers, which are on the Clerks and peoples part to answer; which answers also are to be done not in a hudling, or slubbering fashion, gaping, or scratching the head, or spitting even in the midst of their answer, but gently and pausably, thinking what they say; so that while they answer, *As it was in the beginning* &c., they meditate as they speak, that God hath ever had his people, that have glorified him as wel as now, and that he shall have so for ever. And the like in other answers. This is that which the Apostle cals a reasonable service, Rom. 12. when we speak not as Parrats, without reason, or offer up such sacrifices as they did of old, which was of beasts devoyd of reason; but when we use our reason, and apply our powers to the service of him, that gives them.[1]

This passage may remind us of the existence of qualities in Herbert that have been too often overlooked—shrewd common-sense and humour. In the *Country Parson* they are no less evident than his charity and his essentially practical religion, and they often appear in his poetry, especially in the *Church-porch*, a poem which Herbert prefixed to *The Temple* and which contains some seventy stanzas offering rules and counsels to those who would follow the Christian life. It is far from being the advice of a recluse, or of a spiritual director concerned only with the inner life: we hear the courtier and the man of the world as well as the Rector of Bemerton.

Cheap sins:

> The cheapest sinnes most dearely punisht are;
> Because to shun them also is so cheap:
> For we have wit to mark them, and to spare.
> O crumble not away thy souls fair heap.
> > If thou wilt die, the gates of hell are broad:
> > Pride and full sinnes have made the way a road.[2]

The use of solitude:

> By all means use sometimes to be alone.
> Salute thy self: see what thy soul doth wear.
> Dare to look in thy chest; for 'tis thine own:
> And tumble up and down what thou find'st there.
> > Who cannot rest till he good fellows finde,
> > He breaks up house, turns out of doores his minde.[3]

---

[1] Chap. vi, pp. 18–20. Walton tells us that 'if he were at any time too zealous in his Sermons, it was in reproving the indecencies of the peoples behaviour, in the time of Divine Service' (p. 301).

[2] *The Temple*, 1633, p. 3.   [3] Ibid., p. 6.

Conversation:

> Laugh not too much: the wittie man laughs least:
> For wit is newes onely to ignorance.
> Lesse at thine own things laugh; lest in the jest
> Thy person share, and the conceit advance.
> > Make not thy sport, abuses: for the fly
> > That feeds on dung, is coloured thereby.
>
> Pick out of mirth, like stones out of the ground,
> Profanenesse, filthinesse, abusivenesse.
> These are the scumme, with which coarse wits abound;
> The fine may spare these well, yet not go lesse.
> > All things are bigge with jest: nothing that's plain,
> > But may be wittie, if thou hast the vein. . . .
>
> Entice all neatly to what they know best;
> For so thou dost thy self and him a pleasure:
> (But a proud ignorance will lose his rest,
> Rather than shew his cards) steal from his treasure
> > What to ask further. Doubts well rais'd do lock
> > The speaker to thee, and preserve thy stock.[1]

Going to church:

> Resort to sermons, but to prayers most:
> Praying's the end of preaching. O be drest;
> Stay not for th'other pin: why thou hast lost
> A joy for it worth worlds. Thus hell doth jest
> > Away thy blessings, and extreamly flout thee,
> > Thy clothes being fast, but thy soul loose about thee.[2]

Later I shall have more to say about this peculiar humour of
Herbert's, which runs through almost all his poetry, giving a
rare human tenderness to his adoration and a saving sincerity
to his abnegation, in somewhat the same way as Sidney's
humour colours many of his finest sonnets to Stella, or as
Shakespeare's heroines, in the midst of their distresses, are
able to smile through their tears. Meanwhile here are two
further examples of its simpler and more obvious form:

> ### Giddinesse
>
> Oh, what a thing is man! how farre from power,
> > From settled peace and rest!
> He is some twentie sev'rall men at least
> > Each sev'rall houre.
>
> One while he counts of heav'n, as of his treasure:
> > But then a thought creeps in,
> And calls him coward, who for fear of sinne
> > Will lose a pleasure.

[1] *The Temple*, 1633, pp. 8–11.   [2] Ibid., p. 14.

Now he will sigh it out, and to the warres;
　　Now eat his bread in peace,
And snudge in quiet: now he scorns increase;
　　Now all day spares.

He builds a house, which quickly down must go,
　　As if a whirlwinde blew
And crusht the building: and it's partly true,
　　His minde is so.

O what a sight were Man, if his attires
　　Did alter with his minde;
And like a Dolphins skinne, his clothes combin'd
　　With his desires!

Surely if each one saw anothers heart
　　There would be no commerce,
No sale or bargain passe: all would disperse,
　　And live apart.

Lord, mend or rather make us: one creation
　　Will not suffice our turn:
Except thou make us dayly, we shall spurn
　　Our own Salvation.[1]

Divinitie

As men, for fear the starres should sleep and nod,
　　And trip at night, have spheres suppli'd;
As if a starre were duller then a clod,
　　Which knows his way without a guide:

Just so the other heav'n they also serve,
　　Divinities transcendent skie:
Which with the edge of wit they cut and carve.
　　Reason triumphs, and faith lies by.

Could not that wisdome, which first broacht the wine,
　　Have thicken'd it with definitions?
And jagg'd his seamlesse coat, had that been fine,
　　With curious questions and divisions?

But all the doctrine, which he taught and gave,
　　Was cleare as heav'n, from whence it came.
At least those beams of truth, which onely save,
　　Surpasse in brightnesse any flame.

Love God, and love your neighbour. Watch and pray.
　　Do as ye would be done unto.
O dark instructions; ev'n as dark as day!
　　Who can these Gordian knots undo?

[1] *The Temple,* 1633, p. 119.

But he doth bid us take his bloud for wine.
  Bid what he please; yet I am sure,
To take and taste what he doth there designe,
  Is all that saves, and not obscure.

Then burn thy Epicycles, foolish man;
  Break all thy spheres, and save thy head.
Faith needs no staffe of flesh, but stoutly can
  To heav'n alone both go, and leade.[1]

Nevertheless the habitual tone of Herbert's mind seems to
have been grave and melancholy.

> The Countrey Parson [he says] is generally sad, because he
> knows nothing but the Crosse of Christ, his minde being defixed
> on, and with those nailes wherewith his Master was: or if he
> have any leisure to look off from thence, he meets continually
> with two most sad spectacles, Sin, and Misery; God dishonoured
> every day, and man afflicted.[2]

And here, since it is intimately connected with his character,
is the place to consider briefly the question of the date of
Herbert's poetry. The external evidence is slight. Walton
tells us that the two sonnets to his mother expressing his resolve
to become a religious poet were written in his seventeenth
year, i.e. in 1610. The next date is 1625, when Bacon,
dedicating to him *A Translation of Certain Psalms into English
Verse*, says :'Besides, it being my manner for dedications to
choose those that I hold most fit for the argument, I thought
that in respect of divinity and poesy met—whereof the one is
the matter, the other the stile of this little writing—I could
not make fitter choice'—words which seem to imply that
already Herbert had attained some reputation as a poet. Our
only other evidence is that of the poems themselves, of which
there are two manuscripts, that in the Bodleian, from
which the first edition of *The Temple* was printed in 1633 and
which we may perhaps assume to have been the one sent by
Herbert from his death-bed to Nicholas Ferrar, and that in
Dr. Williams's Library, which contains only 73 of the 169
poems in the Bodleian MS., many of them representing earlier
versions which were subsequently corrected, improved, and
in some cases completely re-written. A comparison of the
two manuscripts teaches us much about Herbert's careful
artistry, but it tells us nothing about the date of the poems or
of the order in which they were written; for while it is obvious

----

[1] *The Temple*, 1633, p. 127.   [2] Chap. xxvii, p. 115.

that many of the 73 poems in the Williams MS. are earlier than the corresponding versions in the Bodleian, it is impossible to decide *how much* earlier, and it is also impossible to decide whether the remaining 96 poems in the Bodleian MS. were written earlier or later than those of which we possess two versions. Partly because he had not sufficiently convinced himself of these facts and partly because he thought that he had detected certain internal evidences of date, Palmer was encouraged to adopt a fanciful chronological arrangement of the poems, as illustrating a spiritual progress from doubt and conflict to settled faith—the one defect in an otherwise admirable edition. This view of *The Temple* as the record of a steady progress from doubt to faith, from hesitation to settled resolution, from conflict to final victory seems to me consistent neither with the poems themselves, with the conception I have been able to form of Herbert's character, nor with the words in which, according to Walton, he commended the manuscript into the hands of Nicholas Ferrar:

> *Sir, I pray deliver this little Book to my dear brother* Farrer, *and tell him, he shall find in it a picture of the many spiritual Conflicts that have past betwixt God and my Soul, before I could subject mine to the will of* Jesus my Master: *in whose service I have now found perfect freedom; desire him to read it: and then, if he can think it may turn to the advantage of any dejected poor Soul, let it be made publick: if not, let him burn it: for* I and it, are less than the least of God's mercies.[1]

The Temple is best regarded not as the record of a progress, but, in Herbert's own words, as 'a picture of *many* spiritual conflicts'—conflicts which, we may suspect, continued until the last days of his life, when he was at last able to withdraw into the 'now' of perfect freedom.

The Countrey Parson knows, that there is a double state of a Christian even in this Life, the one military, the other peaceable. The military is, when we are assaulted with temptations either from within or from without. The Peaceable is, when the Divell for a time leaves us, as he did our Saviour, and the Angels minister to us their owne food, even joy, and peace; and comfort in the holy Ghost. These two states were in our Saviour, not only in the beginning of his preaching, but afterwards also, as *Mat.* 22, 35. He was tempted: And *Luke* 10, 21. He rejoyced in Spirit: And they must be likewise in all that are his.[2]

---

[1] World's Classics ed., p. 314.   [2] Chap. xxxiv, pp. 147–8.

In these words Herbert has left us a picture of his own soul which almost makes further commentary superfluous, and which forms the best possible introduction to his poems.

III

The technical excellence and originality of his poetry are qualities for which Herbert has rarely received due credit. Its metrical variety alone is remarkable, for it has been estimated that, of his 169 poems, 116 are written in metres which are not repeated. Still more important is his mastery of form. He is a poet of poems and not, like so many of his contemporaries and predecessors, of passages. Only 10 of his poems contain more than 50 lines; almost every one of them has a definite beginning, middle, and end, and is confined to the expression and development of a single idea or feeling.

Herbert's verse has this in common with Donne's and with that of the best of Donne's followers, that it is free from the conventional ornaments of poetry and that in rhythm and accent it approaches and suggests the tone of impassioned conversation. Herbert too produces some of his most characteristic effects by means of contrast. He has not Donne's curious detached interest in ideas for their own sakes, and although there are exceptions, his similes are on the whole less ingenious and remote than Donne's; but he often achieves effects of novelty and surprise by the homeliness and familiarity of his epithets and imagery, by the contrast between the dignity of the subject and the homeliness of that with which it is compared or of the language in which it is described, like Donne in such phrases as 'Busie old foole, unruly Sunne', and 'Sawcy pedantique wretch'. This was a device which commended itself to Herbert not only as an artist but as a director of souls—experience had taught him its practical value; for in the *Country Parson* he suggests that in catechizing, when the respondent is puzzled, the parson should suggest the right answer by means of some familiar illustration:

> This is the skill, and doubtlesse the Holy Scripture intends thus much, when it condescends to the naming of a plough, a hatchet, a bushell, leaven, boyes piping and dancing; shewing that things of ordinary use are not only to serve in the way of drudgery, but to be washed, and cleansed, and serve for lights even of Heavenly Truths.[1]

[1] *Country Parson*, chap. xxi, p. 87.

And a new effect of freshness depending on contrast is provided by that gentle humour to which I have already alluded,
that trembling contiguity of smiles and tears which appears
in some of Sidney's sonnets and in some of Donne's love-poems,
but which in religious poetry is peculiar to Herbert.

IV

'. . . and tell him, he shall find in it a picture of the many
spiritual Conflicts that have past betwixt God and my Soul';
'. . . there is a double state of a Christian even in this Life, the
one military, the other peaceable. . . . These two states were
in our Saviour. . . . And they must be likewise in all that are
his.' The passages from which these words are taken form
the best introduction to a study of Herbert's poetry, which
we may begin with two poems in which the central problem,
the struggle to resign, is clearly stated. In the first he tries to
recognize in the various circumstances, especially in that of
his long residence at the University, which seem to be leading
him to the priesthood and withdrawing him from other ways
of life, the hand of Providence; and yet, conscious that other
ambitions, though dormant, are not yet suppressed, doubtful
whether he can achieve that singleness of heart which his
present course demands, he concludes with the passionate cry

> Ah my deare God! though I am clean forgot,
> Let me not love thee, if I love thee not.

In the second, having perhaps finally decided, he tests his
resolution and forces himself to look with clear eyes on the
renunciation of all that his choice involves.

Affliction

> When first thou didst entice to thee my heart,
>   I thought the service brave:
> So many joyes I writ down for my part,
>   Besides what I might have
> Out of my stock of naturall delights,
> Augmented with thy gracious benefits.
>
> I looked on thy furniture so fine,
>   And made it fine to me:
> Thy glorious household-stuffe did me entwine,
>   And 'tice me unto thee.
> Such starres I counted mine: both heav'n and earth
> Payd me my wages in a world of mirth.

What pleasures could I want, whose King I served?
    Where joyes my fellows were.
Thus argu'd into hopes, my thoughts reserved
    No place for grief or fear.
Therefore my sudden soul caught at the place,
And made her youth and fiercenesse seek thy face.

At first thou gav'st me milk and sweetnesses;
    I had my wish and way:
My dayes were straw'd with flow'rs and happinesse;
    There was no moneth but May.
But with my yeares sorrow did twist and grow,
And made a partie unawares for wo.

My flesh began unto my soul in pain,
    Sicknesses cleave my bones;
Consuming agues dwell in ev'ry vein,
    And tune my breath to grones.
Sorrow was all my soul; I scarce beleeved,
Till grief did tell me roundly, that I lived.

When I got health, thou took'st away my life,
    And more; for my friends die:
My mirth and edge was lost; a blunted knife
    Was of more use then I.
Thus thinne and lean without a fence or friend,
I was blown through with ev'ry storm and winde.

Whereas my birth and spirit rather took
    The way that takes the town;
Thou didst betray me to a lingring book,
    And wrap me in a gown.
I was entangled in the world of strife,
Before I had the power to change my life.

Yet, for I threatned oft the siege to raise,
    Not simpring all mine age,
Thou often didst with Academick praise
    Melt and dissolve my rage.
I took thy sweetened pill, till I came neare;
I could not go away, nor persevere.

Yet lest perchance I should too happie be
    In my unhappinesse,
Turning my purge to food, thou throwest me
    Into more sicknesses.
Thus doth thy power crosse-bias me, not making
Thine own gift good, yet me from my wayes taking.

Now I am here, what thou wilt do with me
    None of my books will show:
I reade, and sigh, and wish I were a tree;
    For sure then I should grow
To fruit or shade: at least some bird would trust
Her houshold to me, and I should be just.

Yet, though thou troublest me, I must be meek;
    In weaknesse must be stout.
Well, I will change the service, and go seek
    Some other master out.
Ah my deare God! though I am clean forgot,
Let me not love thee, if I love thee not.[1]

The Pearl. Matth. 13.

I know the wayes of learning; both the head
And pipes that feed the presse, and make it runne;
What reason hath from nature borrowed,
Or of it self, like a good huswife, spunne
In laws and policie; what the starres conspire,
What willing nature speaks, what forc'd by fire;
Both th'old discoveries, and the new-found seas,
The stock and surplus, cause and historie:
All these stand open, or I have the keyes:
                Yet I love thee.

I know the wayes of honour, what maintains
The quick returns of courtesie and wit:
In vies of favours whether partie gains,
When glorie swells the heart, and moldeth it
To all expressions both of hand and eye,
Which on the world a true-love knot may tie,
And bear the bundle, wheresoe're it goes:
How many drammes of spirit there must be
To sell my life unto my friends or foes:
                Yet I love thee.

I know the wayes of pleasure, the sweet strains,
The lullings and the relishes of it;
The propositions of hot bloud and brains;
What mirth and musick mean; what love and wit
Have done these twentie hundred yeares, and more:
I know the projects of unbridled store:
My stuffe is flesh, not brasse; my senses live,
And grumble oft, that they have more in me
Then he that curbs them, being but one to five:
                Yet I love thee.

[1] p. 38.

I know all these, and have them in my hand:
Therefore not sealed, but with open eyes
I flie to thee, and fully understand
Both the main sale, and the commodities;
And at what rate and price I have thy love;
With all the circumstances that may move:
Yet through the labyrinths, not my groveling wit,
But thy silk twist let down from heav'n to me,
Did both conduct and teach me, how by it
                              To climbe to thee.[1]

But even after the choice had been made the seeds of former
ambitions, the attractions of the world he had left and in which
he was so well qualified to shine, still distracted him, tempting
him to regret his decision and preventing that perfect resigna-
tion and purity of heart he would attain.

The Quip

The merrie world did on a day
With his train-bands and mates agree
To meet together, where I lay,
And all in sport to geere at me.

First, Beautie crept into a rose,
Which when I pluckt not, Sir, said she,
Tell me, I pray, Whose hands are those?
But thou shalt answer, Lord, for me.

Then Money came, and chinking still,
What tune is this, poore man? said he:
I heard in Musick you had skill.
But thou shalt answer, Lord, for me.

Then came brave Glorie puffing by
In silks that whistled, who but he?
He scarce allow'd me half an eie.
But thou shalt answer, Lord, for me.

Then came quick Wit and Conversation,
And he would needs a comfort be,
And, to be short, make an oration.
But thou shalt answer, Lord, for me.

Yet when the houre of thy designe
To answer these fine things shall come;
Speak not at large, say, I am thine:
And then they have their answer home.[2]

[1] p. 81.   [2] p. 103.

In this poem the mood is one of gentle melancholy touched by humour. *The Collar* is the record of a severer conflict; it has magnificent passion and dramatic force, and reveals that aspect of Herbert's nature which I have been at some pains to emphasize.

> I struck the board, and cry'd, No more.
> I will abroad.
> What? shall I ever sigh and pine?
> My lines and life are free; free as the rode,
> Loose as the winde, as large as store.
> Shall I be still in suit?
> Have I no harvest but a thorn
> To let me bloud, and not restore
> What I have lost with cordiall fruit?
> Sure there was wine
> Before my sighs did drie it: there was corn
> Before my tears did drown it.
> Is the yeare onely lost to me?
> Have I no bayes to crown it?
> No flowers, no garlands gay? all blasted?
> All wasted?
> Not so, my heart: but there is fruit,
> And thou hast hands.
> Recover all thy sigh-blown age
> On double pleasures: leave thy cold dispute
> Of what is fit and not,[1] forsake thy cage,
> Thy rope of sands,
> Which pettie thoughts have made, and made to thee
> Good cable, to enforce and draw,
> And be thy law,
> While thou didst wink and wouldst not see.
> Away; take heed:
> I will abroad.
> Call in thy deaths head there: tie up thy fears.
> He that forbears,
> To suit and serve his need,
> Deserves his load.
> But as I rav'd and grew more fierce and wilde
> At every word,
> Me thoughts I heard one calling, *Childe*:
> And I reply'd, *My Lord*.[2]

The sense of his own unworthiness engendered by this per-petually renewed struggle leads to the same kind of doubt as we have sometimes noticed in Donne—a doubt as to whether

---

[1] 1633: what is fit, and not   [2] p. 147.

his faith in Christ is strong enough to enable the vicarious
sacrifice to avail for him. The poems in which Donne expresses
this 'sinne of feare' usually end, not on a note of complete assurance, but with a prayer that his faith may be increased, that
Christ may put forth his grace: the two poems in which
Herbert has most perfectly expressed it end with the complete
subjugation of the doubt—love has the last word.

Dialogue

Sweetest Saviour, if my soul
　　Were but worth the having,
Quickly should I then controll
　　Any thought of waving.
But when all my care and pains
Cannot give the name of gains
To thy wretch so full of stains;
What delight or hope remains?

What (childe) is the ballance thine,
　　Thine the poise and measure?
If I say, Thou shalt be mine;
　　Finger not my treasure.
What the gains in having thee
Do amount to, onely he,
Who for man was sold, can see;
That transferr'd th'accounts to me.

But as I can see no merit,
　　Leading to this favour:
So the way to fit me for it,
　　Is beyond my savour.
As the reason then is thine;
So the way is none of mine:
I disclaim the whole designe:
Sinne disclaims and I resigne.

That is all, if that I could
　　Get without repining;
And my clay my creature would
　　Follow my resigning.
That as I did freely part
With my glorie and desert,
Left all joyes to feel all smart——
Ah! no more: thou break'st my heart.[1]

[1] p. 107.

Love

Love bade me welcome: yet my soul drew back,
      Guiltie of dust and sinne.
But quick-ey'd Love, observing me grow slack
      From my first entrance in,
Drew nearer to me, sweetly questioning,
      If I lack'd any thing.

A guest, I answer'd, worthy to be here:
      Love said, you shall be he.
I the unkinde, ungratefull? Ah my deare,
      I cannot look on thee.
Love took my hand, and smiling did reply,
      Who made the eyes but I?

Truth Lord, but I have marr'd them: let my shame
      Go where it doth deserve.
And know you not, sayes Love, who bore the blame?
      My deare, then I will serve.
You must sit down, sayes Love, and taste my meat:
      So I did sit and eat.[1]

Donne insists rather on the awfulness of God, Herbert rather
on his loving-kindnesses and tender mercies.

Discipline

      Throw away thy rod,
      Throw away thy wrath:
                O my God,
      Take the gentle path.

      For my hearts desire
      Unto thine is bent:
                I aspire
      To a full consent.

      Not a word or look
      I affect to own,
                But by book,
      And thy book alone.

      Though I fail, I weep:
      Though I halt in pace,
                Yet I creep
      To the throne of grace.

[1] p. 183.

Then let wrath remove;
Love will do the deed:
　　　　　　　For with love
Stonie hearts will bleed.

Love is swift of foot;
Love's a man of warre,
　　　　　　　And can shoot,
And can hit from farre.

Who can scape his bow?
That which wrought on thee,
　　　　　　　Brought thee low,
Needs must work on me.

Throw away thy rod;
Though man frailties hath,
　　　　　　　Thou art God:
Throw away thy wrath.[1]

Sighs and Grones

O do not use me
After my sinnes! look not on my desert,
But on thy glorie! then thou wilt reform
And not refuse me: for thou onely art
The mightie God, but I a sillie worm;
　　　　O do not bruise me!

O do not urge me!
For what account can thy ill steward make?
I have abus'd thy stock, destroy'd thy woods,
Suckt all thy magazens: my head did ake,
Till it found out how to consume thy goods:
　　　　O do not scourge me!

O do not blinde me!
I have deserv'd that an Egyptian night
Should thicken all my powers; because my lust
Hath still sow'd fig-leaves to exclude thy light:
But I am frailtie, and already dust:
　　　　O do not grinde me!

O do not fill me
With the turn'd viall of thy bitter wrath!
For thou hast other vessels full of bloud,
A part whereof my Saviour empti'd hath,
Ev'n unto death: since he di'd for my good,
　　　　O do not kill me!

[1] p. 173.

But O reprieve me!
For thou hast *life* and *death* at thy command;
Thou art both *Judge* and *Saviour*, *feast*, and *rod*,
Cordiall and *Corrosive*: put not thy hand
Into the bitter box; but O my God,
My God, relieve me![1]

The peace which passeth all understanding seems to have
been granted to Herbert more often than to Donne; yet with
Herbert too it was by no means a perpetual possession. He
is continually striving for it, praying for it, as in that poem
where he compares himself to Aaron, who when he is 'drest',
that is, at peace with himself, can bring peace to his people
and discharge the duties of practical religion. It is one of the
most beautiful and characteristic of Herbert's poems, with
the speaking tone of its verse and the gentle smile at its close.

Aaron

Holinesse on the head,
Light and perfections on the breast,
Harmonious bells below, raising the dead
To leade them unto life and rest.
Thus are true Aarons drest.

Profaneness in my head,
Defects and darknesse in my breast,
A noise of passions ringing me for dead
Unto a place where is no rest.
Poore priest thus am I drest.

Onely another head
I have, another heart and breast,
Another musick, making live not dead,
Without whom I could have no rest:
In him I am well drest.

Christ is my onely head,
My alone onely heart and breast,
My onely musick, striking me ev'n dead;
That to the old man I may rest,
And be in him new drest.

So holy in my head,
Perfect and light in my deare breast,
My doctrine tun'd by Christ, (who is not dead,
But lives in me while I do rest)
Come people; Aaron's drest.[2]

[1] p. 75.   [2] p. 168.

In *Justice* he ponders on this continual alternation between faith and doubt, between confidence in salvation and fear of reprobation, and decides that God has chosen this means to strengthen his faith and to keep it fervid and alive:

> I cannot skill of these thy wayes.
> *Lord, thou didst make me, yet thou woundest me;*
> *Lord, thou dost wound me, yet thou dost relieve me:*
> *Lord, thou relievest, yet I die by thee:*
> *Lord, thou dost kill me, yet thou dost reprieve me.*
>
> But when I mark my life and praise,
> Thy justice me most fitly payes:
> *For, I do praise thee, yet I praise thee not:*
> *My prayers mean thee, yet my prayers stray:*
> *I would do well, yet sinne the hand hath got:*
> *My soul doth love thee, yet it loves delay.*
> I cannot skill of these my wayes.[1]

And in the famous poem *The Pulley* he suggests that the very restlessness of man is part of a divine scheme intended to cause him to return to Him with whom there is no variableness neither shadow of turning:

> When God at first made man,
> Having a glasse of blessings standing by;
> Let us (said he) poure on him all we can:
> Let the worlds riches, which dispersed lie,
>   Contract into a span.
>
> So strength first made a way;
> Then beautie flow'd, then wisdome, honour, pleasure:
> When almost all was out, God made a stay,
> Perceiving that alone of all his treasure
>   Rest in the bottome lay.
>
> For if I should (said he)
> Bestow this jewell also on my creature,
> He would adore my gifts in stead of me,
> And rest in Nature, not the God of Nature.
>   So both should losers be.
>
> Yet let him keep the rest,
> But keep them with repining restlessnesse:
> Let him be rich and wearie, that at least,
> If goodnesse leade him not, yet wearinesse
>   May tosse him to my breast.[2]

[1] p. 88.   [2] p. 153.

What makes Herbert's poetry so intensely human and interesting is that it is the expression of this perpetual struggle after
inward peace, of this unceasing effort to bend a proud and
passionate nature into conformity with a strict conception of
the religious life. The battle has to be continually re-fought
and re-won, and the moods of perfect joy—'port after stormie
seas'—which follow such victories are often expressed with
exquisite freshness and simplicity, as in *The Flower*:

> How fresh, O Lord, how sweet and clean
> Are thy returns! ev'n as the flowers in spring;
> To which, besides their own demean,
> The late-past frosts tributes of pleasure bring.
> Grief melts away
> Like snow in May,
> As if there were no such cold thing.
>
> Who would have thought my shrivel'd heart
> Could have recover'd greenenesse? It was gone
> Quite under ground; as flowers depart
> To see their mother-root, when they have blown;
> Where they together
> All the hard weather,
> Dead to the world, keep house unknown.
>
> These are thy wonders, Lord of power
> Killing and quick'ning, bringing down to hell
> And up to heaven in an houre;
> Making a chiming of a passing-bell.
> We say amisse,
> This or that is:
> Thy word is all, if we could spell.
>
> O that I once past changing were,
> Fast in thy Paradise, where no flower can wither!
> Many a spring I shoot up fair,
> Offring at heav'n, growing and groning thither:
> Nor doth my flower
> Want a spring-showre,
> My sinnes and I joining together:
>
> But while I grow in a straight line,
> Still upwards bent, as if heav'n were mine own,
> Thy anger comes, and I decline:
> What frost to that? What pole is not the zone,
> Where all things burn,
> When thou dost turn,
> And the least frown of thine is shown?

And now in age I bud again,
After so many deaths I live and write;
   I once more smell the dew and rain,
And relish versing: O my onely light,
       It cannot be
       That I am he
On whom thy tempests fell all night.

   These are thy wonders, Lord of love,
To make us see we are but flowers that glide:
   Which when we once can finde and prove,
Thou hast a garden for us, where to bide.
      Who would be more,
      Swelling through store,
Forfeit their Paradise by their pride.[1]

In such a mood, we may believe, the well-known poems *Vertue* and *Life* were composed; and I think it will be agreed that their beauty and significance are increased when they are regarded as pauses and not as final resting-places, as periods of windless calm between the storms which have preceded and those which are yet to come.

Vertue

Sweet day, so cool, so calm, so bright,
The bridall of the earth and skie;
The dew shall weep thy fall to night;
       For thou must die.

Sweet rose, whose hue angrie and brave
Bids the rash gazer wipe his eye:
Thy root is ever in its grave,
       And thou must die.

Sweet spring, full of sweet dayes and roses,
A box where sweets compacted lie;
My musick shows ye have your closes,
       And all must die.

Onely a sweet and vertuous soul,
Like season'd timber, never gives;
But though the whole world turn to coal,
       Then chiefly lives.[2]

[1] p. 160.   [2] p. 80.

Life

I made a posie, while the day ran by:
Here will I smell my remnant out, and tie
    My life within this band.
But time did becken to the flowers, and they
By noon most cunningly did steal away,
    And wither'd in my hand.

My hand was next to them, and then my heart:
I took, without more thinking, in good part
    Times gentle admonition:
Who did so sweetly deaths sad taste convey,
Making my minde to smell my fatall day;
    Yet sugring the suspicion.

Farewell deare flowers, sweetly your time ye spent,
Fit, while ye liv'd, for smell or ornament,
    And after death for cures.
I follow straight without complaints or grief,
Since if my sent be good, I care not, if
    It be as short as yours.[1]

Some of these poems, too, express that radiant joy, that soaring
quality, which, as we shall see, is so characteristic of Vaughan.

Easter

Rise heart; thy Lord is risen. Sing his praise
    Without delayes,
Who takes thee by the hand, that thou likewise
    With him mayst rise:
That, as his death calcined thee to dust,
His life may make thee gold, and much more just.

Awake, my lute, and struggle for thy part
    With all thy art.
The crosse taught all wood to resound his name,
    Who bore the same.
His streched sinews taught all strings, what key
Is best to celebrate this most high day.

Consort both heart and lute, and twist a song
    Pleasant and long:
Or since all musick is but three parts vied
    And multiplied;
O let thy blessed Spirit bear a part,
And make up our defects with his sweet art.

[1] p. 87.

I got me flowers to straw thy way;
I got me boughs off many a tree:
But thou wast up by break of day,
And brought'st thy sweets along with thee.

The Sunne arising in the East,
Though he give light, & th'East perfume;[1]
If they should offer to contest
With thy arising, they presume.

Can there be any day but this,
Though many sunnes to shine endeavour?
We count three hundred, but we misse:
There is but one, and that one ever.[2]

The second part of the poem *Christmas*:

The shepherds sing; and shall I silent be?
    My God, no hymne for thee?
My soul's a shepherd too; a flock it feeds
    Of thoughts, and words, and deeds.
The pasture is thy word: the streams, thy grace
    Enriching all the place.
Shepherd and flock shall sing, and all my powers
    Out-sing the day-light houres.
Then we will chide the sunne for letting night
    Take up his place and right:
We sing one common Lord; wherefore he should
    Himself the candle hold.
I will go searching, till I finde a sunne
    Shall stay, till we have done;
A willing shiner, that shall shine as gladly,
    As frost-nipt sunnes look sadly.
Then we will sing, and shine all our own day,
    And one another pay:
His beams shall cheer my breast, and both so twine,
Till ev'n his beams sing, and my musick shine.[3]

Antiphon

Cho. Let all the world in ev'ry corner sing,
    My God and King.

Vers. The heav'ns are not too high,
    His praise may thither flie:
    The earth is not too low,
    His praises there may grow.

Cho. Let all the world in ev'ry corner sing,
    My God and King.

[1] 'and though the East give perfume.'   [2] p. 33.   [3] p. 73.

Vers. The church with psalms must shout.
No doore can keep them out:
But above all, the heart
Must bear the longest part.

Cho. Let all the world in ev'ry corner sing,
My God and King.[1]

Church-musick

Sweetest of sweets, I thank you: when displeasure
Did through my bodie wound my minde,
You took me thence, and in your house of pleasure
A daintie lodging me assign'd.

Now I in you without a bodie move,
Rising and falling with your wings:
We both together sweetly live and love,
Yet say sometimes, *God help poore Kings.*

Comfort, 'Ile die; for if you poste from me,
Sure I shall do so, and much more:
But if I travell in your companie,
You know the way to heavens doore.[2]

And although the following poem is in a slightly different
mood, it may be quoted here, since, like some of the others,
it has that soaring quality that we shall find again in Vaughan.

Vanitie

Poore silly soul, whose hope and head lies low;
Whose flat delights on earth do creep and grow;
To whom the starres shine not so fair, as eyes;
. Nor solid work, as false embroyderies;
Heark and beware, lest what you now do measure
And write for sweet, prove a most sowre displeasure.

O heare betimes, lest thy relenting
May come too late!
To purchase heaven for repenting
Is no hard rate.
If souls be made of earthly mold,
Let them love gold;
If born on high,
Let them unto their kindred flie:
For they can never be at rest,
Till they regain their ancient nest.
Then silly soul take heed; for earthly joy
Is but a bubble, and makes thee a boy.[3]

[1] p. 45.   [2] p. 57.   [3] p. 104.

V

The preceding poems have been chosen and arranged so
as to give the reader a rapid survey of the depth, variety, and
richness of Herbert's religious experience. They do not record
stages in a progress and they have not the appearance of being
separated from one another by any great interval of time—
they are moments in one complex experience that was for
ever moving between the poles of doubt and faith, through
hesitations, agonies, triumphs, happy meditations, radiant
joys. And perhaps the better we come to know them the
more we shall perceive that the whole experience is really im-
plicit in each of them; for they illuminate each other, and each
gains a new significance when all are studied together. But our
survey has necessarily been rather general, and it is now time
to consider certain aspects of Herbert's poetry in greater detail.

One thing in which, so far as I know, he is unique among
religious poets has perhaps struck the reader's attention—the
extraordinarily intimate and personal nature of his attitude
to God, whom he addresses with the confidence, the familiarity, the playfulness sometimes, of a father, a friend, or a lover.
Indeed, in the poem *Dulnesse* he declares that he would praise
God 'with mirth' and as 'curiously' as a lover praises his mistress:

> Why do I languish thus, drooping and dull,
>   As if I were all earth?
> O give me quicknesse, that I may with mirth
>   Praise thee brim-full!
>
> The wanton lover in a curious strain
>   Can praise his fairest fair;
> And with quaint metaphors her curled hair
>   Curl o're again.
>
> Thou art my lovelinesse, my life, my light,
>   Beautie alone to me:
> Thy bloudy death and undeserv'd, makes thee
>   Pure red and white.
>
> When all perfections as but one appeare,
>   That those thy form doth show,[1]
> The very dust, where thou dost tread and go,
>   Makes beauties here;

[1] I am uncertain of the meaning of these lines, but would suggest: 'And that
one perfection the multitude of perfections which thy form doth show.'

Where are my lines then? my approaches? views?
        Where are my window-songs?
Lovers are still pretending, & ev'n wrongs
        Sharpen their Muse:

But I am lost in flesh, whose sugred lyes
        Still mock me, and grow bold:
Sure thou didst put a minde there, if I could
        Finde where it lies.

Lord, cleare thy gift, that with a constant wit
        I may but look towards thee:
Look onely; for to *love* thee, who can be,
        What angel fit?[1]

The peculiarity of this poem is not so much that it offers God
the adoration of a lover—other religious poets and mystics
have done that—as that on Herbert's lips such language
sounds perfectly natural and appropriate, suggesting neither
an uncommon state of mystical exaltation nor a tendency to
weakness or sentimentality. There is that same blend of wit
and tenderness which is characteristic of some of the best
love-poetry of his age—even that conceit about red and white,
which many would find offensive, seems to me, I must admit,
entirely in keeping with the whole tone of the poem, and not
at all extravagant.

In *Unkindnesse* he thinks of God as a friend to whom he has
been ungrateful:

        Lord, make me coy and tender to offend:
        In friendship, first I think if that agree,
                Which I intend,
                Unto my friends intent and end.
        I would not use a friend, as I use Thee.

        If any touch my friend, or his good name;
        It is my honour and my love to free
                His blasted fame
                From the least spot or thought of blame.
        I could not use a friend, as I use Thee.

        My friend may spit upon my curious floore:
        Would he have gold? I lend it instantly;
                But let the poore,
                And thou within them starve at doore.
        I cannot use a friend, as I use Thee.

                        [1] p. 108.
3886   T

When that my friend pretendeth to a place,
I quit my interest, and leave it free:
    But when thy grace
    Sues for my heart, I thee displace,
Nor would I use a friend, as I use Thee.

Yet can a friend what thou hast done fulfill?
O write in brasse, *My God upon a tree*
    His bloud did spill
    Onely to purchase my good-will:
Yet use I not my foes, as I use thee.[1]

And in *Sinne*, as in many other poems, God appears as a
gracious providence, a father who is ever seeking the love of
his children:

Lord, with what care hast thou begirt us round!
    Parents first season us: then schoolmasters
    Deliver us to laws; they send us bound
To rules of reason, holy messengers.

Pulpits and sundayes, sorrow dogging sinne,
    Affections sorted, anguish of all sizes,
    Fine nets and strategems to catch us in,
Bibles laid open, millions of surprises,

Blessings beforehand, tyes of gratefulnesse,
    The sound of glorie ringing in our eares:
    Without our shame; within, our consciences;
Angels and grace, eternall hopes and fears.

    Yet all these sences and their whole aray
    One cunning bosome-sinne blows quite away.[2]

In short, Herbert tries to love God with his *whole* heart, with
the love proper to *every* personal relationship. Consider the
inimitable blend of adoration and gentle humour in the
following poem, especially in the beautiful 'countrey-aires'
of the sixth stanza. In all the greatest English love-poetry,
notably in that of Sidney, Shakespeare (particularly in his
dramatic love-poetry) and Donne, there is humour—a recognition of the smallness and insignificance of the personality on
which such an experience has been thrust, of the incongruity
between them; and yet withal a laughing affirmation of this
personality, in spite of its insignificance—an attempt to
separate the personality of the beloved from the experience
which its approach has kindled, and with which it tends to

---

    [1] p. 86.   [2] p. 37.

become identified, by dwelling on what is familiar, weak, pitiful, by clinging to particulars—a perpetual revolution between the universal and the particular, the personal and the impersonal or suprapersonal. These moments, I think, may be detected in Herbert's poetry too: its humour, its peculiar tenderness are the expression of a desire, perhaps subconscious, to remain, while surrendering himself to God, intensely aware both of God's personality and of his own.

Gratefulnesse

Thou that hast giv'n so much to me,
Give one thing more, a gratefull heart.
See how thy beggar works on thee
              By art.

He makes thy gifts occasion more,
And sayes, If he in this be crost,
All thou hast giv'n him heretofore
              Is lost.

But thou didst reckon, when at first
Thy word our hearts and hands did crave,
What it would come to at the worst
              To save.

Perpetuall knockings at thy doore,
Tears sullying thy transparent rooms,
Gift upon gift, much would have more,
              And comes.

This not withstanding, thou wentst on,
And didst allow us all our noise:
Nay thou hast made a sigh and grone
              Thy joyes.

Not that thou hadst not still above
Much better tunes, then grones can make;
But that these countrey-aires thy love
              Did take.

Wherefore I crie, and crie again;
And in no quiet canst thou be,
Till I a thankfull heart obtain
              Of thee:

Not thankfull, when it pleaseth me;
As if thy blessings had spare dayes:
But such a heart, whose pulse may be
              Thy praise.[1]

[1] p. 116.

Herbert loves to draw his metaphors and illustrations from those humble, homely, and familiar things which, like the ox and the ass and the Shepherds in old pictures of the Nativity, seem to make God more human and more near. Thus in *Even-song*, after reflecting on man's indifference to God's perpetual care, he continues:

> Yet still thou goest on,
> And now with darknesse closest wearie eyes,
> Saying to man, *It doth suffice:*
> *Henceforth repose; your work is done.*
>
> Thus in thy Ebony box
> Thou dost inclose us, till the day
> Put our amendment in our way,
> And give new wheels to our disorder'd clocks.[1]

Indeed, due partly perhaps, as is suggested by the passage already quoted from the *Country Parson*, to his practical experience as a pastor, Herbert seems deliberately to have moved towards greater simplicity of style, as he records in the second poem entitled *Jordan*, a poem which it is most interesting to compare with Sidney's famous sonnet concluding

Foole saide My muse to mee, looke in thy heart and write.

> When first my lines of heav'nly joyes made mention,
> Such was their lustre, they did so excell,
> That I sought out quaint words, and trim invention;
> My thoughts began to burnish, sprout, and swell,
> Curling with metaphors a plain intention,
> Decking the sense, as if it were to sell.
>
> Thousands of notions in my brain did runne,
> Off'ring their service, if I were not sped:
> I often blotted what I had begunne;
> This was not quick enough, and that was dead.
> Nothing could seem too rich to clothe the sunne,
> Much lesse those joyes which trample on his head.
>
> As flames do work and winde, when they ascend,
> So did I weave my self into the sense.
> But while I bustled, I might heare a friend
> Whisper, *How wide is all this long pretence!*
> *There is in love a sweetnesse readie penn'd:*
> *Copie out onely that, and save expense.*[2]

[1] p. 56.   [2] p. 95.

Several of his poems are almost entirely composed of a list
of racy and realistic similes:

Dotage

False glozing pleasures, casks of happinesse,
Foolish night-fires, womens and childrens wishes,
Chases in Arras, guilded emptinesse,
Shadows well mounted, dreams in a career,
Embroider'd lyes, nothing between two dishes;
  These are the pleasures here.

True earnest sorrows, rooted miseries,
Anguish in grain, vexations ripe and blown,
Sure-footed griefs, solid calamities,
Plain demonstrations, evident and cleare,
Fetching their proofs ev'n from the very bone;
  These are the sorrows here.

But oh the folly of distracted men,
Who griefs in earnest, joyes in jest pursue;
Preferring, like brute beasts, a lothsome den
Before a court, ev'n that above so cleare,
Where are no sorrows, but delights more true,
  Then miseries are here![1]

Simplicity and naturalness of style are characteristic of almost
all the poems I have quoted, but perhaps these qualities are
most *obvious*, and certainly the extreme homeliness and
familiarity of Herbert's imagery is most apparent, in some of
his remarkable allegorical poems.

Redemption

Having been tenant long to a rich Lord,
 Not thriving, I resolved to be bold,
 And make a suit unto him, to afford
A new small-rented lease, and cancell th'old.

In heaven at his manour I him sought:
 They told me there, that he was lately gone
 About some land, which he had dearly bought
Long since on earth, to take possession.

I straight return'd, and knowing his great birth,
 Sought him accordingly in great resorts;
 In cities, theatres, gardens, parks, and courts:
At length I heard a ragged noise and mirth

 Of theeves and murderers: there I him espied,
 Who straight, *Your suit is granted*, said, & died.[2]

---

[1] p. 161.   [2] p. 31.

The Church-floore

Mark you the floore? that square & speckled stone,
    Which looks so firm and strong,
                Is *Patience:*
And th'other black and grave, wherewith each one
    Is checker'd all along,
                Humilitie:
The gentle rising, which on either hand
    Leads to the Quire above,
                Is *Confidence:*
But the sweet cement, which in one sure band
    Ties the whole frame, is *Love*
                And *Charitie.*

  Hither sometimes Sinne steals, and stains
  The marbles neat and curious veins:
But all is cleansed when the marble weeps.
  Sometimes Death, puffing at the doore,
  Blows all the dust about the floore:
But while he thinks to spoil the room, he sweeps.
  Blest be the *Architect*, whose art
  Could build so strong in a weak heart.[1]

The World

Love built a stately house; where *Fortune* came,
And spinning phansies, she was heard to say,
That her fine cobwebs did support the frame,
Whereas they were supported by the same:
But *Wisdome* quickly swept them all away.

Then *Pleasure* came, who liking not the fashion,
Began to make *Balcones, Terraces,*
Till she had weakened all by alteration:
But rev'rend *laws*, and many a *proclamation*
Reformed all at length with menaces.

Then enter'd *Sinne*, and with that Sycomore,
Whose leaves first sheltered man from drought & dew,
Working and winding slily evermore,
The inward walls and Sommers cleft and tore:
But *Grace* shor'd these, and cut that as it grew.

Then *Sinne* combin'd with *Death* in a firm band
To rase the building to the very floore:
Which they effected, none could them withstand.
But *Love* and *Grace* took *Glorie* by the hand,
And built a braver Palace then before.[2]

[1] p. 58.   [2] p. 76.

Peace

Sweet Peace, where dost thou dwell? I humbly crave,
    Let me once know.
  I sought thee in a secret cave,
    And ask'd, if Peace were there.
A hollow winde did seem to answer, No:
    Go seeke elsewhere.

I did; and going did a rainbow note:
    Surely, thought I,
  This is the lace of Peaces coat:
    I will search out the matter.
But while I lookt, the clouds immediately
    Did break and scatter.

Then went I to a garden, and did spy
    A gallant flower,
  The crown Imperiall: Sure, said I,
    Peace at the root must dwell.
But when I digg'd, I saw a worm devoure
    What show'd so well.

At length I met a rev'rend good old man,
    Whom when for Peace
  I did demand; he thus began:
    There was a Prince of old
At Salem dwelt, who liv'd with good increase
    Of flock and fold.

He sweetly liv'd; yet sweetnesse did not save
    His life from foes.
  But after death out of his grave
    There sprang twelve stalks of wheat:
Which many wondring at, got some of those
    To plant and set.

It prosper'd strangely, and did soon disperse
    Through all the earth:
  For they that taste it do rehearse,
    That vertue lies therein,
A secret vertue bringing peace and mirth
    By flight of sinne.

Take of this grain, which in my garden grows,
    And grows for you;
  Make bread of it: and that repose
    And peace which ev'ry where
With so much earnestnesse you do pursue,
    Is onely there.[1]

[1] p. 117.

The Pilgrimage

I travell'd on, seeing the hill, where lay
    My expectation.
A long it was and weary way.
The gloomy cave of Desperation
I left on th'one, and on the other side
    The rock of Pride.

And so I came to phansies medow strow'd
    With many a flower:
Fain would I here have made abode,
But I was quicken'd by my houre.
So to cares cops I came, and there got through
    With much ado.

That led me to the wilde of passion, which
    Some call the wold;
A wasted place, but sometimes rich.
Here I was robb'd of all my gold,
Save one good Angell, which a friend had ti'd
    Close to my side.

At length I got unto the gladsome hill,
    Where lay my hope,
Where lay my heart; and climbing still,
When I had gain'd the brow and top,
A lake of brackish waters on the ground
    Was all I found.

With that abash'd and struck with many a sting
    Of swarming fears,
I fell, and cry'd, Alas my King;
Can both the way and end be tears?
Yet taking heart I rose, and then perceiv'd
    I was deceiv'd:

My hill was further: so I flung away,
    Yet heard a crie
Just as I went, *None goes that way*
And lives: If that be all, said I,
After so foul a journey death is fair,
    And but a chair.[1]

[1] p. 135.

HENRY VAUGHAN

I

HENRY VAUGHAN and his twin brother Thomas were
born at Newton St. Bridget, Brecknockshire, in 1621 or
1622. In 1638 they both entered Jesus College, Oxford.
Thomas was presented, in 1640, with the living of St.
Bridget's, Brecknockshire, but was deprived of this on
account of his adherence to the royalist side during the Civil
War, and about 1647 he returned to Oxford, where he had
been elected a fellow of his college, and applied himself to
chemical researches and to curious and rather fantastic
speculations which he called divine magic, inspired by the
writings of his hero, Cornelius Agrippa. He published several
books full of enthusiasm for what seemed to him new truths
of the first importance, in which, together with much that is
fantastic and absurd, there is a mystical strain which sometimes reminds us of his brother's poems. He died in 1665–6.
Henry did not remain long at Oxford. In a letter dated
'Breckon June the 15th —73', to John Aubrey, who was
collecting materials for his friend Wood's *Athenae Oxonienses*,
he says:

> I stayed not att Oxford to take any degree, butt was sent to
> London, beinge then designed by my father for the study of
> the Law, wch the sudden eruption of our late civil warres wholie
> frustrated. . . .
> My profession allso is physic, wch I have practised now for
> many years with good successe (I thank god!) & a repute big
> enough for a person of greater parts than my selfe.[1]

About 1643 he began to practise as a physician at Brecknock,
and in 1646 he published his first volume of poems, with the
title *Poems, with the tenth Satyre of Iuvenal Englished*. There is
little that is distinctively 'metaphysical' in the style of these
poems—most of them are in the sprightly manner of the
popular Cambridge poet, Thomas Randolph, and other
members of the Tribe of Ben; although there are two poems
which seem to have been inspired by Donne's *Valediction:
forbidding mourning*, especially by the following stanzas of that
poem:

---

[1] *The Works of Henry Vaughan*, ed. Martin, pp. 667–8.

Dull sublunary lovers love
(Whose soule is sense) cannot admit
Absence, because it doth remove
Those things which elemented it.

But we by a love, so much refin'd,
That our selves know not what it is,
Inter-assured of the mind,
Care lesse, eyes, lips, and hands to misse.

To Amoret gone from him

Fancy, and I, last Evening walkt,
And, *Amoret*, of thee we talkt;
The West just then had stolne the Sun,
And his last blushes were begun:
We sate, and markt how every thing
Did mourne his absence; How the Spring
That smil'd, and curl'd about his beames,
Whilst he was here, now check'd her streames:
The wanton Eddies of her face
Were taught lesse noise, and smoother grace;
And in a slow, sad channell went,
Whisp'ring the banks their discontent:
The careless ranks of flowers that spread
Their perfum'd bosomes to his head,
And with an open, free Embrace,
Did entertaine his beamy face;
Like absent friends point to the West,
And on that weake reflection feast.
If Creatures then that have no sence,
But the loose tye of influence,
(Though fate, and time each day remove
Those things that element their love)
At such vast distance can agree,
   Why, *Amoret*, why should not wee.[1]

To Amoret, of the difference 'twixt him, and other Lovers, and what true Love is

Marke, when the Evenings cooler wings
  Fanne the afflicted ayre, how the faint Sunne,
      Leaving undone,
      What he begunne,
Those spurious flames suckt up from slime, and earth
      To their first, low birth,
      Resignes, and brings.

[1] p. 8.

They shoot their tinsill beames, and vanities,
   Thredding with those false fires their way;
            But as you stay
            And see them stray,
You loose the flaming track, and subt'ly they
            Languish away,
            And cheate your Eyes.

Just so base, Sublunarie Lovers hearts
   Fed on loose prophane desires,
            May for an Eye,
            Or face comply:
But those removed, they will as soone depart,
            And shew their Art,
            And painted fires.

Whil'st I by pow'rfull Love, so much refin'd,
   That my absent soule the same is,
            Carelesse to misse,
            A glaunce, or kisse,
Can with those Elements of lust and sence,
            Freely dispence,
            And court the mind.

Thus to the North the Loadstones move,
   And thus to them th'enamour'd steel aspires:
            Thus, *Amoret*,
            I doe affect;
And thus by winged beames, and mutuall fire,
            Spirits and Stars conspire,
            And this is L O V E.[1]

Another poem in this volume must come as a surprise to those
who only know Vaughan as the author of *Silex Scintillans*. It
is called *A Rhapsodie. Occasionally written upon a meeting with
some of his friends at the Globe Taverne*. The following description of London at night is admirable, and reminiscent of
Donne in his realistic vein:

   Should we goe now awandring, we should meet
   With Catchpoles, whores, & Carts in ev'ry street:
   Now when each narrow lane, each nooke & Cave,
   Signe-posts, & shop-doors, pimp for ev'ry knave,
   When riotous sinfull plush, and tell-tale spurs
   Walk Fleet street, & the Strand, when the soft stirs
   Of bawdy, ruffled Silks, turne night to day;
   And the lowd whip, and Coach scolds all the way;

[1] p. 12.

When lust of all sorts, and each itchie bloud
From the Tower-wharfe to Cymbelyne, and Lud,
Hunts for a Mate, and the tyr'd footman reeles
'Twixt chaire-men, torches, & the hackny wheels.[1]

And he concludes with a rollicking catch:

Lets laugh now, and the prest grape drinke,
Till the drowsie Day-Starre winke;
And in our merry, mad mirth run
Faster, and further then the Sun;
And let none his Cup forsake,
Till that Starre againe doth wake;
So we men below shall move
Equally with the gods above.[2]

Vaughan does not seem to have remained long at Brecknock, but to have removed to his native Newton St. Bridget, where he spent the rest of his life; for the dedication of his next volume of poems, *Olor Iscanus*, is dated 'Newton by Usk this 17, of Decemb. 1647'. The history of this volume is somewhat obscure; the dedication to Lord Kildare Digby bears the date 1647, but it was not published until 1651, apparently by Vaughan's brother Thomas, and without the author's consent, for in an address by 'The Publisher to the Reader' we are told that 'the Author had long agoe condemn'd these Poems to Obscuritie, and the Consumption of that Further Fate, which attends it'. In the interval between composition and publication there must have occurred that strange and sudden conversion to which we must soon refer. In style and spirit this volume is akin to its predecessor. The author is in complete sympathy with contemporary literature: there are commendatory verses on Mrs. Katherine Philips ('the Match-less Orinda'), on Davenant's *Gondibert*, and on the plays of Fletcher and Cartwright—'wit in Cartwright at her Zenith was'. There is also a very pleasant, witty poem *To his retired friend, an invitation to Brecknock*, in which he describes the miserable condition of Brecknock, whose walls had been pulled down by its inhabitants to prevent the town from being occupied:

. . . and in the *Shire-*
-Hall furs of an old *Saxon Fox* appear,
With brotherly Ruffs and Beards, and a strange sight
Of high Monumentall Hats ta'ne at the fight
Of *Eighty eight*; while ev'ry *Burgesse* foots
The mortall *Pavement* in eternall boots.

[1] p. 11.   [2] p. 12.

'Come then', he concludes,

> Come then! and while the slow Isicle hangs
> At the stiffe thatch, and Winters frosty pangs
> Benumme the year, blith (as of old) let us
> 'Midst noise and War, of Peace, and mirth discusse.
> This portion thou wert born for: why should wee
> Vex at the times ridiculous miserie?
> An age that thus hath fool'd it selfe, and will
> (Spite of thy teeth and mine) persist so still.[1]

Another poem, *Upon a Cloke lent him by Mr. J. Ridsley*, suggests that Vaughan took some part in the fighting. He implies that he was one of the garrison who left Beeston Castle on its surrender to the Parliamentary forces in 1645, and he wishes that he had had the cloak, which seems to have been of very ample dimensions, from the beginning of his military career:

> O that thou hadst it when this Jugling fate
> Of Souldierie first seiz'd me! at what rate
> Would I have bought it then, what was there but
> I would have giv'n for the *Compendious hutt*?[2]

The profound spiritual revolution which Vaughan underwent about this time is revealed by the publication in 1650 of *Silex Scintillans*. The work was reissued in 1655 with a second part, containing additional poems, and a preface, in which Vaughan expresses profound dissatisfaction with contemporary literature and with his own earlier performances. His attitude to the wits, whom, as we have seen, he had imitated and commended, has completely changed. 'That this Kingdom hath abounded with those ingenious persons, which in the late notion are termed *Wits*, is too well known. Many of them having cast away all their fair portion of time, in no better employments, then a deliberate search, or excogitation of *idle words*, and a most vain, insatiable desire to be reputed *Poets*.' He keenly regrets his own efforts in this kind: 'And here, because I would prevent a just *censure* by my free *confession*, I must remember, that I my self have for many years together, languished of this very *sickness*; and it is no long time since I have recovered.' He has suppressed his 'greatest follies', and although he thinks those which escaped were fairly harmless, he declares that his guilt in writing them

---

[1] pp. 46–7.   [2] p. 54.

'can never be expiated without *special sorrows*'. 'The true remedy', he concludes,

> lies wholly in their bosoms, who are the gifted persons, by a wise exchange of *vain* and *vitious subjects*, for *divine Themes* and *Celestial praise*. . . . The first, that with any effectual success attempted a *diversion* of this foul and overflowing *stream*, was the blessed man, Mr. George Herbert, whose holy *life* and *verse* gained many pious Converts, (of whom I am the least) . . . He that desires to excel in this kinde of *Hagiography*, or holy writing, must strive (by all means) for *perfection* and true *holyness*, that a *door may be opened to him in heaven*, Rev. 4.1. and then he will be able to write (with *Hierotheus* and holy Herbert) A true Hymn.

How can we explain this sudden and complete change of outlook? Some allusions in *Silex Scintillans*, especially the beautiful poem *Silence, and stealth of days*, seem to connect it with the death of that brother who is also referred to by Thomas Vaughan at the conclusion of his *Anthroposophia Theomagica*, where, apologizing for the defects of his book, he says that it was 'compos'd in *Haste*, and in my *Dayes of Mourning*, on the *sad Occurence* of a *Brother's Death*'.[1] The book was published in 1650, but the Latin dedication is dated 'Oxonii 48'.

Then, too, there came a time when Vaughan was no longer able to dismiss the confusion and troubles of the Civil War in the same light-hearted and contemptuous way as at the conclusion of his *Invitation to Brecknock*. As with others of his contemporaries, they led him to turn his thoughts heavenward and suggested to him that 'the fashion of this world passeth away'. In the *Mount of Olives*, a volume of devotions, published in 1652, and of which the dedication bears the date October 1651, he declares:

> We could not have lived in an age of more instruction, had we been left to our own choice. We have seen such vicissitudes and examples of humane frailty, as the former world (had they happened in those ages) would have judged prodigies. We have seen Princes brought to their graves by a new way, and the highest order of humane honours trampled upon by the lowest. We have seene Judgement beginning at Gods Church, and (what hath beene never heard of, since it was redeem'd and established by his blessed Son,) we have seen his Ministers cast out of the Sanctuary, & barbarous persons without *light* or

---

[1] p. 65.

perfection, usurping holy offices. A day, an hour, a minute (saith *Causabone*) is sufficient to over-turn and extirpate the most settled Governments, which seemed to have been founded and rooted in Adamant. Suddenly do the high things of this world come to an end, and their delectable things passe away, for when they seem to be in their *flowers* and full strength, they perish to astonishment; And sure the ruine of the most goodly peeces seems to tell, that the dissolution of the whole is not far off.[1]

We have already noticed similar reflections in Donne's *Anniversaries* and in Reynolds's *Mythomystes*.

Whether the feelings and reflections aroused by his brother's death and by the spectacle of the Civil War actually caused Vaughan's conversion or were themselves largely directed by that fact it is impossible to say. The connexion between great spiritual experiences and particular events, even when much detailed knowledge is available, must always remain obscure; for, after all, the spirit bloweth where it listeth.

It is probable that sickness visited him about this time, for the *Flores Solitudinis*, a volume of translations from various devotional works, published in 1654, though the preface 'To the Reader' bears the date April 17, 1652, carries the sub-title 'Collected in his Sicknesse and Retirement'. In his dedication to Sir Charles Egerton he says:

> The incertainty of life, and a peevish, inconstant state of health would not suffer me to stay for greater performances, or a better season;[2]

and in his address to the reader he says:

> It may be thy spirit is such a popular, phantastick *flye*, as loves to gad in the *shine* of this world; if so, this *light* I live by in the *shade*, is too great for thee. I send it abroad to bee a companion of those wise *Hermits*, who have withdrawne from the present generation, to confirme them in their solitude, and to make that rigid *necessity* their pleasant *Choyse*.[3]

We have now been able to form some picture of the author of *Silex Scintillans*. Illuminated by some profound spiritual experience, saddened by death, sickness, and the misery and confusion of the world around him, he has resolved to spend the rest of his days in his native village on the banks of his beloved Usk, devoting his practical energies to the relief of sickness,

[1] pp. 170-1.   [2] p. 215.   [3] p. 216.

and his thoughts to the contemplation of the mercies and mysteries of God—listening for those divine intimations which he cannot hear amid the noises of the busy world, but which come to him in solitude, especially among the sights and sounds of nature, where, as in the days of his childhood —that childhood when he seemed nearest to God and immortality,—he is able to detect

some shadows of eternity.

II

Let us consider some of the characteristics of his poems. They are full of the imagery of light and darkness. To him the world is no abiding home, but a place of pilgrimage and trial, in general a somewhat dark and unfamiliar place except when illuminated by flashes of divine love, reminding man of the place from whence he has come and to which he is journeying. In one of the meditations in the *Mount of Olives* he says:

> When thou art to go from home, remember that thou art to come forth into the *World*, and to Converse with an Enemy; And what else is the World but a Wildernesse? A darksome, intricate wood full of *Ambushes* and dangers; A Forrest where spiritual hunters, principalities and powers spread their nets, and compasse it about.[1]

And again:

> Let sensual *natures* judge as they please, but for my part, I shall hold it no *Paradoxe* to affirme, *there are no pleasures in this world*. Some *coloured griefes* and *blushing woes* there are, which look so clear as if they were *true complexions*; but it is a very sad and a tryed truth that they are but *painted*. To draw then to an end, let us looke alwayes upon this *Day-Lilie* of life, as if the *Sun* were already *set*.[2]

Over and over again in these meditations his favourite text and image of the light shining in darkness appears. In his prayer 'When thou dost awake' he exclaims:

> O God the Father! who saidst in the beginning, *Let there be light*, and it was so; *Inlighten my Eyes that I never sleepe* in death: lest at any time my Enemy should say, *I have prevailed against him*.
>
> O God the Sonne! light of light; the most true and perfect

[1] p. 146.   [2] pp. 185–6.

light, from whom this light of the Sun, and the day had their beginning; thou, that art the light shining in darknesse, In-lightning every one that cometh into this world, expell from me all Clouds of Ignorance, and give me true understanding, that in thee, and by thee I may know the *Father*; whom to know is to live, and to serve is to reigne.[1]

And in the course of his 'Meditation before the receiving of the holy Communion' he exclaims:

O light of light, the all-seeing light that shineth in darknesse, and the darknesse comprehendeth it not, what will become of me, when I shall appear before thy glorious and searching Eye![2]

Elsewhere:

It is an observation of some *spirits*, that *the night is the mother of thoughts*. And I shall adde, that those thoughts are *Stars*, the *Scintillations* and *lightnings* of the soul strugling with *darknesse*.[3]

'The Contemplation of *death*', he declares,

is an obscure, melancholy *walk*, an Expatiation in *shadows* & *solitude*, but it leads unto *life*, & he that sets forth at *midnight*, will sooner meet the *Sunne*, then he that sleeps it out betwixt his curtains.[4]

Finally, at the conclusion of his preface to *Flores Solitudinis* he says:

All that may bee objected is, that I write unto thee out of a land of darknesse, out of that unfortunate region, where the Inhabitants sit in the shadow of death: where destruction passeth for propagation,[5] and a thick black night for the glorious day-spring. If this discourage thee, be pleased to remember, that there are bright starrs under the most palpable clouds, and light is never so beautifull as in the presence of darknes.[6]

His poems, as I have said, are full of this imagery. At the conclusion of *Resurrection and Immortality* the soul says to the body:

So shalt thou then with me
(Both wing'd and free,)
Rove in that mighty, and eternall light
Where no rude shade, or night
Shall dare approach us; we shall there no more
Watch stars, or pore

---

[1] pp. 143-4.   [2] p. 160.   [3] p. 169.   [4] p. 169.
[5] Here Vaughan is probably referring to the Act for the Propagation of the Gospel in Wales (1649) under which his brother and his friend Thomas Powell were ejected from their livings.   [6] p. 217.

Through melancholly clouds, and say
Would it were Day!
One everlasting *Saboth* there shall runne
Without *Succession*, and without a *Sunne*.[1]

There is that exquisite poem in which he is referring to his brother's death:

Silence, and stealth of dayes! 'tis now
Since thou art gone,
Twelve hundred houres, and not a brow
But Clouds hang on.
As he that in some Caves thick damp,
Lockt from the light,
Fixeth a solitary lamp
To brave the night,
And walking from his Sun, when past
That glim'ring Ray,
Cuts through the heavy mists in haste
Back to his day:
So o'r fled minutes I retreat
Unto that hour
Which shew'd thee last, but did defeat
Thy light, and pow'r.
I search, and rack my soul to see
Those beams again,
But nothing but the snuff to me
Appeareth plain:
That, dark and dead, sleeps in its known
And common urn,
But those, fled to their Makers throne,
There shine, and burn.
O could I track them! but souls must
Track one the other,
And now the spirit, not the dust
Must be thy brother.
Yet I have one *Pearle* by whose light
All things I see,
And in the heart of Earth, and night
Find Heaven, and thee.[2]

And there is this poem's companion, the beautiful *Ascension Hymn*:

They are all gone into the world of light!
And I alone sit lingring here;
Their very memory is fair and bright,
And my sad thoughts doth clear.

---

[1] p. 402.   [2] p. 425. I have ventured to re-punctuate this poem.

It glows and glitters in my cloudy brest
   Like stars upon some gloomy grove,
Or those faint beams in which this hill is drest,
   After the Sun's remove.

I see them walking in an Air of glory,
   Whose light doth trample on my days:
My days, which are at best but dull and hoary,
   Meer glimering and decays.

O holy hope! and high humility,
   High as the Heavens above!
These are your walks, and you have shew'd them me
   To kindle my cold love.

Dear, beauteous death! the Jewel of the Just,
   Shining no where, but in the dark;
What mysteries do lie beyond thy dust;
   Could man outlook that mark!

He that hath found some fledg'd birds nest, may know
   At first sight, if the bird be flown;
But what fair Well, or Grove he sings in now,
   That is to him unknown.

And yet, as Angels in some brighter dreams
   Call to the soul, when man doth sleep:
So some strange thoughts transcend our wonted theams,
   And into glory peep.

If a star were confin'd into a Tomb
   Her captive flames must needs burn there;
But when the hand that lockt her up, gives room,
   She'l shine through all the sphære.

O Father of eternal life, and all
   Created glories under thee!
Resume thy spirit from this world of thrall
   Into true liberty.

Either disperse these mists, which blot and fill
   My perspective (still) as they pass,
Or else remove me hence unto that hill,
   Where I shall need no glass.[1]

Then there is that poem where he describes how in time's book
he saw, amid many disordered lives, the fair white page of his
brother's. The verses convey a marvellous impression of *lux*

---

[1] p. 483.

in tenebris. Vaughan resembles Donne in his power of creating emotional atmosphere, although his reverie, his intense contemplation, burning like a steady flame, is quite unlike Donne's feverish intellectual activity.

> As time one day by me did pass
>   Through a large dusky glasse
>   He held, I chanc'd to look
>   And spyed his curious book
> Of past days, where sad Heav'n did shed
> A mourning light upon the dead.
>
> Many disordered lives I saw
>   And foul records which thaw
>   My kinde eyes still, but in
>   A fair, white page of thin
> And ev'n, smooth lines, like the Suns rays,
> Thy name was writ, and all thy days.
>
> O bright and happy Kalendar!
>   Where youth shines like a star
>   All pearl'd with tears, and may
>   Teach age, *The Holy way*;
> Where through thick pangs, high agonies
> Faith into life breaks, and death dies.
>
> As some meek *night-piece* which day quails,
>   To candle-light unveils:
>   So by one beamy line
>   From thy bright lamp did shine,
> In the same page thy humble grave
> Set with green herbs, glad hopes and brave.
>
> Here slept my thoughts dear mark! which dust
>   Seem'd to devour, like rust;
>   But dust (I did observe)
>   By hiding doth preserve,
> As we for long and sure recruits,
> Candy with sugar our choice fruits.
>
> O calm and sacred bed where lies
>   In deaths dark mysteries
>   A beauty far more bright
>   Then the noons cloudless light
> For whose dry dust green branches bud
> And robes are bleach'd in the *Lambs* blood.

Sleep happy ashes! (blessed sleep!)
 While haplesse I still weep;
 Weep that I have out-liv'd
 My life, and unreliev'd
Must (soul-lesse shadow!) so live on,
Though life be dead, and my joys gone.[1]

Above all, there is *The Night*, one of the most exquisitely
tender and sensitive of all religious poems, suggested by St.
John's phrase about Nicodemus, 'The same came unto him by
night'. Notice the speaking tone of the verses, their 'still,
soft call'. One of Donne's innovations was to make the rhythm
of lyric poetry approach more nearly to that of impassioned
colloquial speech, and Vaughan nobly carried on the tradition.

  Through that pure *Virgin-shrine*,
That sacred vail drawn o'r thy glorious noon
That men might look and live as Glo-worms shine,
  And face the Moon:
 Wise *Nicodemus* saw such light
 As made him know his God by night.

  Most blest believer he!
Who in that land of darkness and blinde eyes
Thy long expected healing wings could see,
  When thou didst rise,
 And what can never more be done,
 Did at mid-night speak with the Sun!

  O who will tell me, where
He found thee at that dead and silent hour!
What hallow'd solitary ground did bear
  So rare a flower,
 Within whose sacred leafs did lie
 The fulness of the Deity.

  No mercy-seat of gold,
No dead and dusty *Cherub*, nor carv'd stone,
But his own living works did my Lord hold
  And lodge alone;
 Where *trees* and *herbs* did watch and peep
 And wonder, while the *Jews* did sleep.

  Dear night! this worlds defeat;
The stop to busie fools; cares check and curb;
The day of Spirits; my souls calm retreat
  Which none disturb!
 Christs progress, and his prayer time;
 The hours to which high Heaven doth chime.

   [1] p. 512.

Gods silent, searching flight:
When my Lords head is fill'd with dew, and all
His locks are wet with the clear drops of night;
    His still, soft call;
His knocking time; The souls dumb watch,
When Spirits their fair kinred catch.

Were all my loud, evil days
Calm and unhaunted as is thy dark Tent,
Whose peace but by some *Angels* wing or voice
    Is seldom rent;
Then I in Heaven all the long year
Would keep, and never wander here.

But living where the Sun
Doth all things wake, and where all mix and tyre
Themselves and others, I consent and run
    To ev'ry myre,
And by this worlds ill-guiding light,
Erre more then I can do by night.

There is in God (some say)
A deep, but dazling darkness; As men here
Say it is late and dusky, because they
    See not all clear;
O for that night! where I in him
Might live invisible and dim.[1]

Finally, there is that truly remarkable poem *The World*.
Vaughan quotes at its conclusion 1 John, ii. 16–17.

> All that is in the world, the lust of the flesh, the lust of the
> Eys, and the pride of life, is not of the father, but is of the world.
> And the world passeth away, and the lusts thereof, but he
> that doth the will of God abideth for ever.

It is possible, however, that Vaughan had also in mind a
famous passage in the *Timaeus* (37d), where Plato describes
how God or the Demiurge created time:

> He conceived the idea of making a moving image of eternity,
> and accordingly when he ordered the heavens he made an
> image of eternity, in such fashion that while eternity itself
> remained unmoved, the image thereof had a motion according
> to number; and this image we call time.

It is interesting to observe how naturally the thought and
language of the *Timaeus* combine with Vaughan's mystical
Christianity. And it is the truest and highest kind of mysticism,
not cloudy and obscure, but concrete and clear, where con-

[1] p. 522.

ceptions have the intensity and vividness of perceptions. Here
is a poet thinking through the senses, exercising in a wonderful
way that power which Carew recognized in Donne, when he
said that Donne could

> the deepe knowledge of darke truths so teach,
> As sense might judge, what phansie could not reach.

I saw Eternity the other night
Like a great *Ring* of pure and endless light,
 All calm, as it was bright,
And round beneath it, Time in hours, days, years
  Driv'n by the spheres
Like a vast shadow mov'd, In which the world
 And all her train were hurl'd;
The doting Lover in his queintest strain
  Did their Complain,
Neer him, his Lute, his fancy, and his flights,
  Wits sour delights,
With gloves, and knots the silly snares of pleasure
  Yet his dear Treasure
All scatter'd lay, while he his eys did pour
  Upon a flowr.

2.

The darksome States-man hung with weights and woe
Like a thick midnight-fog mov'd there so slow
  He did nor stay, nor go;
Condemning thoughts (like sad Ecclipses) scowl
  Upon his soul,
And Clouds of crying witnesses without
  Pursued him with one shout.
Yet dig'd the Mole, and lest his ways be found
  Workt under ground,
Where he did Clutch his prey, but one did see
  That policie,
Churches and altars fed him, Perjuries
  Were gnats and flies,
It rain'd about him bloud and tears, but he
  Drank them as free.

3.

The fearfull miser on a heap of rust
Sate pining all his life there, did scarce trust
  His own hands with the dust,
Yet would not place one peece above, but lives
  In feare of theeves.
Thousands there were as frantick as himself
  And hug'd each one his pelf,

The down-right Epicure plac'd heav'n in sense
  And scornd pretence
While others slipt into a wide Excesse
  Said little lesse;
The weaker sort slight, triviall wares Inslave
  Who think them brave,
And poor, despised truth sate Counting by
  Their victory.

4.

Yet some, who all this while did weep and sing,
And sing, and weep, soar'd up into the *Ring*,
  But most would use no wing.
O fools (said I,) thus to prefer dark night
  Before true light,
To live in grots, and caves, and hate the day
  Because it shews the way,
The way which from this dead and dark abode
  Leads up to God,
A way where you might tread the Sun, and be
  More bright than he.
But as I did their madnes so discusse
  One whisper'd thus,
This Ring the Bride-groome did for none provide
  But for his bride.[1]

About most of these poems there is something brooding and
meditative; they seem to have been composed at night; they
suggest one sitting in darkness and celebrating the divine
illumination that has visited him there; but Vaughan has also
written some exquisite morning hymns, penetrated with a
radiant and lyric joy.

The Morning-watch

O Joyes! Infinite sweetnes! with what flowres,
And shoots of glory, my soul breakes, and buds!
  All the long houres
  Of night, and Rest
  Through the still shrouds
  Of sleep, and Clouds,
  This Dew fell on my Breast;
  O how it *Blouds*,
And *Spirits* all my Earth! heark! In what Rings,
And *Hymning Circulations* the quick world
  Awakes, and sings;
  The rising winds,
  And falling springs,

[1] p. 466.

Birds, beasts, all things
Adore him in their kinds.
Thus all is hurl'd
In sacred *Hymnes*, and *Order*, The great *Chime*
And *Symphony* of nature. Prayer is
The world in tune,
A spirit-voyce,
And vocall joyes
Whose *Eccho* is heav'ns blisse.
O let me climbe
When I lye down! The Pious soul by night
Is like a clouded starre, whose beames though sed
To shed their light
Under some Cloud
Yet are above,
And shine, and move
Beyond that mistie shrowd.
So in my Bed
That Curtain'd grave, though sleep, like ashes, hide
My lamp, and life, both shall in thee abide.[1]

Here are some lines from *The Dawning*:

Ah! what time wilt thou come? when shall that crie
The *Bridegroome's Comming*! fil the sky?
Shall it in the Evening run
When our words and works are done?
Or wil thy all-surprizing light
Break at midnight?
When either sleep, or some dark pleasure
Possesseth mad man without measure;
Or shal these early, fragrant hours
Unlock thy bowres?
And with their blush of light descry
Thy locks crown'd with eternitie;
Indeed, it is the only time
That with thy glory doth best chime,
All now are stirring, ev'ry field
Ful hymns doth yield,
The whole Creation shakes off night,
And for thy shadow looks the light.[2]

The Revival:

Unfold, unfold! take in his light,
Who makes thy Cares more short than night.
The Joys, which with his *Day-star* rise,
He deals to all, but drowsy Eyes:

[1] p. 424.   [2] p. 451.

And what the men of this world miss,
Some *drops* and *dews* of future bliss.
    Hark! how his *winds* have chang'd their *note*,
And with warm *whispers* call thee out.
The *frosts* are past, the *storms* are gone:
And backward *life* at last comes on.
The lofty *groves* in express Joyes
Reply unto the *Turtles* voice,
And here in *dust* and *dirt*, O here
The *Lilies* of his love appear![1]

No poet, not even Shelley, has written more beautifully of light, or better expressed the sacramental significance of dawn. Vaughan's brother too, in spite of his many odd notions, shared this mystical feeling for light:

> And if we may behold in any one Creature any spark of that Eternal Fire, or any farr-off dawning of Gods brightness, the same in the beauty and vertue of this Light may be best discerned.[2]

III

Let us now proceed to the consideration of another characteristic feeling or idea in Vaughan's poetry. As we have seen, he has, like many of his contemporaries, a strong conviction that the world has grown old and out of joint and that it has travelled far away from God. This conviction often leads him to meditate on the youth of the world, on the days when angels mingled with men, and heaven and earth seemed nearer together. This is the theme of the poem *Corruption*:

> Sure, It was so. Man in those early days
>   Was not all stone, and Earth,
> He shin'd a little, and by those weak Rays
>   Had some glimpse of his birth.
> He saw Heaven o'r his head, and knew from whence
>   He came (condemned,) hither,
> And, as first Love draws strongest, so from hence
>   His mind sure progress'd thither.
> Things here were strange unto him: Swet and till,
>   All was a thorn, or weed,
> Nor did those last, but (like himself,) dyed still
>   As soon as they did *Seed*,
> They seem'd to quarrel with him; for that Act
>   That fel him, foyl'd them all,
> He drew the Curse upon the world, and Crackt
>   The whole frame with his fall.

---

[1] p. 643.   [2] *A Brief Natural History*, 1669, p. 34.

This made him long for *home*, as loath to stay
    With murmurers, and foes;
He sigh'd for *Eden*, and would often say
    Ah! what bright days were those?
Nor was Heav'n cold unto him; for each day
    The vally, or the Mountain
Afforded visits, and still *Paradise* lay
    In some green shade, or fountain.
Angels lay *Leiger* here; Each Bush, and Cel,
    Each Oke, and high-way knew them,
Walk but the fields, or sit down at some *wel*,
    And he was sure to view them.
Almighty *Love*! where art thou now? mad man
    Sits down, and freezeth on,
He raves, and swears to stir nor fire, nor fan,
    But bids the thread be spun.
I see, thy Curtains are Close-drawn; Thy bow
    Looks dim too in the Cloud,
Sin triumphs still, and man is sunk below
    The Center, and his shrowd;
All's in deep sleep, and night; Thick darknes lyes
    And hatcheth o'r thy people;
But hark! what trumpets that? what Angel cries
    Arise! Thrust in thy sickle.[1]

The same thought is expressed in the poem *Religion*:

> My God, when I walke in those groves,
> And leaves thy spirit doth still fan,
> I see in each shade that there growes
> An Angell talking with a man.
>
> Under a *Juniper*, some house,
> Or the coole *Mirtles* canopie,
> Others beneath an *Oakes* greene boughs,
> Or at some *fountaines* bubling Eye;
>
> Here *Jacob* dreames, and wrestles; there
> *Elias* by a Raven is fed,
> Another time by th'Angell, where
> He brings him water with his bread;
>
> In *Abr'hams* Tent the winged guests
> (O how familiar then was heaven!)
> Eate, drinke, discourse, sit downe, and rest
> Untill the Coole, and shady *Even*;

[1] p. 440.

Nay thou thy selfe, my God, in *fire*,
Whirle-winds, and *Clouds*, and the *soft voice*
Speak'st there so much, that I admire
We have no Conf'rence in these daies;

Is the truce broke? or 'cause we have
A mediatour now with thee,
Doest thou therefore old Treaties wave
And by appeales from him decree?

Or is't so, as some green heads say
That now all miracles must cease?
Though thou hast promis'd they should stay
The tokens of the Church, and peace;

No, no; Religion is a Spring
That from some secret, golden Mine
Derives her birth, and thence doth bring
Cordials in every drop, and Wine;

But in her long, and hidden Course
Passing through the Earths darke veines,
Growes still from better unto worse,
And both her taste, and colour staines. . . .[1]

It is interesting to note that in each of the two following
poems the phrase 'white days' occurs. In *The Search*, an
allegorical description of the search for divine truth, we have
the lines:

Tyr'd here, I come to *Sychar*; thence
To *Jacobs wel*, bequeathed since
Unto his sonnes, (where often they
In those calme, golden Evenings lay
Watring their flocks, and having spent
Those white dayes, drove home to the Tent
Their *well-fleec'd* traine;)[2]

And in *Isaacs Marriage*, noticing the fact that Isaac prayed
for his bride, instead of using oaths and compliments, he
exclaims:

. . . happy those
White dayes, that durst no impious mirth expose![3]

And of course there is the famous line in *The Retreate* where he
regrets the

white, Celestiall thought

of his childhood.

[1] p. 404.   [2] p. 406.   [3] p. 408.

When he looks at *The Rain-bow* he thinks of its first appearance:

> Still yong and fine! but what is still in view
> We slight as old and soil'd, though fresh and new.
> How bright wert thou, when *Shems* admiring eye
> Thy burnisht, flaming *Arch* did first descry!
> When *Terah, Nahor, Haran, Abram, Lot,*
> The youthful worlds gray fathers in one knot,
> Did with intentive looks watch every hour
> For thy new light, and trembled at each shower![1]

Finally, there is the beautiful little poem *The dwelling-place*, suggested by St. John's words: 'They came, therefore, and saw where he abode; and they abode with him that day.'

> What happy, secret fountain,
>   Fair shade, or mountain,
> Whose undiscover'd virgin glory
> Boasts it this day, though not in story,
> Was then thy dwelling? did some cloud
> Fix'd to a Tent, descend and shrowd
> My distrest Lord? or did a star
> Becken'd by thee, though high and far,
> In sparkling smiles haste gladly down
> To lodge light, and increase her own?
> My dear, dear God! I do not know
> What lodgd thee then, nor where, nor how;
> But I am sure, thou dost now come
> Oft to a narrow, homely room,
> Where thou too hast but the least part,
> My God, I mean *my sinful heart.*[2]

In these poems, then, Vaughan muses on the early days of the world and of Christianity in much the same way as Spenser and other poets had mused on the traditional legend of a Golden Age and on the days of Chivalry.

> O! goodly usage of those antique tymes,
> In which the sword was servaunt unto right;
> When not for malice and contentious crymes,
> But all for prayse, and proofe of manly might,
> The martiall brood accustomed to fight:
> Then honour was the meed of victory,
> And yet the vanquished had no despight.
> Let later age that noble use envy,
> Vyle rancor to avoid and cruel surquedry.[3]

---

[1] p. 509.   [2] p. 516.   [3] *The Faerie Queene*, III. i. 13.

> So oft as I with state of present time
> The image of the antique world compare,
> When as mans age was in his freshest prime,
> And the first blossome of faire vertue bare;
> Such oddes I finde twixt those, and these which are,
> As that, through long continuance of his course,
> Me seemes the world is runne quite out of square
> From the first point of his appointed sourse;
> And being once amisse growes daily wourse and wourse.[1]

The difference is that, while the ideal with which Spenser
unfavourably contrasted his own age was formed from the
romances and the classic poets, Vaughan's was formed from
Scripture. But these reflections on the world's decay also
suggested to Vaughan another line of meditation which, I
think, is to be found in the works of only one other of his
contemporaries, Thomas Traherne. He returned, not only
to the early days of the world, but to his own early days, to the
days of his childhood, in which, so it seemed to him, his soul,
not yet corrupted by the ways of the world or dulled by the
lethargy of custom, had looked upon the Creation as God
intended all men to look upon it, as a wonderful and glorious
thing, the garment of God. This idea is expressed in the most
amous of all his poems, *The Retreate*:

> Happy those early dayes! when I
> Shin'd in my Angell-infancy.
> Before I understood this place
> Appointed for my second race,
> Or taught my soul to fancy ought
> But a white, Celestiall thought,
> When yet I had not walkt above
> A mile, or two, from my first love,
> And looking back (at that short space,)
> Could see a glimpse of his bright-face;
> When on some *gilded Cloud*, or *flowre*
> My gazing soul would dwell an houre,
> And in those weaker glories spy
> Some shadows of eternity;
> Before I taught my tongue to wound
> My Conscience with a sinfull sound,
> Or had the black art to dispence
> A sev'rall sinne to ev'ry sence,
> But felt through all this fleshly dresse
> Bright *shootes* of everlastingnesse.

[1] *The Faerie Queene*, Proem to Bk. v. i.

O how I long to travell back
And tread again that ancient track!
That I might once more reach that plaine,
Where first I left my glorious traine,
From whence th'Inlightned spirit sees
That shady City of Palme trees;
But (ah!) my soul with too much stay
Is drunk, and staggers in the way.
Some men a forward motion love,
But I by backward steps would move,
And when this dust falls to the urn
In that state I came return.[1]

And in another poem, entitled *Childe-hood*, he exclaims:

I cannot reach it; and my striving eye
Dazles at it, as at eternity.
    Were now that Chronicle alive,
Those white designs which children drive,
And the thoughts of each harmless hour,
With their content too in my pow'r,
Quickly would I make my path even,
And by meer playing go to Heaven. . . .

And yet the *Practice*[2] worldlings call
Business and weighty action all,
Checking the poor childe for his play,
But gravely cast themselves away.

    Dear, harmless age! the short, swift span,
Where weeping virtue parts with man;
Where love without lust dwells, and bends
What way we please, without self-ends.

An age of mysteries! which he
Must live twice, that would Gods face see;
Which *Angels* guard, and with it play,
Angels! which foul men drive away.

How do I study now, and scan
Thee, more then ere I studyed man,
And onely see through a long night
Thy edges, and thy bordering light!
O for thy Center and mid-day!
For sure that is the *narrow way*.[3]

Only in these two poems does Vaughan reveal to us that he
had made the new and thrilling discovery of the divinity of

[1] p. 419.   [2] Pragmatic.   [3] p. 520.

childhood—that discovery which forms the basis of all the thinking of his contemporary Traherne. To be able to look upon the world as something wonderfully fresh and beautiful and fascinating, to feel that it all belongs to you and yet to have no desire to call anything in it your own, but to be content to possess it by loving it and understanding it, and thus to create in your own mind a second creation more glorious than the first, because you have given it a voice to praise God and have thus helped him to realize his design in the first creation— this, declares Traherne, is the secret of childhood, and we must recapture it if we are to attain true felicity. 'Certainly Adam in Paradise had not more sweet and curious apprehensions of the world, than I when I was a child', he exclaims; and this is how he describes them:

> The corn was orient and immortal wheat, which never should be reaped, nor was ever sown. I thought it had stood from everlasting to everlasting. The dust and stones of the street were as precious as gold: the gates were at first the end of the world. The green trees when I saw them first through one of the gates transported and ravished me; their sweetness and unusual beauty made my heart to leap, and almost mad with ecstasy, they were such strange and wonderful things. The Men! O what venerable and reverend creatures did the aged seem! Immortal Cherubims! And young men glittering and sparkling Angels, and maids strange seraphic pieces of life and beauty! Boys and girls tumbling in the street, and playing, were moving jewels. I knew not that they were born or should die: But all things abided eternally as they were in their proper places. Eternity was manifest in the Light of the Day, and something infinite behind everything appeared: which talked with my expectation and moved my desire. The city seemed to stand in Eden, or to be built in Heaven. The streets were mine, the temple was mine, the people were mine, their clothes and gold and silver were mine, as much as their sparkling eyes, fair skins and ruddy faces. The skies were mine, and so were the sun and moon and stars, and all the World was mine; and I the only spectator and enjoyer of it. I knew no churlish proprieties, nor bounds, nor divisions: but all proprieties and divisions were mine: all treasures and the possessors of them. So that with much ado I was corrupted, and made to learn the dirty devices of this world. Which now I unlearn, and become, as it were, a little child again that I may enter into the Kingdom of God.

One of the most fascinating things about the study of seventeenth-century literature is that here and there new and strange ways of thinking and feeling appear for a moment; they seem to go underground and remain buried during the rationalistic and common-sensical eighteenth century, and then, perhaps in a rather different form, some of them emerge again. Wordsworth, perplexed almost to despair by the failure of those hopes for mankind which the French Revolution had aroused in him, able to find no comfort or illumination in contemporary philosophy, driven back upon himself, at last, like Vaughan and Traherne, found inspiration in remembering the great moments of childhood; and, when he tried to look upon the world as he had looked upon it then, it again took on, no less than when he had wandered with Beaupuy on the banks of the Loire, 'the attraction of a country in romance'.

We do not attach enough importance to spiritual discoveries. This discovery of Vaughan and Traherne was quite as important as any of those made by the members of the Royal Society; but unfortunately it remained for a long time unknown and unacted upon and had to be made again. That age in general neither understood nor appreciated childhood. On January 27, 1658, John Evelyn records in his diary that

> After six fits of a quartan ague with which it pleased God to visit him, died my deare son Richard, to our inexpressible griefe and affliction, 5 yeares and 3 days old onely, but at that tender age a prodigy for witt and understanding; for beauty of body a very angel; for endowment of mind of incredible and rare hopes.

And he goes on to reveal, as Mrs. Meynell noticed in a charming essay, that the child 'was chiefly precious to him inasmuch as he was, too soon, a likeness of the man he never lived to be'. 'To give onely a little taste of some of them', continues Evelyn, referring to those 'incredible and rare hopes',

> To give onely a little taste of some of them, and thereby glory to God, who out of the mouthes of babes and infants does sometimes perfect his praises: at 2 yeares and a halfe old he could perfectly reade any of the English, Latine, French, or Gothic letters, pronouncing the three first languages exactly. He had before the 5th yeare, or in that yeare, not onely skill to reade most written hands, but to decline all the nouns, conjugate the verbs regular, and most of the irregular; learn'd out Puerilis, got by heart almost the entire vocabularie of Latine and French primitives and words, could make congruous syntax, turne English into Latine, and *vice versa*, construe and

3886   z

prove what he read, and did the government and use of relatives, verbs, substantives, elipses, and many figures and tropes, and made a considerable progress in Comenius's Janua; began himselfe to write legibly, and had a strong passion for Greeke.

This is only 'a little taste' of Evelyn's record of the poor child's attainments, but it is sufficient to show that, as Mrs. Meynell observes, it was the fact that he did them out of the course of nature that was, to Evelyn, so exquisite. 'They thought their little boy strangely hopeful', she continues,

> because he was so quick on his way to be something else. They lost the timely perfection the while they were so intent upon their hopes. And yet it is our own modern age that is charged with haste! . . . Our fathers valued change for the sake of its results; we value it in the act. . . . All their literature dealing with children is bent upon this haste, this suppression of the approach to what seemed then the only time of fulfilment. The way was without rest to them. And this because they had the illusion of a rest to be gained at some later point of this unpausing life.
>
> Evelyn and his contemporaries dropped the very word child as soon as might be, if not sooner. When a poor little boy came to be eight years old they called him a youth. The diarist himself had no cause to be proud of his own early years, for he was so far indulged in idleness by an 'honoured grandmother' that he was 'not initiated into any rudiments' till he was four years of age. He seems even to have been a youth of eight before Latin was seriously begun; but this fact he is evidently, in later years, with a total lack of a sense of humour, rather ashamed of, and hardly acknowledges. It is difficult to imagine what childhood must have been when nobody, looking on, saw any fun in it; when everything that was proper to five years old was defect. A strange good conceit of themselves and of their own ages had those fathers.[1]

IV

Let us now pass on to another characteristic of Vaughan's poetry. We often find in Vaughan, as we sometimes find in Herbert, an antithesis between nature and man, between the calm, orderly, and obedient behaviour of nature, and the restlessness, self-will, and disobedience of man. Vaughan, like his brother Thomas and many of his contemporaries, believed that the world was the manifestation of a divine

[1] 'That Pretty Person' in *Essays*, 1918.

spirit, was penetrated by that spirit, but that while animals
and plants and inanimate things always instinctively, naturally, inevitably obeyed the laws and motions of that spirit,
man alone, having the power of choice or free will, was able
to resist these motions and laws; and accordingly he often
exhorts man to do voluntarily and reasonably what the rest
of the creation do naturally and instinctively—like Wordsworth, though with a difference, he bids him learn from
nature. His brother Thomas in his *Lumen de Lumine: or A new
magicall Light discovered and communicated to the World* (1651),
speaking of the correspondences between heaven and earth,
declares:

> Suppose then we should *dilapidat* or *discompose* some *Artificiall
> Building*, stone by stone: There is no *question* but we should
> come at *last* to the *Earth* whereupon it is *founded*. It is just so in
> *Magic*: if we open any *Naturall Body*, and *separate* all the *parts*
> thereof *one* from *another*, we shall come at *last* to the *Prester*,
> which is the *Candle*, and *secret Light* of God. . . .
> Hee shall know the *secret Love* of *Heaven* and Earth, and the
> sense of that deep *Cabalism*, *Non est planta hic inferiùs cui non est
> stella in Firmamento superiùs, & ferit eam stella, & dicit ei Cresce.*
> There is not an *Herb* here *below*, but he hath a *star* in *Heaven
> above*, and the *star* strikes him with her *Beame*, and sayes to him,
> *Grow*.[1]

In a poem to which he has prefixed a paraphrase of a text
from Romans viii. 19, 'Etenim res Creatae exerto Capite
observantes expectant revelationem Filiorum Dei', Vaughan
moralizes on this theme. Observe how, under the inspiration of St. Paul, Vaughan suggests that the obedience of the
creatures is not dictated merely by natural instincts and laws
and by the influence of the stars, but also by some obscure
and latent will to Good.

> And do they so? have they a Sense
>   Of ought but Influence?
> Can they their heads lift, and expect,
>   And grone too? why th'Elect
> Can do no more: my volumes sed
>   They were all dull, and dead,
> They judg'd them senslesse, and their state
>   Wholly Inanimate.
> Go, go; Seal up thy looks,
>   And burn thy books.

[1] p. 88.

2

I would I were a stone, or tree,
    Or flowre by pedigree,
Or some poor high-way herb, or Spring
    To flow, or bird to sing!
Then should I (tyed to one sure state,)
    All day expect my date;
But I am sadly loose, and stray
    A giddy blast each way;
    O let me not thus range!
        Thou canst not change.

3

Sometimes I sit with thee, and tarry
    An hour, or so, then vary.
Thy other Creatures in this Scene
    Thee only aym, and mean;
Some rise to seek thee, and with heads
    Erect peep from their beds;
Others, whose birth is in the tomb,
    And cannot quit the womb,
    Sigh there, and grone for thee,
        Their liberty.

4

O let not me do lesse! shall they
    Watch, while I sleep, or play?
Shall I thy mercies still abuse
    With fancies, friends, or newes?
O brook it not! thy bloud is mine,
    And my soul should be thine;
O brook it not! why wilt thou stop
    After whole showres one drop?
    Sure, thou wilt joy to see
        Thy sheep with thee.[1]

And again in *Christs Nativity* he declares how the creatures
praise God and observe his law:

Awake, glad heart! get up, and Sing,
It is the Birth-day of thy King,
        Awake! awake!
        The Sun doth shake
Light from his locks, and all the way
Breathing Perfumes doth spice the day.

[1] p. 432.

Awak, awak! heark, how th'*wood* rings,
Winds whisper, and the busie *springs*
    A Consort make;
    Awake, awake!
Man is their high-priest, and should rise
To offer up the sacrifice.

I would I were some *Bird*, or Star,
Flutt'ring in woods, or lifted far
    Above this *Inne*
    And Rode of sin!
Then either Star, or *Bird*, should be
Shining, or singing still to thee. . . .[1]

And in the poem *Man* he reflects on what seems to him the contrast between the steadfastness of nature and the restlessness of man in a way that is reminiscent of Herbert's *Pulley*:

Weighing the stedfastness and state
Of some mean things which here below reside,
Where birds like watchful Clocks the noiseless date
    And Intercourse of times divide,
Where Bees at night get home and hive, and flowrs
        Early, aswel as late,
Rise with the Sun, and set in the same bowrs;

2

I would (said I) my God would give
The staidness of these things to man! for these
To his divine appointments ever cleave,
    And no new business breaks their peace;
The birds nor sow, nor reap, yet sup and dine,
        The flowres without clothes live,
Yet *Solomon* was never drest so fine.

3

Man hath stil either toyes, or Care,
He hath no root, nor to one place is ty'd,
But ever restless and Irregular
    About this Earth doth run and ride,
He knows he hath a home, but scarce knows where,
        He sayes it is so far
That he hath quite forgot how to go there.

[1] p. 442.

4

He knocks at all doors, strays and roams,
Nay hath not so much wit as some stones have
Which in the darkest nights point to their homes,
    By some hid sense their Maker gave;
Man is the shuttle, to whose winding quest
            And passage through these looms
God order'd motion, but ordain'd no rest.[1]

And this is how he moralizes on *Cock-crowing*:

Father of lights! what Sunnie seed,
What glance of day hast thou confin'd
Into this bird? To all the breed
This busie Ray thou hast assign'd;
        Their magnetisme works all night,
        And dreams of Paradise and light.

Their eyes watch for the morning hue,
Their little grain expelling night
So shines and sings, as if it knew
The path unto the house of light.
        It seems their candle, howe'r done,
        Was tinn'd and lighted at the sunne.

If such a tincture, such a touch,
So firm a longing can impowre
Shall thy own image think it much
To watch for thy appearing hour?
        If a meer blast so fill the sail,
        Shall not the breath of God prevail? . . .

If joyes, and hopes, and earnest throws,
And hearts, whose Pulse beats still for light
Are given to birds; who, but thee, knows
A love-sick souls exalted flight?
        Can souls be track'd by any eye
        But his, who gave them wings to flie?

Onely this Veyle which thou hast broke,
And must be broken yet in me,
This veyle, I say, is all the cloke
And cloud which shadows thee from me.
        This veyle thy full-ey'd love denies,
        And onely gleams and fractions spies.

[1] p. 477.

O take it off! make no delay,
But brush me with thy light, that I
May shine unto a perfect day,
And warme me at thy glorious Eye!
    O take it off! or till it flee,
    Though with no Lilie, stay with me![1]

Finally, in his last volume of verse, *Thalia Rediviva* (1678), he has a delightful poem called *The Bee* in which he calls up a picture of the hermit living alone with nature and joining in creation's hymn:

Haile happy harmless solitude,
Our Sanctuary from the rude
And scornful world: the calm recess
Of faith, and hope and holiness!
Here something still like *Eden* looks,
Hony in Woods, *Julips* in Brooks:
And *Flow'rs*, whose rich, unrifled *Sweets*
With a chast kiss the cool dew greets.
When the toyls of the Day are done
And the tir'd world sets with the Sun,
Here *flying* winds and *flowing* Wells
Are the wise, watchful Hermits *Bells*;
Their buisie *murmurs* all the night
To *praise* or *prayer* do invite,
And with an awful sound arrest
And piously employ his breast.
    When in the *East* the Dawn doth blush,
Here cool, fresh *Spirits* the air brush;
Herbs (strait) get up, *Flow'rs* peep and spread:
Trees whisper praise, and bow the head.
Birds from the shades of night releast
Look round about, then quit the neast,
And with united gladness sing
The glory of the morning's King.
The *Hermit* hears, and with meek voice
Offers his own up, and their Joys:
Then prays, that all the world may be
Blest with as sweet an unity. . . .

    O purer years of light, and grace!
The *diff'rence* is great, as the *space*
'Twixt you and us: who blindly run
After *false-fires*, and leave the *Sun*.
Is not fair *Nature* of her self
Much richer than dull *paint*, or *pelf*?

[1] p. 488.

And are not *streams* at the *Spring-head*
More sweet than in carv'd *Stone*, or *Lead*?
But *fancy* and some *Artist's* tools
Frame a Religion for fools. . . .

   O lead me, where I may be free
In *truth* and *Spirit* to serve thee!
Where undisturb'd I may converse
With thy great self, and there rehearse
Thy gifts with thanks, and from thy store
Who art all blessings, beg much more!

Give me the Wisdom of the *Bee*,
And her unwearied Industry:
That from the *wild Gourds* of these days
I may extract Health and thy praise;
Who can'st turn darkness into light,
And in my weakness shew thy might![1]

V

But not only does Vaughan insist on this contrast between the orderliness and obedience of nature and the caprice and self-will of man; he would also have us regard Nature as a system of divine hieroglyphs, revealing to the loving and careful observer something of the will and power of God; he would have us recognize in natural laws real and not merely casual analogies with spiritual laws. This way of regarding nature was in a sense very old. From the earliest times, influenced doubtless by the magnificent poetry of the Psalms, the Church had taught that knowledge of God was to be sought not only in the Bible, the *Liber Revelationis*, but also in Nature, the *Liber Creaturarum*. Nevertheless, its appeals to Nature had generally been trite and conventional: the old Bestiaries, where the lion appears as the symbol of strength, the fox of cunning, &c., are a good example of its method. Moreover, those who pushed their inquiries into the secrets of nature too far were regarded with suspicion and often treated as sorcerers or magicians. Bacon, in the *Advancement of Learning*, reviews the discredits which learning has received from divines:

I hear the former sort say, that knowledge is of those things which are to be accepted of with great limitation and caution: that the aspiring to overmuch knowledge was the original temptation and sin whereupon ensued the fall of man: that

[1] p. 652.

knowledge hath in it somewhat of the serpent, and therefore
when it entereth into a man it makes him swell; 'Scientia
inflat': that Salomon gives a censure, 'That there is no end of
making books, and that much reading is weariness of the flesh';
and again in another place, 'That in spacious knowledge there
is much contristation, and that he that increaseth knowledge
increaseth anxiety': that Saint Paul gives a caveat, 'That we
be not spoiled through vain philosophy': that experience
demonstrates how learned men have been arch-heretics, how
learned times have been inclined to atheism, and how the
contemplation of second causes doth derogate from our depen-
dence upon God, who is the first cause.

Bacon replies that true knowledge does not lead to atheism
and pride but to humility and adoration:

> For in the entrance of philosophy, When the second causes,
> which are next unto the senses, do offer themselves to the mind
> of man, if it dwell and stay there it may induce some oblivion
> of the highest cause; but when a man passeth on further, and
> seeth the dependence of causes, and the works of Providence,
> then, according to the allegory of the poets, he will easily
> believe that the highest link of nature's chain must needs be
> tied to the foot of Jupiter's chair.

Too often, as in Macaulay's famous essay, Bacon has been
represented as a mere utilitarian, interested in science only
for the sake of the material benefits it was to confer; but
although he certainly does insist on these, and condemns Aris-
totelianism for its unfruitfulness, he never loses sight of his
great conception of science as an attempt to penetrate the
secrets of God. Most of his followers, however, in what was
called 'new philosophy', ceased to emphasize this aspect, and
concentrated their attention on the solution of definite problems and on practical applications. Perhaps this was ine-
vitable: the old medieval ideal of a harmony of the sciences,
metaphysics, natural philosophy, and divinity, with divinity
as their queen, was doomed to perish. Nevertheless, many
sixteenth- and seventeenth-century thinkers could not bring
themselves to abandon this ideal. They shared in the revived
enthusiasm for the investigation of nature, but they insisted
on regarding it as the handmaid of divinity. They despised
what seemed to them the mean utilitarianism of the experimental method, and still insisted that the true method was that
of analogy—that all spiritual laws had their counterparts in
natural laws, and that the one was to be used to discover and

illuminate the other. Men like Cornelius Agrippa and his humble disciple Thomas Vaughan approached chemistry with a kind of mystical enthusiasm: they pursued it, not for the sake of any material or practical end, but because it seemed to enable them in some small measure to repeat the processes of creation. Indeed, they called it 'natural magic'.

This tendency of thought had been greatly stimulated by the *Heptaplus* of Pico della Mirandula, a work in which that ardent humanist tried to fortify and recommend his conviction that all human doctrine and belief was part of one original revelation of God to man by proposing a sevenfold method of interpreting the Mosaic account of the creation—an attempt that was closely imitated, a hundred years later, by Henry More in his *Conjectura Cabbalistica*. 'In explaining the harmony between Plato and Moses', says Pater, in his delightful essay,

> Pico lays hold on every sort of figure and analogy, on the double meaning of words, the symbols of the Jewish ritual, the secondary meanings of obscure stories in the later Greek mythologists. Everywhere there is an unbroken system of correspondences. Every object in the terrestrial world is an analogue, a symbol or counterpart, of some higher reality in the starry heavens, and this again of some law of the angelic life in the world beyond the stars. There is the element of fire in the material world; the sun is the fire of heaven; and in the super-celestial world there is the fire of the seraphic intelligence. 'But behold how they differ! The elementary fire burns, the heavenly fire vivifies, the super-celestial fire loves.' In this way, every natural object, every combination of natural forces, every accident in the lives of men, is filled with higher meanings. Omens, prophecies, supernatural coincidences, accompany Pico himself all through life. There are oracles in every tree and mountain-top, and a significance in every accidental combination of the events of life.

In order to understand Vaughan and many of his contemporaries it is most important to recognize that this attitude to the study of nature, this belief in the method of analogy, was still very common. For example, John Smith, one of the most famous of the Cambridge Platonists, and a fellow of Queens' College from 1644 to 1652, declares in his *Select Discourses*:

> God made the Universe and all the Creatures contained therein as so many Glasses wherein he might reflect his own Glory: He hath copied forth himself in the Creation; and in this Outward World we may read the lovely characters of the Divine Goodness, Power and Wisdom. . . . Though Good men, all of them,

are not acquainted with all those Philosophical notions touching the relation between Created and Uncreated Being; yet may they easily find every Creature pointing out to that Being whose image and superscription it bears, and climb up from those darker resemblances of the Divine Wisdome and Goodness shining out in different degrees upon several Creatures, ὥσπερ ἀναβαθμοῖς τισί, as the Antients speak, till they sweetly repose themselves in the bosom of the Divinity: and while they are thus conversing with this lower World, and are viewing *the invisible things of God in the things that are made,* in this visible and outward Creation, they find God many times secretly flowing into their Souls, and leading them silently out of the Court of the Temple into the Holy Place.[1]

'Thus', he continues:

may a Good man walk up and down the World as in a Garden of Spices, and suck a Divine Sweetness out of every flower. There is a Twofold meaning in every Creature, as the Jews speak of their Law, a *Literal,* and a *Mystical,* and the one is but the ground of the other. . . . It is the drowsie and muddy spirit of Superstition which, being lull'd asleep in the lap of worldly delights, is fain to set some Idol at its elbow, something that may jogg it and put it in mind of God. Whereas true Religion never finds it self out of the Infinite Sphere of the Divinity, and whereever it finds *Beauty, Harmony, Goodness, Love, Ingenuity, Wisdome, Holiness, Justice,* and the like, it is ready to say, *Here* and *There is God*: wheresoever any such Perfections shine out, an holy Mind climbs up by these Sun-beams, and raises up it self to God. . . . A Good man finds every place he treads upon *Holy ground*; to him the World is God's Temple; he is ready to say with *Jacob*, Gen. 28. *How dreadfull is this place! this is none other but the House of God.*[2]

And he concludes with an expression of regret for that separation of the sciences to which I have referred:

To conclude, It was a degenerous and unworthy Spirit in that Philosophy which first separated and made such distances between *Metaphysical* Truths & the Truths of *Nature*; whereas the First and most antient Wisdome amongst the Heathens was indeed a Philosophical Divinity, or a Divine Philosophy; which continued for divers ages, but as men grew worse, their queazy stomachs began to loath it: which made the truly-wise *Socrates* complain of the Sophisters of that Age which began now to corrupt and debase it; whereas heretofore the Spirit of Philosophy was more generous and divine, and did more purifie and

---

[1] 1660, pp. 430–1.   [2] pp. 433–4.

ennoble the Souls of Men, commending Intellectual things to them, and taking them off from settling upon Sensible and Material things here below, and still exciting them to endeavour after the nearest resemblance of God the Supreme Goodness and Loveliness, and an intimate Conjunction with him; which, according to the strain of that Philosophy, was the true Happiness of Immortal Souls.[1]

Thomas Vaughan, in his *Lumen de Lumine* (1651), also laments this separation of the sciences:

> In the past, and more Knowing years of the world, when Magic was better, and more generally understood, the Professors of this Art divided it into three parts, Elementall, Cælestiall, and Spirituall. The Elementall part contained all the Secrets of Physic, the Cælestiall those of Astrologie, and the Spirituall those of Divinitie. Every one of these by it self was but a Branch or Lim, but being united all Three, they were the Pandects of the Science. Now in these thy dayes there is no man can shew thee any reall Physic, or Astrologie, neither have they any more, than a Tong-and-Book Divinitie. The Reason of it is this; In Process of time these three Sciences (which work no wonders without a mutuall essentiall Union) were by misinterpretation dismembred, and set apart, so that every one of them was held to be a Facultie by it self.[2]

Sir Thomas Browne, in that curious work *The Garden of Cyrus, Or, the Quincunciall, Lozenge, or net-work plantations of the ancients, artificially, naturally, and mystically considered* (1658), observes towards the close of his discourse:

> Studious Observators may discover more analogies in the orderly book of nature, and cannot escape the Elegancy of her hand in other correspondencies.[3]

And he mentions a few analogies which he thinks might be profitably investigated:

> If any shall further quæry . . . why Geomancers do imitate the Quintuple Figure, in their Mother Characters of Acquisition and Amission *etc.* somewhat answering the Figures in the Lady or speckled Beetle. . . . He shall not fall on trite or triviall disquisitions. And these we invent and propose unto acuter enquirers, nauseating crambe verities and questions over-queried. Flat and flexible truths are beat out by every hammer; But *Vulcan* and his whole forge sweat to work out *Achilles* his armour. A large field is yet left unto sharper discerners to enlarge upon

---

[1] pp. 434–5.   [2] p. 16.   [3] Sayle's ed., iii, pp. 183–4.

this order, to search out the *quaternio's* and figured draughts of
this nature, and moderating the study of names, and meer
nomenclature of plants, to erect generalities, disclose unobserved
proprieties, not only in the vegetable shop, but in the whole
volume of nature.[1]

'To erect generalities', to 'disclose unobserved proprieties',
that is to say, the method of analogy, was to these men the only
profitable way of investigating nature. Henry Reynolds in
his *Mythomystes*, published about 1633, strongly disapproves of
the experimental philosophy and of what seem to him its low
and vulgar aims.

> 'What one of a million of our Scollers or writers among vs',
> he exclaims, 'vnderstands, or cares to be made vnderstand,
> scarse the lowest and triuiallest of Natures wayes, much lesse
> seekes to draw (by wisely obseruing her higher and more hidden
> workings) any profitable vse or benefit from them, for their
> owne, or the publike good, then perhaps to make an Almanack
> or a diuing-bote to take butts or crabs vnder water with, or else
> some Douch water-bellowes, by rarefying water into a comprest
> ayre to blow the fire withall?'

Whereas a live knowledge of Nature would enable us

> not sawcily to leap, but by the linkes of that golden chaine of
> *Homer*, that reaches from the foote of *Iupiters* throne to the Earthe,
> more knowingly and consequently more humbly climbe vp to
> him, who ought to bee indeed the only end and period of all
> our knowledge and vnderstanding.[2]

And Thomas Vaughan, as I have remarked, approaches
chemistry with a kind of mystical enthusiasm. In his *Lumen de
Lumine*, after describing the first matter or 'Moysaycall Earth',
which he takes to be virgin sulphur, he continues:

> This *earth* must be *dissolved* into *water*, and that *water* must
> be *coagulated* again into *earth*. This is done by a certaine Naturall
> *Agent*, which the Philosophers call their *secret fire*.[3]

He then describes this 'fire' in the same enthusiastic and meta-
phorical way as he has described the 'Moysaycall Earth'. What
is the point of it all? What has provoked all this confused
exaltation? What is the end in view? He tells us, in a passage

[1] Ibid., pp. 208–9.
[2] *Critical Essays of the Seventeenth Century*, ed. Spingarn, vol. i, pp. 172–4.
[3] 1651, p. 57.

which follows his account of how the dissolution and coagulation are to be effected:

> Doe this, and thou hast placed *Nature in Horizonte Aeternitatis*: Thou hast performed that *Command* of the *Cabalist, Fige finem in Principio, sicut Flammam prunae Conjunctam: quia Dominus SUPER-LATIVE unus, & non tenet secundum*. . . . Consider then what you seek: you seek an *Indissoluble, miraculous, transmuting, uniting union*, but such a *tye* cannot be without the *first unitie; Creare enim* (saith one) *atque intrinsecùs transmutare absque violentià, Munus est proprium duntaxat Primae Potentiae, Primae sapientiae, Primi amoris*. To *Create*, and *Transmute essentially*, and *naturally* or without any *violence*, is the only proper office of the *first power*, the *first Wisdome*, and the *first love*. Without this *love* the *Elements* will never be *maried*, they will never *inwardly* and *essentially unite*, which is the *end* and *perfection* of *Magic*. Study then to understand this, and when thou hast perform'd, I will allow thee that *Test* of the *Mekkubalim: Intellexisti in sapientià, & sapuisti in Intellegentia, statuisti Rem super Puritates suas, & Creatorem in Throno suo collocâsti*.[1]

That is to say, the proper reason for studying chemistry is that it enables us in some measure to repeat the processes of God in the Creation.

Thus, during the greater part of the seventeenth century there were two distinct attitudes towards the study of nature. The one was critical and scientific, confining itself to the investigation of particular problems, sometimes with a practical end in view. This attitude has continued almost until our own day. It assumes that the physical world consists of something called matter, and that matter is governed by mechanical laws. In its later developments it became very remote from the comprehension, interests, and intuitions of the ordinary man, but in its earlier stages it was not quite so exclusive. Men of ordinary culture were able to appreciate its theories and methods, which were very congenial to an age that was seeking for laws and norms in every department of human activity. In fact, the 'new philosophy' as it was called played a most important part in building up the 'Weltanschauung' of the Age of Prose and Reason. It was one of the manifestations of a new tendency of thought, and it also reinforced and confirmed that tendency. It encouraged and justified the desire to find and establish laws in every department—in metaphysics and moral philosophy, in politics, in taste. Its influence was

[1] 1651, pp. 63–4.

on the whole hostile to poetry and imagination, for what could not be clearly and simply explained—could not, according to the Cartesian formula, be clearly and distinctly conceived —was too often dismissed as unreal, illusory, extravagant, romantic, *enthusiastic.*

The other view of nature, fantastic and uncritical as it appears at first sight, was not altogether unreasonable. It over-simplified things by assuming, as the medieval Church had assumed, that every spiritual law had its analogy in the world of natural law; but on the whole it was right in refusing to regard the universe as mechanical and God as a kind of clock-maker. It insisted that there was

> a divine flame burning in all things:

it regarded what was dogmatically called matter as a manifestation of spirit; its world was a living organism, interpenetrated by God, and revealing God. It made possible that poetic and imaginative attitude to nature which we find in Henry Vaughan, in Traherne, sometimes in Henry More, and which reappeared like a new and authentic inspiration in German philosophy, in Wordsworth, and in the Romantic poets.

Thomas Vaughan, in his *Anima Magica Abscondita* (1650), exclaims:

> In the *Summer* translate thy self to the Fields, where all are green with the Breath of God, and fresh with the Powers of heaven. Learn to refer all Naturals to their Spirituals *per viam Secretioris Analogiae*; for this is the way the *Magicians* went, and found out Miracles.[1]

His brother, in a poem called *Rules and Lessons*, gives the same advice:

> Walk with thy fellow-creatures: note the *hush*
> And *whispers* amongst them. There's not a *Spring*,
> Or *Leafe* but hath his *Morning-hymn*; Each *Bus*
> And *Oak* doth know *I AM*; canst thou not sing?
>   O leave thy Cares, and follies! go this way
>   And thou art sure to prosper all the day. . . .
>
> To highten thy *Devotions*, and keep low
> All mutinous thoughts, what busines e'r thou hast
> Observe God in his works; here *fountains* flow,
> *Birds* sing, *Beasts* feed, *Fish* leap, and th'*Earth* stands fast;
>   Above are restles *motions*, running *Lights*,
>   Vast Circling *Azure*, giddy *Clouds*, days, nights.

[1] p. 52.

When *Seasons* change, then lay before thine Eys
His wondrous *Method*; mark the various *Scenes*
In heav'n; *Hail, Thunder, Rain-bows, Snow*, and *Ice*,
Calmes, Tempests, Light, and *darknes* by his means;
  Thou canst not misse his *Praise*; Each *tree, herb, flowre*
  Are shadows of his *wisedome*, and his Pow'r.[1]

And in the poem *Vanity of Spirit* he tells how in his efforts to know God he

  summoned nature: peirc'd through all her store,
Broke up some seales, which none had touch'd before.[2]

In *The Tempest* he declares:

Sure, mighty love foreseeing the discent
 Of this poor Creature, by a gracious art
 Hid in these low things snares to gain his heart,
And layd surprizes in each Element.

All things here shew him heaven; *Waters* that fall
 Chide, and fly up; *Mists* of corruptest fome
 Quit their first beds & mount; trees, herbs, flowres, all
Strive upwards stil, and point him the way home.[3]

In *The Constellation* he seems to insist that what we should call the scientific study of nature is mere idle curiosity, and that the true method is the analogical. He says to the stars:

Silence, and light, and watchfulnes with you
 Attend and wind the Clue,
No sleep, nor sloth assailes you, but poor man
 Still either sleeps, or slips his span. . . .

Perhaps some nights hee'l watch with you, and peep
 When it were best to sleep,
Dares know Effects, and Judge them long before,
 When th'herb he treads knows much, much more.

But seeks he your *Obedience, Order, Light*,
 Your calm and wel-train'd flight,
Where, though the glory differ in each star,
 Yet is there peace still, and no war?[4]

In the life of nature he is continually finding intimations and confirmations of spiritual truths. There is a very charming poem which seems to have been inspired by his grief for that

---

[1] p. 436.   [2] p. 418.   [3] p. 461.   [4] p. 469.

brother's death to which we have detected other allusions. Looking for a favourite flower in winter he was unable to find it, but after digging about the familiar spot

> ... I saw the warm Recluse alone to lie
>   Where fresh and green
>   He lived of us unseen.
>
> Many a question Intricate and rare
>   Did I there strow,
> But all I could extort was, that he now
>   Did there repair
> Such losses as befel him in this air
>   And would e'r long
>   Come forth most fair and young.
>
> This past, I threw the Clothes quite o'r his head,
>   And stung with fear
> Of my own frailty dropt down many a tear
>   Upon his bed,
> Then sighing whisper'd, *Happy are the dead!*
>   *What peace doth now*
>   *Rock him asleep below?*
>
> And yet, how few believe such doctrine springs
>   From a poor root
> Which all the Winter sleeps here under foot
>   And hath no wings
> To raise it to the truth and light of things,
>   But is stil trod
>   By ev'ry wandring clod.
>
> O thou! whose spirit did at first inflame
>   And warm the dead,
> And by a sacred Incubation fed
>   With life this frame
> Which once had neither being, forme, nor name,
>   Grant I may so
>   Thy steps track here below,
>
> That in these Masques and shadows I may see
>   Thy sacred way,
> And by those hid ascents climb to that day
>   Which breaks from thee
> Who art in all things, though invisibly;
>   Shew me thy peace,
>   Thy mercy, love, and ease,

And from this Care, where dreams and sorrows raign
    Lead me above
Where Light, Joy, Leisure, and true Comforts move
    Without all pain,
There, hid in thee, shew me his life again
    At whose dumbe urn
Thus all the year I mourn.[1]

Finally, there is that exquisite poem *The Water-fall*. The
water seems to pause on the brink of the fall, and seems afraid,
just as the soul is afraid when it approaches death. Nevertheless, the soul, like the water, will

rise to a longer course more bright and brave.

Read the first stanza carefully. There is more loving natural
description in Vaughan than in any other seventeenth-century
poet, except, perhaps, Marvell; but then Marvell rarely ven-
tures beyond his garden.

With what deep murmurs through times silent stealth
Doth thy transparent, cool and watry wealth
        Here flowing fall,
        And chide, and call,
As if his liquid, loose Retinue staid
Lingring, and were of this steep place afraid,
        The common pass
        Where, clear as glass,
        All must descend
        Not to an end:
But quickned by this deep and rocky grave,
Rise to a longer course more bright and brave.

Dear stream! dear bank, where often I
Have sate, and pleas'd my pensive eye,
Why, since each drop of thy quick store
Runs thither, whence it flow'd before,
Should poor souls fear a shade or night,
Who came (sure) from a sea of light?
Or since those drops are all sent back
So sure to thee, that none doth lack,
Why should frail flesh doubt any more
That what God takes, hee'l not restore?
O useful Element and clear!
My sacred wash and cleanser here,
My first consigner unto those
Fountains of life, where the Lamb goes?

[1] p. 478.

What sublime truths, and wholesome themes,
Lodge in thy mystical, deep streams!
Such as dull man can never finde
Unless that Spirit lead his minde,
Which first upon thy face did move,
And hatch'd all with his quickning love.
As this loud brooks incessant fall
In streaming rings restagnates all,
Which reach by course the bank, and then
Are no more seen, just so pass men.
O my invisible estate,
My glorious liberty, still late!
Thou art the Channel my soul seeks,
Not this with Cataracts and Creeks.[1]

[1] p. 537.

THOMAS TRAHERNE

ALMOST our whole knowledge of the outward life of Thomas Traherne is contained in the following brief notice in Wood's *Athenae Oxonienses*:

> Thomas Traherne, a shoemaker's son of Hereford, was entred a Commoner of Brasen-n. college on the first day of March 1652, took one degree in arts, left the house for a time, entred into the sacred function, and in 1661 he was actually created Master of Arts. About that time he became rector of Credinhill commonly called Crednell near to the city of Hereford, afterwards domestic chaplain to S. Orlando Bridgman lord keeper of the great seal, and minister of Tuddington, called by some Teddington, near Hampton Court in Middlesex, and in 1669 bach. of divinity. He hath written,
> *Roman Forgeries: or, a true Account of false Records discovering the Impostures and counterfeit Antiquities of the Church of Rome.* Lond. 1673. oct.
> *Christian Ethics: or divine Morality, opening the Way to Blessedness, by the Rules of Virtue and Reason.* Lond. 1675. oct.
> He died at Teddington before-mention'd, in the house of S. Orl. Bridgman, and was buried on the tenth day of October in the church there, under the reading desk, in sixteen hundred seventy and four. This person, who always led a single and devout life, was well read in primitive antiquity as in the councils, fathers, &c.[1]

To this list of Traherne's published writings must be added *A Serious and Patheticall Contemplation of the Mercies of God, in several most Devout and Sublime Thanksgivings for the same. Published by the Reverend Doctor Hickes at the request of a friend of the Authors,* which appeared in 1699. It was the fact that Hickes mentions that his friend had been chaplain to Sir Orlando Bridgman which enabled the late Mr. Bertram Dobell to discover that his name was Thomas Traherne, and it was a poem in this volume, *These sweeter far than Lillies are,* which convinced him that Traherne was also the author of the anonymous manuscripts of poems and prose meditations which he had acquired and which he published in 1903 and 1908. His conviction was finally justified by Mr. H. J. Bell's accidental discovery, in the British Museum, of Burney MS. 392, *Poems of*

---

[1] Ed. Bliss, vol. iii, p. 1016.

Felicity, containing Divine Reflections on the Native Objects of an Infant-Ey. By Tho. Traheron. B. D. Author of the Roman Forgeries, and Christian Ethiks, a volume which had apparently been prepared for publication by Traherne's brother Philip, and which contains, with textual variations, many of the poems in Dobell's MS., together with thirty-eight poems not found in that collection. This manuscript was edited and published by Mr. Bell in 1910. The poems from both these manuscripts have recently been very carefully edited by Miss Gladys Wade, who in the preface to her edition gives very strong reasons for believing that the *Meditations on the Creation* and *Meditations and Devotions on the Life of Christ*, being the first and second parts of *A Collection of Meditations and Devotions in Three Parts*, published in 1717 by Nathaniel Spinckes and erroneously attributed by the Dr. Hickes already mentioned to a certain Mrs. Susanna Hopton of Hereford, were in fact written for this lady by Thomas Traherne.

I

That sense of the divinity of childhood which occasionally appears in Vaughan is the central intuition around which all Traherne's poems and Meditations revolve; it is the 'masterlight of all his seeing'.

'The counsel which our Saviour giveth in the Revelation to the Church of Ephesus', he declares in the *Centuries of Meditations*,

is by all Churches, and by every Soul diligently to be observed: *Remember from whence thou art fallen, and repent*. Which intimates our duty of remembering our happiness in the estate of innocence. For without this we can never prize our Redeemer's love: He that knows not to what he is redeemed cannot prize the work of redemption. The means cannot there be valued, where the end is despised. Since therefore by the Second Adam, we are restored to that we lost in the first: unless we value that we lost in the first, we cannot truly rejoice in the second.[1]

Well! for Traherne that state of innocence from which Adam fell is enjoyed by all of us—and, alas! by most of us too early lost!—in our childhood.

Will you see the infancy of this sublime and celestial greatness? Those pure and virgin apprehensions I had from the

[1] 2nd Cent. 5, p. 81.

womb, and that divine light wherewith I was born are the best unto this day, wherein I can see the Universe. By the Gift of God they attended me into the world, and by His special favour I remember them till now. Verily they seem the greatest gifts His wisdom could bestow, for without them all other gifts had been dead and vain. They are unattainable by book, and therefore I will teach them by experience. Pray for them earnestly: for they will make you angelical, and wholly celestial. Certainly Adam in Paradise had not more sweet and curious apprehensions of the world, than I when I was a child.

All appeared new, and strange at first, inexpressibly rare and delightful and beautiful. I was a little stranger, which at my entrance into the world was saluted and surrounded with innumerable joys. My knowledge was Divine. I knew by intuition those things which since my Apostasy, I collected again by the highest reason. My very ignorance was advantageous. I seemed as one brought into the Estate of Innocence. All things were spotless and pure and glorious: yea, and infinitely mine, and joyful and precious. I knew not that there were any sins, or complaints or laws. I dreamed not of poverties, contentions or vices. All tears and quarrels were hidden from mine eyes. Everything was at rest, free and immortal. I knew nothing of sickness or death or rents or exaction, either for tribute or bread. In the absence of these I was entertained like an Angel with the works of God in their splendour and glory, I saw all in the peace of Eden; Heaven and Earth did sing my Creator's praises, and could not make more melody to Adam, than to me. All Time was Eternity, and a perpetual Sabbath. Is it not strange, that an infant should be heir of the whole World, and see those mysteries which the books of the learned never unfold?

The corn was orient and immortal wheat, which never should be reaped, nor was ever sown. I thought it had stood from everlasting to everlasting. The dust and stones of the street were as precious as gold: the gates were at first the end of the world. The green trees when I saw them first through one of the gates transported and ravished me; their sweetness and unusual beauty made my heart to leap, and almost mad with ecstasy, they were such strange and wonderful things. The Men! O what venerable and reverend creatures did the aged seem! Immortal Cherubims! And young men glittering and sparkling Angels, and maids strange seraphic pieces of life and beauty! Boys and girls tumbling in the street, and playing, were moving jewels. I knew not that they were born or should die: But all things abided eternally as they were in their proper places. Eternity was manifest in the Light of the Day, and something infinite behind everything appeared: which talked with my expectation and moved my desire. The city seemed to stand in

Eden, or to be built in Heaven. The streets were mine, the temple was mine, the people were mine, their clothes and gold and silver were mine, as much as their sparkling eyes, fair skins and ruddy faces. The skies were mine, and so were the sun and moon and stars, and all the World was mine; and I the only spectator and enjoyer of it. I knew no churlish proprieties, nor bounds, nor divisions: but all proprieties and divisions were mine: all treasures and the possessors of them. So that with much ado I was corrupted, and made to learn the dirty devices of this world. Which now I unlearn, and become, as it were, a little child again that I may enter into the Kingdom of God.[1]

Our Saviour's meaning, when He said, *He must be born again and become a little child that will enter into the Kingdom of Heaven* is deeper far than is generally believed. It is not only in a careless reliance upon Divine Providence, that we are to become little children, or in the feebleness and shortness of our anger and simplicity of our passions, but in the peace and purity of all our soul. Which purity also is a deeper thing than is commonly apprehended. For we must disrobe ourselves of all false colours, and unclothe our souls of evil habits; all our thoughts must be infant-like and clear; the powers of our soul free from the leaven of this world, and disentangled from men's conceits and customs. Grit in the eye or yellow jaundice will not let a man see those objects truly that are before it. And therefore it is requisite that we should be as very strangers to the thoughts, customs, and opinions of men in this world, as if we were but little children. So those things would appear to us only which do to children when they are first born. Ambitions, trades, luxuries, inordinate affections, casual and accidental riches invented since the fall, would be gone, and only those things appear, which did to Adam in Paradise, in the same light and in the same colours: God in His works, Glory in the light, Love in our parents, men, ourselves, and the face of Heaven: Every man naturally seeing those things, to the enjoyment of which he is naturally born.[2]

The first Light which shined in my Infancy in its primitive and innocent clarity was totally eclipsed: insomuch that I was fain to learn all again. If you ask me how it was eclipsed? Truly by the customs and manners of men, which like contrary winds blew it out: by an innumerable company of other objects, rude, vulgar, and worthless things, that like so many loads of earth and dung did overwhelm and bury it: by the impetuous torrent of wrong desires in all others whom I saw or knew that carried me away and alienated me from it: by a whole sea of other matters and concernments that covered and drowned it: finally by the evil influence of a bad education that did not foster and cherish it. All men's thoughts and words were about

[1] 3rd Cent. 1–3, pp. 151–3.   [2] 3rd Cent. 5, pp. 155–6.

other matters. They all prized new things which I did not dream
of. I was a stranger and unacquainted with them; I was little
and reverenced their authority; I was weak, and easily guided
by their example: ambitious also, and desirous to approve myself unto them. And finding no one syllable in any man's mouth
of those things, by degrees they vanished, my thoughts (as indeed what is more fleeting than a thought?) were blotted out;
and at last all the celestial, great, and stable treasures to which
I was born, as wholly forgotten, as if they had never been.[1]

In his insistence that in our early childhood we all, in some
measure, enjoy that state of innocence from which Adam fell,
Traherne recognizes that he is being slightly heterodox on the
doctrine of original sin. Thus, after venturing the opinion

> that our misery proceedeth ten thousand times more from the
> outward bondage of opinion and custom, than from any inward
> corruption or depravation of Nature: And that it is not our
> parents' loins, so much as our parents' lives, that enthrals and
> blinds us

he hastens to add:

> Yet is all our corruption derived from Adam: inasmuch as
> all the evil examples and inclinations of the world arise from
> his sin.

'But', he continues, returning to his obstinate conviction,

> But I speak it in the presence of God and of our Lord Jesus
> Christ, in my pure primitive virgin Light, while my apprehen-
> sions were natural, and unmixed, I cannot remember but that
> I was ten thousand times more prone to good and excellent
> things than evil. But I was quickly tainted and fell by others.[2]

Christ has indeed restored the state of innocence, but to
enter Christ's Kingdom we must become as little children; and
Traherne interprets the Christian exhortation to forsake the
world as a command to leave 'artificial' things for 'natural'
things, the things that made our pleasure in childhood.

> To contemn the world and to enjoy the world are things con-
> trary to each other. How then can we contemn the world, which
> we are born to enjoy? Truly there are two worlds. One was
> made by God, the other by men. That made by God was great
> and beautiful. Before the Fall it was Adam's joy and the Temple
> of his Glory. That made by men is a Babel of Confusions: In-
> vented Riches, Pomps and Vanities, brought in by Sin. Give

[1] 3rd Cent. 7, p. 157.   [2] 3rd Cent. 8, p. 158.

all (saith Thomas à Kempis) for all. Leave the one that you may enjoy the other.[1]

The works of darkness are Repining, Envy, Malice, Covetousness, Fraud, Oppression, Discontent and Violence. All which proceed from the corruption of Men and their mistake in the choice of riches: for having refused those which God made, and taken to themselves treasures of their own, they invented scarce and rare, insufficient, hard to be gotten, little, movable and useless treasures.[2]

Would one think it possible for a man to delight in gauderies like a butterfly, and neglect the Heavens? Did we not daily see it, it would be incredible. They rejoice in a piece of gold more than in the Sun; and get a few little glittering stones and call them jewels. And admire them because they be resplendent like the stars, and transparent like the air, and pellucid like the sea. But the stars themselves which are ten thousand times more useful, great, and glorious they disregard. Nor shall the air itself be counted anything, though it be worth all the pearls and diamonds in ten thousand worlds. A work of God so Divine by reason of its precious and pure transparency, that all worlds would be worth nothing without such a treasure.[3]

πολλὰ καὶ ἀνόσια περὶ τὸ τῶν πολλῶν νόμισμα γέγονεν—we are irresistibly reminded of Plato's words about those Guardians who are to be forbidden the use of gold and silver:

Tell them they have divine gold and silver in their souls for ever; that they need no money stamped of men—neither may they otherwise than impiously mingle the gathering of the divine with the mortal treasure, for through that which the law of the multitude has coined, endless crimes have been done and suffered; but in theirs is neither pollution nor sorrow.[4]

Traherne frequently expresses the same idea in his poems, most perfectly perhaps in *Thanksgivings for the Beauty of his Providence*, a poem to which Dobell gave the title of *The Ways of Wisdom*, and which convinced him that the author of the *Serious and Pathetical Contemplation*, in which it occurs, was also the author of the anonymous manuscripts.

> These sweeter far than Lillies are,
> No Roses may with these compare!
>   How these excel
>   No Tongue can tell!
> Which he that well and truly knows,
>   With praise and joy he goes.

[1] 1st Cent. 7, p. 6.   [2] 1st Cent. 33, pp. 21–2.
[3] 1st Cent. 34, pp. 22–3.
[4] *Republic*, 416 e, translated by Ruskin in *Munera Pulveris*, § 89.

How great and happy's he, that knows his Ways,
    To be divine and heavenly Joys!
    To whom each City is more brave,
Than Walls of Pearl, and Streets which Gold doth pave:
        Whose open eyes
        Behold the Skies;
    Who loves their Wealth and Beauty more,
        Than Kings love golden Ore!

Who sees the heavenly antient Ways,
Of GOD the Lord, with Joy and Praise;
        More than the Skies,
        With open Eyes,
    Doth prize them all: yea more than Gems
            And Regal Diadems.
That more esteemeth Mountains as they are,
    Than if they Gold and Silver were:
    To whom the *SUN* more pleasure brings,
Than Crowns and Thrones, and Palaces, to Kings.
        That knows his Ways,
        To be the Joys,
And Way of God. These things who knows,
    With Joy and Praise he goes![1]

II

These reflections on his own early experiences lead Traherne
to certain profound convictions or intuitions, to a conception
of God, Man, and Nature which is both intensely philosophic
and intensely poetic. He insists that God can only be known
through the creation; that the creation only becomes signifi-
cant, only reaches its $\tau\grave{o}$ $\tau\acute{\iota}$ $\mathring{\eta}\nu$ $\epsilon\mathring{\iota}\nu\alpha\iota$ when it is mirrored and re-
created by the mind of a man, which is more divine than its
object; that man's duty is perpetually to recreate the world and
to present it as an acceptable offering to God; and that happiness, felicity, consists in seeing the world as God sees it, feeling
that all things are working together for good.

Like that of Plato, the attitude of the Christian Church towards the external world had never been entirely satisfactory
or consistent. The commandment to forsake the world was
literally interpreted; the world was regarded chiefly as a place
of trial and pilgrimage and all sensible things, appearances,
were regarded as in some measure illusory. The Renaissance
has often been regarded as a worldly, a secular movement; and
certainly the active spirits of that age, with their intense interest

[1] *Poetical Works*, ed. Wade, p. 236.

in physical science, their discoveries of new lands, and their passionate love of beauty were not disposed to reject as illusory the world of appearances. They desired to 'save phenomena', and to find some explanation of the cosmic process more satisfying than that commonly provided by traditional theology. We can see this general tendency of thought, which we may perhaps describe as an attempt to substitute a dynamic for a static explanation of the world, working in different ways in many very different minds: in Nicholas of Cusa, the last of the great schoolmen, with his conception of the universe as the *explicatio Dei*; in Raymond de Sabunde with his insistence on the *liber creaturarum* and his doctrine that man's duty is to unite the creation with God; in the cosmosophists, Paracelsus and Cornelius Agrippa, with their strange amalgam of conceptions drawn from alchemy, Neoplatonism, and the Cabbala, yet permeated with a sense of 'the one spirit's plastic stress'; in Giordano Bruno, with his doctrine of the divinity of matter and of an ensouled universe; in the humble and unlearned Philosophus Teutonicus, with his gradual progress from the conventional notion of the Trinity to the conception of a God in whom the conflict of opposites is the principle of being; in Pico della Mirandula, who took all knowledge for his province and who deduced all wisdom from one original revelation of God to man; in poets such as Spenser who found in a kind of Christian Platonism a justification for their worship of beauty. As I have already remarked in speaking of Vaughan, it is a great misfortune that the spiritual or poetic element in this movement of thought quickly left the main stream, which during the latter part of the seventeenth and most of the eighteenth century took the form of an intensely progressive but emphatically materialistic application of reason in physical science, politics, and taste, and of a philosophy and theology which insisted indeed that the world was the creation of a 'divine artificer', but which, because of its distrust of 'enthusiasm' and its lack of profound emotional experience, easily degenerated into the self-complacency and the rather greasy optimism of Pangloss.

Traherne sometimes suggests that the cause and purpose of the creation was to satisfy a want and therefore, in a sense, to remove an imperfection, in the nature of God himself. This view had occasionally been expressed by earlier writers, but the orthodox explanation was nearer to that given by Plato in the *Timaeus* (29 *e*), that God created the world, not in order to perfect himself, since he was already perfect, but in order to communicate his goodness. The difference of emphasis is important, for according to the view suggested, though not positively affirmed, by Traherne, the creation is more organic-ally and essentially related to the creator, and therefore more divine.

> God did infinitely for us, when He made us to want like Gods, that like Gods we might be satisfied. The heathen Deities wanted nothing, and were therefore unhappy, for they had no being. But the Lord God of Israel, the Living and True God, was from all Eternity, and from all Eternity wanted like a God. He wanted the communication of His divine essence, and per-sons to enjoy it. He wanted Worlds, He wanted Spectators, He wanted Joys, He wanted Treasures. He wanted, yet He wanted not, for He had them.
> This is very strange that God should want. For in Him is the fulness of all Blessedness: He overfloweth eternally. His wants are as glorious as infinite: perfective needs that are in His nature, and ever Blessed, because always satisfied. He is from eternity full of want, or else He would not be full of Treasure. Infinite want is the very ground and cause of infinite treasure. It is incredible, yet very plain. Want is the fountain of all His fulness. Want in God is treasure to us. For had there been no need He would not have created the World, nor made us, nor manifested His wisdom, nor exercised His power, nor beautified Eternity, nor prepared the Joys of Heaven. But He wanted Angels and Men, Images, Companions: And these He had from all Eternity.[1]
> He willed the Creation not only that He might Appear but Be: wherein is seated the mystery of the Eternal Generation of His Son.[2]

He continually insists that the world is the manifestation of God:

> Ancient philosophers have thought God to be the Soul of the World. Since therefore this visible World is the body of God, not His natural body, but which He hath assumed; let us see how glorious His wisdom is in manifesting Himself thereby. It hath not only represented His infinity and eternity which we thought impossible to be represented by a body, but His beauty also, His wisdom, goodness, power, life and glory, His righteous-ness, love, and blessedness: all which as out of a plentiful treasury, may be taken and collected out of this world.[3]

[1] 1st Cent. 41–2, pp. 27–8.
[2] 1st Cent. 53, p. 35.   [3] 2nd Cent. 21, p. 91.

Here, again, as in his attitude to the doctrine of original sin and in his view of the cause and purpose of the creation, Traherne's fundamental intuitions, his fidelity to his own experience, seem to drive him beyond the bounds of orthodox Christianity. At times he seems very near to Pantheism, that doctrine which the Church has always looked upon with extreme disfavour, since its logical consequence is that good and evil are equally manifestations of God, and that God himself is no more than the *rerum natura*, the nature of things. Traherne, however, is able to preserve the conception of a God who is both immanent and transcendent; he never admits or recognizes the existence of any necessary evil in the creation, and moral evil he attributes entirely to man's misuse of his free will, often explicitly declaring that Heaven and Hell are within us:

> 'Tis not the change of place, but glorious principles well practised that establish Heaven in the life and soul. An angel will be happy anywhere, and a devil miserable, because the principles of the one are always good, of the other, bad. From the centre to the utmost bounds of the everlasting hills all is Heaven before God, and full of treasure; and he that walks like God in the midst of them, blessed.[1]

As we shall see later, Traherne never really faces the problem of evil, but he contrives to avoid both Pantheism and Dualism.

God, then, is both immanent and transcendent, but we can only come to love him and know him through his works:

> Wouldst thou love God alone? God alone cannot be beloved. He cannot be loved with a finite love, because He is infinite. Were He beloved alone, His love would be limited. He must be loved in all with an illimited love, even in all His doings, in all His friends, in all His creatures. Everywhere in all things thou must meet His love.[2]
>
> All things were made to be yours, and you were made to prize them according to their value: which is your office and duty, the end for which you were created, and the means whereby you enjoy. The end for which you were created, is that by prizing all that God hath done, you may enjoy yourself and Him in Blessedness.[3]
>
> You never enjoy the world aright, till you see how a sand exhibiteth the wisdom and power of God. . . . You never enjoy the world aright, till the Sea itself floweth in your veins, till you are clothed with the heavens, and crowned with the stars: and

[1] 4th Cent. 37, p. 252.   [2] 1st Cent. 72, p. 52.   [3] 1st Cent. 12, p. 8.

perceive yourself to be the sole heir of the whole world, and
more than so, because men are in it who are every one sole heirs
as well as you. Till you can sing and rejoice and delight in God,
as misers do in gold, and Kings in sceptres, you never enjoy the
world.[1]

This conception of man as a link between the Creation and
the Creator is closely connected with that conception of Man
the Microcosm which appears in the writings of many Renaissance philosophers, notably in the discourse *De Hominis Digni-
tate* of Pico della Mirandula, which Traherne enthusiastically
praises and the substance of which he renders into his own
incomparable prose.[2] Pater, in his essay on Pico in *The Renaissance*, has some delightful and appropriate remarks on this
discourse:

> The oration which Pico composed for the opening of this
> philosophical tournament still remains; its subject is the dignity
> of human nature, the greatness of man. In common with nearly
> all mediaeval speculation, much of Pico's writing has this for
> its drift; and in common also with it, Pico's theory of that dignity
> is founded on a misconception of the place in nature both of the
> earth and of man. For Pico the earth is the centre of the uni-
> verse: and around it, as a fixed and motionless point, the sun
> and moon and stars revolve, like diligent servants or ministers.
> And in the midst of all this is placed man, *nodus et vinculum mundi*,
> the bond or copula of the world, and the 'interpreter of nature':
> that famous expression of Bacon's really belongs to Pico. *Tritum
> est in scholis*, he says, *esse hominem minorem mundum, in quo mixtum
> ex elementis corpus et spiritus coelestis et plantarum anima vegetalis et
> brutorum sensus et ratio et angelica mens et Dei similitudo conspicitur:—*
> 'It is a commonplace of the schools that Man is a little world,
> in which we may discern a body mingled of earthy elements,
> and ethereal breath, and the vegetable life of plants, and the
> senses of the lower animals, and reason, and the intelligence of
> angels, and a likeness to God.'
> A commonplace of the schools! But perhaps it had some new
> significance and authority, when men heard one like Pico re-
> iterate it; and, false as its basis was, the theory had its use. For
> this high dignity of man, thus bringing the dust under his feet
> into sensible communion with the thoughts and affections of the
> angels, was supposed to belong to him, not as renewed by a
> religious system, but by his own natural right. The proclama-
> tion of it was a counterpoise to the increasing tendency of
> mediaeval religion to depreciate man's nature, to sacrifice this
> or that element in it, to make it ashamed of itself, to keep the

[1] 1st Cent. 27 and 29, pp. 18–19.   [2] 4th Cent. 74–7, pp. 280–4.

degrading or painful accidents of it always in view. It helped man onward to that reassertion of himself, that rehabilitation of human nature, the body, the senses, the heart, the intelligence, which the Renaissance fulfils.

III

Traherne, however, develops this conception of Man the Microcosm in a way that anticipates much of the work of Berkeley and later idealism and which has the freshness and power of an original intuition, often reminding us of some of the finest moments in the *Prelude*. Over and over again he insists that God, Man, and Nature are essentially, organically, dynamically related; that the creation, God's manifestation of himself, only becomes significant, only really exists, through the mind of man, and that accordingly God's purpose in the Creation can only be realized in and through the co-operation of man, whose duty it is to understand and delight in all that he perceives, thereby continually re-creating and returning to God a second Creation more glorious than the first. And like the German mystics, Eckhart, Tauler, and Jakob Böhme, Traherne connects God's manifestation of himself in the Creation with the 'mystery of the eternal generation of his son'.

Christ dwelling in our hearts by Faith is an Infinite Mystery, which may thus be understood: An object seen, is in the faculty of seeing it, and by that in the Soul of the seer, after the best of manners. Whereas there are eight manners of in-being, the in-being of an object in a faculty is the best of all. Dead things are in a room containing them in a vain manner; unless they are objectively in the Soul of a seer. The pleasure of an enjoyer is the very end why things are in any place. The place and the thing placed in it, being both in the understanding of a spectator of them. Things dead in dead place effect nothing. But in a living Soul, that seeth their excellencies, they excite a pleasure answerable to their value, a wisdom to embrace them, a courage not to forsake them, a love of their Donor, praises and thanksgivings; and a greatness and a joy equal to their goodness.[1]

We could easily show that the idea of Heaven and Earth in the Soul of Man, is more precious with God than the things themselves and more excellent in nature. Which because it will surprise you a little, I will. What would Heaven and Earth be worth, were there no spectator, no enjoyer? As much therefore as the end is better than the means, the thought of the World whereby it is enjoyed is better than the World. So is the idea of it in the Soul of Man, better than the World in the esteem of

[1] 1st Cent. 100, p. 75.

God: it being the end of the World, without which Heaven and Earth would be vain. . . . The world within you is an offering returned, which is infinitely more acceptable to God Almighty, since it came from Him, that it might return unto Him. Wherein the mystery is great. For God hath made you able to create worlds in your own mind which are more precious unto Him than those which He created; and to give and offer up the world unto Him, which is very delightful in flowing from Him, but much more in returning to Him. Besides all which in its own nature also a Thought of the World, or the World in a Thought, is more excellent than the World, because it is spiritual and nearer unto God. The material world is dead and feeleth nothing, but this spiritual world, though it be invisible, hath all dimensions, and is a divine and living Being, the voluntary Act of an obedient Soul.[1]

These ideas are expressed in one of Traherne's most successful poems:

Thoughts. II.

I

A Delicate and Tender Thought
The Quintessence is found of all he Wrought.
It is the fruit of all his Works,
Which we conceive,
Bring forth, and Give,
Yea and in which the Greater Value lurks.
It is the fine and Curious Flower,
Which we return, and offer evry hour:
So Tender in our Paradice
That in a Trice
It withers strait, and fades away,
If we but ceas its Beautie to display.

2

Why Things so Precious, should be made
So Prone, so Easy, and so Apt to fade
It is not easy to declare.
But God would have
His Creatures Brave
And that too by their own Continual Care.
He gave them Power evry Hour,
Both to Erect, and to Maintain a Tower,
Which he far more in us doth Prize
Then all the Skies.
That we might offer it to Him,
And in our Souls be like the Seraphim.

[1] 2nd Cent. 90, pp. 138–9.

3

That Temple David did intend,
Was but a Thought, and yet it did transcend
King Solomons. A Thought we know
Is that for which
God doth Enrich
With Joys even Heaven above, and Earth below.
For that all Objects might be seen
He made the Orient Azure and the Green:
That we might in his Works delight.
And that the Sight
Of those his Treasures might Enflame
The Soul with Love to him, he made the same.

4

This Sight which is the Glorious End
Of all his Works, and which doth comprehend
Eternity, and Time, and Space,
Is far more dear,
And far more near
To him, then all his Glorious Dwelling Place.
It is a Spiritual World within.
A LIVING WORLD, and nearer far of Kin
To God, then that which first he made.
While that doth fade
This therfore ever shall Endure,
Within the Soul as more Divine and Pure.[1]

IV

To maintain this 'Circulation', as he calls it in one of his
poems, to exercise the creative and priestly office of media-
tion between the creation and the creator, and at the same
time to cherish the sabbatical conviction that the whole
creation is good, and that all things are working together for
good with them that love God—this, according to Traherne,
is happiness, felicity; and to pursue happiness is not only a
natural instinct but a religious duty.

Is it not the shame and reproach of Nature, that men should
spend so much time in studying trades, and be so ready skilled
in the nature of clothes, of grounds, of gold and silver &c., and
to think it much to spend a little time in the study of God,
themselves, and happiness? What have men to do in this world,
but to make themselves happy? Shall it ever be praised, and

[1] *Poetical Works*, ed. Wade, p. 70.

despised? Verily, happiness being the sovereign and supreme
of our concerns, should have the most peculiar portion of our
time, and other things what she can spare.[1]

The best of all possible ends is the Glory of God, but happiness was that I thirsted after. And yet I did not err, for the
Glory of God is to make us happy.[2]

When I came into the country, and being seated among silent
trees, and meads and hills, had all my time in mine own hands,
I resolved to spend it all, whatever it cost me, in search of happiness, and to satiate that burning thirst which Nature had en-
kindled in me from my youth. In which I was so resolute,
that I chose rather to live upon ten pounds a year, and to go in
leather clothes, and feed upon bread and water, so that I might
have all my time clearly to myself, than to keep many thousands
per annum in an estate of life where my time would be devoured
in care and labour. And God was so pleased to accept of that
desire, that from that time to this, I have had all things plenti-
fully provided for me, without any care at all, my very study
of Felicity making me more to prosper, than all the care in the
whole world. So that through His blessing I live a free and a
kingly life as if the world were turned again into Eden, or much
more, as it is at this day.[3]

The image of God implanted in us, guided me to the manner
wherein we were to enjoy. For since we were made in the similitude of God, we were made to enjoy after His similitude. Now
to enjoy the treasures of God in the similitude of God, is the
most perfect blessedness God could devise. . . . I no sooner dis-
cerned this but I was (as Plato saith, In *summa Rationis arce quies
habitat*) seated in a throne of repose and perfect rest. All things
were well in their proper places, I alone was out of frame and
had need to be mended. For all things were God's treasures
in their proper places, and I was to be restored to God's Image.
Whereupon you will not believe, how I was withdrawn from all
endeavours of altering and mending outward things. They lay
so well, methought, they could not be mended: but I must be
mended to enjoy them.[4]

When things are ours in their proper places, nothing is need-
ful but prizing to enjoy them. God therefore hath made it
infinitely easy to enjoy, by making everything ours, and us able
so easily to prize them. Everything is ours that serves us in its
place. The Sun serves us as much as is possible, and more than
we could imagine. The Clouds and Stars minister unto us, the
World surrounds us with beauty, the Air refresheth us, the Sea
revives the earth and us. The Earth itself is better than gold
because it produceth fruits and flowers. And therefore in the

[1] 4th Cent. 7, p. 233.   [2] 3rd Cent. 39, p. 180.
[3] 3rd Cent. 46, p. 186.   [4] 3rd Cent. 59 and 60, pp. 195-6.

beginning, was it made manifest to be mine, because Adam alone was made to enjoy it. By making one, and not a multitude, God evidently shewed one alone to be the end of the World and every one its enjoyer. For every one may enjoy it as much as He.[1]

You never enjoy the World aright, till you see all things in it so perfectly yours, that you cannot desire them any other way: and till you are convinced that all things serve you best in their proper places.[2]

It is true that there is a superficial resemblance between these meditations and the famous argument from design so popular with those eighteenth-century optimists and deists who demonstrated *ad nauseam* that the world was manifestly the work of a divine artificer, and that *tout est bien dans le plus beau monde possible*. The resemblance, however, is no more than superficial. Traherne's accent is joyful and childlike and comes to us, as I have said, with the freshness and power of an original intuition, while that of the eighteenth-century deists is generally smug and complacent. The creation to which they direct their readers' attention is dead—'inanimate nature'; the happiness which it is supposed to promote is usually commonplace and material; and the creator who mechanically constructed it is represented as a kind of clock-maker who, having wound up his clock, refuses to interfere with it until it has run down. The arguments are similar, but the experiences from which they arise and which they also communicate are worlds apart; and as Plato insists in the *Phaedrus*, we can only determine the worth of an argument after we have traced it back to the fundamental ideas or convictions on which it rests.

This, then, is Traherne's conception of the happiness which it is our duty to seek; and he insists that the true Christian will not willingly defer his happiness until another life.

There are Christians that place and desire all their happiness in another life, and there is another sort of Christians that desire happiness in this. The one can defer their enjoyment of Wisdom till the World to come, and dispense with the increase and perfection of knowledge for a little time: the other are instant and impatient of delay, and would fain see that happiness here, which they shall enjoy hereafter. Not the vain happiness of this world, falsely called happiness, truly vain: but the real joy and glory of the blessed, which consisteth in the enjoyment of the whole world in communion with God; not this only, but the

---

[1] 1st Cent. 14, pp. 9–10.   [2] 1st Cent. 38, p. 25.

invisible and eternal, which they earnestly covet to enjoy immediately: for which reason they daily pray *Thy Kingdom come*, and
travail towards it by learning Wisdom as fast as they can.
Whether the first sort be Christians indeed, look you to that.
They have much to say for themselves. Yet certainly they that
put off felicity with long delays are to be much suspected. For
it is against the nature of love and desire to defer. Nor can any
reason be given why they should desire it at last, and not now.
If they say because God hath commanded them, that is false:
for He offereth it now, now they are commanded to have their
conversation in Heaven, now they may be full of joy and full of
glory. *Ye are not straitened in me, but in your own bowels.* Those
Christians that can defer their felicity may be contented with
their ignorance.[1]

It is instructive to turn from this to Donne's great meditation on the Death of Ecstasy:

> The contemplation of God, and heaven, is a kinde of buriall,
> and Sepulchre, and rest of the soule; and in this death of rapture,
> and exstasie, in this death of the Contemplation of my interest
> in my Saviour, I shall finde my self, and all my sins enterred,
> and entombed in his wounds, and like a Lily in Paradise, out of
> red earth, I shall see my soule rise out of his blade, in a candor,
> and in an innocence, contracted there, acceptable in the sight
> of his Father.

As Grierson remarks:

> This is the highest level that Donne ever reached in eloquence
> inspired by the vision of the joy and not the terror of the Chris-
> tian Faith.

It is the only passage of its kind I can remember. Donne does
not speak of this state of ecstasy as the natural condition of
every true Christian; it is the final reward of a long series of
battles against worldliness and sin, and indeed the conviction
of sin forgiven, the joy of escape from sin, is the central flame.
In Traherne the sense of sin, so powerful and omnipresent in
Donne, is hardly apparent. The sin of which he accuses his
early youth, after he had lost the visions of childhood, is rather
ignorance than moral evil in the ordinary sense, and what he
asks for is not forgiveness but illumination. In some ways he is
nearer to Plato and Aristotle than to Christianity. For him,
as for Plato and Socrates, we might almost say that virtue is
knowledge and vice ignorance, and the condition towards
which he aspires is nearer to Aristotle's θεωρία than to that of

---

[1] 4th Cent. 9, pp. 235–6.

the saints. There are many passages in the *Meditations* which remind us of the *Ethics*, and it is worth remembering that Traherne connects his rediscovery and interpretation of his early experiences with his residence at Oxford.

Having been at the University, and received there the taste and tincture of another education, I saw that there were things in this world of which I never dreamed; glorious secrets, and glorious persons past imagination. There I saw that Logic, Ethics, Physics, Metaphysics, Geometry, Astronomy, Poesy, Medicine, Grammar, Music, Rhetoric, all kinds of Arts, Trades, and Mechanisms that adorned the world pertained to felicity; at least there I saw those things, which afterwards I knew to pertain unto it: and was delighted in it . . . and those things which my nurses, and parents, should have talked of there were taught unto me.[1]

It is true that even at the University

some things were defective too. There was never a tutor that did professly teach Felicity, though that be the mistress of all other sciences. . . . Howbeit there we received all those seeds of knowledge that were afterwards improved; and our souls were awakened to a discerning of their faculties, and exercise of their powers.[2]

It seems clear that Traherne received some very fruitful 'seeds of knowledge' from 'the Philosopher', who taught that the end of all human action was happiness, εὐδαιμονία; that happiness consisted in a virtuous activity of the soul, ψυχῆς ἐνέργεια κατ' ἀρετήν; that the highest of human activities was reason, and the highest kind of reason that impassioned contemplation, θεωρία, which may fitly be ascribed to the gods, and in which man also, in virtue of some divine spark within him, may participate and thereby make himself in some measure like unto the gods —ἐφ' ὅσον ἐνδέχεται ἀθανατίζειν.

I saw moreover that it did not so much concern us what objects were before us, as with what eyes we beheld them, with what affections we esteemed them, and what apprehensions we had about them. All men see the same objects, but do not equally understand them. Intelligence is the tongue that discerns and tastes them, Knowledge is the Light of Heaven, Love is the Wisdom and Glory of God, Life extended to all objects is the sense that enjoys them. So that Knowledge, Life, and Love are the very means of all enjoyment, which above all things we must seek for and labour after. All objects are in God Eternal:

[1] 3rd Cent. 36, p. 179.   [2] 3rd Cent. 37, p. 179.

which we by perfecting our faculties are made to enjoy. Which then are turned into Act, when they are exercised about their objects; but without them are desolate and idle; or discontented and forlorn. Whereby I perceived the meaning of the definition wherein Aristotle describeth Felicity, when he saith, *Felicity is the perfect exercise of perfect virtue in a perfect Life.* For that life is perfect when it is perfectly extended to all objects, and perfectly sees them, and perfectly loves them: which is done by a perfect exercise of virtue about them.[1]

In expressing his idea of what seems to him the highest happiness of which human nature is capable Aristotle is not troubled by the reflection that the majority of men are unlikely to attain it, for the doctrine that all souls are equal in the sight of the gods had no place in Greek philosophy. The Christian Church, on the other hand, has generally set before men a less exclusive and aristocratic happiness, insisting that all men, even the humblest, may obtain it by the exercise of will and faith, and by the grace of God. Traherne sometimes speaks rather harshly of the *domus angusta*, of the lives and ways of poor and simple folk, and with an accent that is more Hellenic than Christian;[2] and he draws a distinction between perfect and imperfect Christians, insisting that a perfect Christian must also be a philosopher.

> Is not a Philosopher a lover of wisdom? That is the significa-
> tion of the very word, and sure it is the essence of a Christian,
> or very near it, to be a lover of wisdom. Can a Christian be so
> degenerate as to be a lover of imperfection? Does not your very
> nature abhor imperfection? 'Tis true a Christian so far as he
> is defective and imperfect may be ignorant, yet still he is a lover
> of wisdom and a studier of it. He may be defective, but so far
> as he is defective he is no Christian, for a Christian is not a
> Christian in his blemishes, but his excellencies. Nor is a man
> indeed a man in his ignorances, but his wisdom. Blemishes may
> mar a man, and spoil a Christian, but they cannot make him.
> Defects may be in him and cleave unto him, but they are to be
> shaken off and repented. Every man therefore according to his
> degree, so far forth as he is a Christian, is a Philosopher.[3]

And of St. Paul's commandment, 'Be men in understanding', he says:

> This plainly shows, that though a weak Christian may believe
> great things by an implicit faith, yet it is very desirable his faith
> should be turned into assurance, and that cannot be but by the
> riches of knowledge and understanding.[4]

[1] 3rd Cent. 68, pp. 201–2. [2] cp. 3rd Cent. 28, ad fin., pp. 173–4.
[3] 4th Cent. 5, pp. 231–2. [4] 4th Cent. 6, p. 232.

In many ways, then, Traherne's conception of felicity, his interpretation of the commandment 'Be ye perfect, even as your Father in Heaven is perfect', differs from that of orthodox Christianity. Illumination rather than victory in a moral conflict, union with God through impassioned contemplation and recreation of his works, through renunciation of self, or rather through discovery of the real self, which, as he is never tired of affirming, contains God and the whole world—it is for these that he prays; and his attitude to the Incarnation and Passion is akin to that of the German mystics and to some of the Cambridge Platonists, notably John Smith, for whom Christ is less an historical person than a spirit and a life. He has little sense of sin, and his life, though simple, seems to have been sheltered and congenial, and supplied with that modicum of 'external goods' without which, as Aristotle admits, $\theta\epsilon\omega\rho\acute{\iota}a$ is impossible. He is unorthodox, perhaps, but let us remember that many of the saints have been unorthodox, that there have been contemplative as well as active saints, and that in its highest manifestations the religious consciousness can rise to a point that transcends morality, and where there is no further need for conflict, because it has been all swallowed up in victory.

Nevertheless, these distinctions must not be taken to imply that Traherne's writings in general reveal a want of human sympathy and affection. He declares indeed that

> Had we not loved ourselves at all, we could never have been obliged to love anything. So that self-love is the basis of all love.[1]

But remembering the 'new commandment' and the beautiful saying, 'the friend is another self', which Aristotle took over from Pythagoras, he also declares that

> He was ten years studying before he could satisfy his self-love. And now finds nothing more easy than to love others better than oneself: and that to love mankind so is the comprehensive method to all Felicity.[2]

And again:

> The world is best enjoyed and most immediately while we converse blessedly and wisely with men. I am sure it were desirable that they could give and receive infinite treasures: and perhaps they can. For whomsoever I love as myself, to him I give myself, and all my happiness, which I think is infinite: and I receive him and all his happiness.[3]

[1] 4th Cent. 55, p. 266.   [2] Ibid.   [3] 4th Cent. 19, p. 242.

He had another saying—He lives most like an Angel that lives upon least himself, and doth most good to others. For the Angels neither eat nor drink, and yet do good to the whole world. Now a man is an incarnate Angel. And he that lives in the midst of riches as a poor man himself, enjoying God and Paradise, or Christendom which is better, conversing with the poor, and seeing the value of their souls through their bodies, and prizing all things clearly with a due esteem, is arrived here to the estate of immortality.[1]

And thus the θεωρία which for Traherne, as for Aristotle, is the highest felicity, is interpenetrated by a spirit that was unknown to 'the Philosopher'—'all light and love'.

Felicity

Prompted to seek my Bliss abov the Skies,
    How often did I lift mine Eys
        Beyond the Spheres!
Dame Nature told me *there* was endless Space
Within my Soul; I spy'd its very face:
        Sure it not for nought appears.
    What is there wch a Man may see
        Beyond the Spheres?
        FELICITY.

There in the Mind of God, that Sphere of Lov,
    (In nature, hight, extent, abov
        All other Spheres,)
A Man may see Himself, the World, the Bride
Of God *His Church*, wch as they there are ey'd
        Strangely exalted each appears:
        His Mind is higher than the Space
            Abov the Spheres,
            Surmounts all Place.

No empty Space; it is all full of Sight,
    All Soul & Life, an Ey most bright,
        All Light & Lov;
Which doth at once all things possess and giv,
Heven & Earth, with All that therin liv;
        It rests at quiet, & doth mov;
        Eternal is, yet Time includes;
            A Scene abov
            All Interludes.[2]

---

[1] 4th Cent. 29, p. 248.   [2] *Poems of Felicity*, ed. Bell, p. 22.

Indeed, as with Wordsworth, Traherne's early 'love of nature' seems to have led gradually to 'love of man'.

I remember once the first time I came into a magnificent or noble dining-room, and was left there alone, I rejoiced to see the gold and state and carved imagery, but when all was dead, and there was no motion, I was weary of it, and departed dissatisfied. But afterwards, when I saw it full of lords and ladies, and music and dancing, the place which once seemed not to differ from a solitary den, had now entertainment, and nothing of tediousness but pleasure in it. By which I perceived (upon a reflection made long after) that men and women are when well understood a principal part of our true felicity.[1]

And in one of the most childlike and delightful of his poems he tells how when he heard of 'Christendom' he tried to conceive of it as a definite place, some wonderful country beyond the seas, and how he tried to people it with the best of all he knew. The scene grew more and more familiar until at last the truth broke upon him that the Kingdom of God is in no strange land.

> Things Native sweetly grew,
> Which there mine Ey did view,
> Plain, simple, cheap, on either side the Street,
> Which was exceeding fair & wide;
> Sweet Mansions there mine Eys did meet;
> Green Trees the shaded Doors did hide:
> My chiefest Joys
> Were Girls & Boys
> That in those Streets still up & down did play,
> Which crown'd the Town with constant Holiday.
>
> A sprightly pleasant Time,
> (Ev'n Summer in its prime),
> Did gild the Trees, the Houses, Children, Skies,
> And made the City all divine;
> It ravished my wondring Eys
> To see the Sun so brightly shine:
> The Heat & Light
> Seem'd in my sight
> With such a dazling Lustre shed on them,
> As made me think 'twas th'*New Jerusalem*.

[1] 3rd Cent. 22, pp. 167–8.

Beneath the lofty Trees
I saw, of all Degrees,
Folk calmly sitting in their doors; while som
Did standing with them kindly talk,
Som smile, som sing, or what was don
Observ, while others by did walk;
They view'd the Boys
And Girls, their Joys,
The Streets adorning with their Angel-faces,
Themselvs diverting in those pleasant Places.

The Streets like Lanes did seem,
Not pav'd with Stones, but green,
Which with red Clay did partly mixt appear;
'Twas Holy Ground of great Esteem;
The Spring's choice Liveries did wear
Of verdant Grass that grew between
The purling Streams,
Which golden Beams
Of Light did varnish, coming from the Sun,
By wch to distant Realms was Service don.

In fresh & cooler Rooms
Retir'd they dine: Perfumes
They wanted not, having the pleasant Shade,
And Peace to bless their House within,
By sprinkled Waters cooler made,
For those incarnat Cherubin.
This happy Place,
With all the Grace
The Joy & Beauty which did it beseem,
Did ravish me & highten my Esteem.

That here to rais Desire
All Objects do conspire,
Peeple in Years, & Yong enough to play,
Their Streets of Houses, comon Peace,
In one continued Holy day
Whose gladsom Mirth shall never cease:
Since these becom
My *Christendom*,
What learn I more than that *Jerusalem*
Is *mine*, as 'tis *my Maker's*, choicest Gem.

Before I was aware
Truth did to me appear,
And represented to my Virgin-Eys

Th'unthought of Joys & Treasures
Wherin my Bliss & Glory lies;
My God's Delight, (wch givs me Measure)
His Turtle Dov,
Is Peace & Lov
In Towns: for holy Children, Maids, & Men
Make up the King of Glory's Diadem.[1]

V

The reader must already have been struck by a remarkable
resemblance between some of the fundamental intuitions and
experiences of Wordsworth and Traherne. Wordsworth, like
Traherne, after a period of doubt and disillusion and dissatisfaction found the secret of happiness, the *via salutis*, in his
recollections of early childhood—of that time when

. . . meadow, grove, and stream,
The earth, and every common sight,
To me did seem
Apparell'd in celestial light,
The glory and the freshness of a dream.

And again, like Traherne, it was not merely in the sensible
happiness of childhood that he found this secret, but in those
strange moments when the soul felt itself to be on the verge of
some great discovery—

those obstinate questionings
Of sense and outward things,
Fallings from us, vanishings;
Blank misgivings of a Creature
Moving about in worlds not realized,
High instincts before which our mortal Nature
Did tremble like a guilty Thing surprised:
But for those first affections,
Those shadowy recollections,
Which, be they what they may,
Are yet the fountain light of all our day,
Are yet the master-light of all our seeing;
Uphold us, cherish, and have power to make
Our noisy years seem moments in the being
Of the eternal Silence.[2]

Dumb yearnings, hidden appetites, are ours,
And *they must* have their food. Our childhood sits,
Our simple childhood, sits upon a throne

[1] *Poems of Felicity*, ed. Bell, pp. 45–7.   [2] *Intimations of Immortality.*

That hath more power than all the elements.
I guess not what this tells of Being past,
Nor what it augurs of the life to come;
But so it is.[1]

Traherne also finds significance in these 'dumb yearnings'.

When I heard any news I received it with greediness and
delight, because my expectation was awakened with some hope
that my happiness and the thing I wanted was concealed in it.
Glad tidings, you know, from a far country brings us our
salvation: and I was not deceived. In Jury was Jesus killed,
and from Jerusalem the Gospel came. Which when I once
knew, I was very confident that every Kingdom contained like
wonders and causes of joy, though that was the fountain of
them. As it was the first fruits, so was it the pledge of what I
shall receive in other countries. Thus also when any curious
cabinet, or secret in chemistry, geometry or physic was offered
to me, I diligently looked in it, but when I saw it to the bottom
and not my happiness I despised it. These imaginations and
this thirst of news occasioned these reflections.

On News

I

News from a forein Country came,
As if my Treasures & my Joys lay there;
So much it did my Heart enflame!
'Twas wont to call my Soul into mine Ear;
Which thither went to meet
Th' approaching Sweet,
And on the Threshold stood
To entertain the secret Good;
It hover'd there
As if 'twould leav mine Ear,
And was so eager to embrace
Th' expected Tidings, as they came,
That it could change its dwelling-Place,
To meet the voice & Fame.

2

As if new Tidings were the Things,
Which did comprise my wished unknown Treasure,
Or els did bear them on their wings;
With so much Joy they came, with so much Pleasure,
My Soul stood at the Gate
To recreäte

[1] *The Prelude*, v. 506.

It self with Bliss, & woo
Its speedier Approach; a fuller view
It fain would take,
Yet Journeys back would make
Unto my Heart, as if 'twould fain
Go out to meet, yet stay within,
Fitting a place to entertain,
And bring the Tidings in.

3

What Sacred Instinct did inspire
My Soul in Childhood with an hope so strong?
What secret Force mov'd my Desire
T' Expect my Joys beyond the Seas, so yong?
Felicity I knew
Was out of view;
And being left alone,
I thought all Happiness was gon
From Earth: for this
I long'd-for absent Bliss,
Deeming that sure beyond the Seas,
Or els in som thing near at hand
Which I knew not since nought did pleas
I knew, my Bliss did stand.

4

But little did the Infant dream
That all the Treasures of the World were by,
And that himself was so the Cream
And Crown of all which round about did ly.
Yet thus it was! The Gem,
The Diadem,
The Ring enclosing all
That stood upon this Earthen Ball;
The Hev'nly Ey,
Much wider than the Sky,
Wherin they all included were;
The Love, the Soul, that was the King
Made to possess them, did appear
A very little Thing![1]

Again, although Traherne, like Wordsworth, makes a sharp distinction between 'natural' and 'artificial', glorifies the senses, and praises a 'wise passiveness', he also, like Wordsworth, insists that his visions depended on his own 'creative sensibility', and he is never tired of meditating on the mystery

[1] 3rd Cent. 25, 26, pp. 170–2; *Poems of Felicity*, ed. Bell, p. 20.

and infinity of the mind. Thus, in *The Præparative*, he declares
that
simple Sense
Is Lord of all created Excellence;
but later in the same poem he exclaims:
'Tis not the Object, but the Light,
That maketh Hev'n: 'Tis a clearer Sight.
Felicity
Appears to none but them that purely see.[1]
And the following meditation expresses most clearly, perhaps,
his conception, which has already been profusely illustrated,
of the nobility and power of the human mind:

The true exemplar of God's infinity is that of your understanding, which is a lively pattern and idea of it. It excludeth nothing,
and containeth all things, being a power that permitteth all
objects to be, and is able to enjoy them. Here is a profitable
endlessness of infinite value, because without it infinite joys and
blessings would be lost, which by it are enjoyed. How great
doth God appear, in wisely preparing such an understanding
to enjoy His creatures; such an endless, invisible, and mysterious
receiver! And how blessed and divine are you, to whom God
hath not only simply appeared, but whom He hath exalted as
an Immortal King among all His creatures![2]

Indeed, it is perhaps of those passages in the *Prelude* where
Wordsworth emphasizes the part played by his 'creative sensi-
bility' that Traherne most reminds us—passages such as that
where, after describing how he loved nature in his schooldays,
he adds:
But let this
Be not forgotten, that I still retained
My first creative sensibility;
That by the regular action of the world
My soul was unsubdued. A plastic power
Abode with me; a forming hand, at times
Rebellious, acting in a devious mood;
A local spirit of his own, at war
With general tendency, but, for the most,
Subservient strictly to external things
With which it communed.[3]

Or that where he describes how, during his first summer vaca-
tion, he had
hopes and peace
And swellings of the spirit, was rapt and soothed,
Convers'd with promises, had glimmering views
How Life pervades the undecaying mind,

[1] *Poems of Felicity*, ed. Bell, p. 15.
[2] 2nd Cent. 24, pp. 95–6.   [3] *The Prelude*, ii. 358 ff.

How the immortal Soul with God-like power
Informs, creates, and thaws the deepest sleep
That time can lay upon her; how on earth
Man, if he do but live within the light
Of high endeavours, daily spreads abroad
His being with a strength that cannot fail.[1]

Or that where, after recalling some of the great moments of
childhood and youth, he exclaims:

Oh! mystery of Man, from what a depth
Proceed thy honours! I am lost, but see
In simple childhood something of the base
On which thy greatness stands, but this I feel,
That from thyself it is that thou must give,
Else never canst receive. The days gone by
Come back upon me from the dawn almost
Of life: the hiding-places of my power
Seem open; I approach, and then they close;
I see by glimpses now; when age comes on,
May scarcely see at all, and I would give,
While yet we may, as far as words can give,
A substance and a life to what I feel:
I would enshrine the spirit of the past
For future restoration.[2]

Above all, that passage where he describes the effect upon him
of the news that he and his companion 'had crossed the Alps'
—news which, since the stream and the road, the rocks and the
sky of Italy did not differ from those of Switzerland, could
derive from the imagination alone its thrilling and apocalyptic
significance.

Imagination—here the Power so called
Through sad incompetence of human speech,
That awful Power rose from the mind's abyss
Like an unfathered vapour that enwraps,
At once, some lonely traveller. I was lost;
Halted without an effort to break through;
But to my conscious soul I now can say—
'I recognize thy glory': in such strength
Of usurpation, when the light of sense
Goes out, but with a flash that has revealed
The invisible world, doth greatness make abode,
There harbours; whether we be young or old
Our destiny, our being's heart and home,

[1] *The Prelude*, iv. 152 ff., A text (1805).   [2] Ibid. xi. 329 ff., A text (1805).

Is with infinitude, and only there;
With hope it is, hope that can never die,
Effort, and expectation, and desire,
And something evermore about to be.[1]

Not Chaos, not
The darkest pit of lowest Erebus,
Nor aught of blinder vacancy, scooped out
By help of dreams—can breed such fear and awe
As fall upon us often when we look
Into our Minds, into the Mind of Man—
My haunt, and the main region of my song.[2]

Finally, after describing that journey over Salisbury Plain
during which he began to compose *Guilt and Sorrow*, he reminds
Coleridge that he remarked, after reading that poem,

That also then I must have exercised
Upon the vulgar forms of present things
And actual world of our familiar days,
A higher power, have caught from them a tone,
An image, and a character, by books
Not hitherto reflected. Call we this
But a persuasion taken up by Thee
In friendship; yet the mind is to herself
Witness and judge, and I remember well
That in life's every-day appearances
I seem'd about this period to have sight
Of a new world, a world, too, that was fit
To be transmuted and made visible
To other eyes, as having for its base
That whence our dignity originates,
That which both gives it being and maintains
A balance, an ennobling interchange
Of action from within and from without,
The excellence, pure spirit, and best power
Both of the object seen, and eye that sees.[3]

The tragedy of Wordsworth's life is that he was unable to
maintain this balance, and that he tried to live entirely upon
the strength of past emotions, both giving and receiving less.
Traherne, on the other hand, though a much less powerful
spirit than Wordsworth, seems, ever since he rediscovered it,
to have retained with unabated freshness that 'creative sensibility' which presented a world of glories to his 'Infant-Ey'.

---

[1] *The Prelude*, vi. 592 ff.   [2] *The Recluse*, 1888, p. 52.
[3] *The Prelude*, xii. 360 ff., A text (1805).

Wordsworth also, like Traherne, believed that 'all that we behold'—and not merely, as Bradley has reminded us, 'a good deal that we behold'—'is full of blessings'.

> To unorganic natures I transferr'd
> My own enjoyments, or, the power of truth
> Coming in revelation, I convers'd
> With things that really are, I, at this time
> Saw blessings spread around me like a sea.
> Thus did my days pass on, and now at length
> From Nature and her overflowing soul
> I had receiv'd so much that all my thoughts
> Were steeped in feeling; I was only then
> Contented when with bliss ineffable
> I felt the sentiment of Being spread
> O'er all that moves, and all that seemeth still,
> O'er all, that, lost beyond the reach of thought
> And human knowledge, to the human eye
> Invisible, yet liveth to the heart;
> O'er all that leaps, and runs, and shouts, and sings,
> Or beats the gladsome air, o'er all that glides
> Beneath the wave, yea, in the wave itself
> And mighty depth of waters. Wonder not
> If such my transports were; for in all things now
> I saw one life, and felt that it was joy.[1]

Not only is there a remarkable general similarity between these two experiences; there are also many curious and interesting resemblances in detail. Thus, the following stanza from Traherne's poem *Wonder*—and a similar passage from the *Centuries*[2] has been already quoted—

> Harsh rugged Objects were conceal'd,
> Oppressions, Tears, & Cries,
> Sins, Griefs, Complaints, Dissentions, weeping Eys,
> Were hid: And only things reveal'd
> Which hevenly Spirits & the Angels prize.[3]

reminds us of Wordsworth's thanksgiving for the fact that shepherds became associated with his early love of nature, so that he started with a prepossession in favour of man's capacity for goodness and nobility which no later experience of his frequent meanness and selfishness could shake.

> Call ye these appearances—
> Which I beheld of shepherds in my youth,
> This sanctity of Nature given to man—
> A shadow, a delusion, ye who pore

---

[1] Ibid., ii. 410 ff., A text (1805). [2] 3rd Cent. 2.
[3] *Poems of Felicity*, ed. Bell, p. 4.

F f

On the dead letter, miss the spirit of things,
Whose truth is not a motion or a shape
Instinct with vital functions, but a block
Or waxen image which yourselves have made,
And ye adore! But blessed be the God
Of Nature and of Man that this was so;
That men before my inexperienced eyes
Did first present themselves thus purified,
Removed, and to a distance that was fit:
And so we all of us in some degree
Are led to knowledge, wheresoever led,
And howsoever; were it otherwise,
And we found evil fast as we find good
In our first years, or think that it is found,
How could the innocent heart bear up and live![1]

Since Traherne was unknown until the present century, it is fortunately unnecessary to prove that Wordsworth either had or had not read him. It is here a question of more refreshing 'sources' than those commonly tapped for us by historians of literature—sources of deep and original experience, which sprang up independently in two poets widely separated by time and circumstance, each of whom confirms the reality of the other's inspiration.

VI

The reader will remember that Carew, in his great *Elegy*, praised Donne's pulpit-eloquence because it did

the deepe knowledge of darke truths so teach,
As sense might judge, what phansie could not reach,

and his poetry because it renounced 'servile imitation' and conventional ornaments—'The silenc'd tales o' th' Metamorphoses'. These, certainly, are two of the most important characteristics of 'metaphysical' poetry, and are shared by all the writers of this school, however different their genius. It is therefore remarkably interesting that in the verses *The Author to the Critical Peruser* Traherne should claim just these qualities for his own poetry—that it makes mysteries apparent to sense and that it renounces commonplace metaphors.

The naked Truth in many faces shewn,
Whose inward Beauties very few hav known,
A Simple Light, transparent Words, a Strain
That lowly creeps, yet maketh Mountains plain,

[1] *The Prelude*, viii. 293 ff.

Brings down the highest Mysteries to sense
And keeps them there; that is Our Excellence:
At that we aim; to th'end thy Soul might see
With open Eys thy Great *Felicity*,
Its Objects view, and trace the glorious Way
Wherby thou may'st thy Highest Bliss enjoy.

No curling Metaphors that gild the Sence,
Nor Pictures here, nor painted Eloquence;
No florid Streams of Superficial Gems,
But real Crowns & Thrones & Diadems!
That Gold on Gold should hiding shining ly
May well be reckon'd baser Heraldry.

An easy Stile drawn from a native vein,
A clearer Stream than that wch Poets feign,
Whose bottom may, how deep so'ere, be seen,
Is that wch I think fit to win Esteem:
Els we could speak *Zamzummim* words, & tell
A Tale in tongues that sound like *Babel-Hell*;
In Meteors speak, in blazing Prodigies,
Things that amaze, but will not make us wise.

On Shining Banks we could nigh *Tagus* walk;
In flow'ry Meads of rich *Pactolus* talk;
Bring in the *Druids*, & the *Sybills* view;
See what the Rites are wch the *Indians* do;
Derive along the channel of our Quill
The Streams that flow from high *Parnassus* hill;
Ransack all Nature's Rooms, & add the things
Which *Persian* Courts enrich; to make Us Kings:
To make us Kings indeed! Not verbal Ones,
But reall Kings, exalted unto Thrones;
And more than Golden Thrones! 'Tis this I do,
Letting Poëtick Strains & Shadows go.[1]

Traherne, then, both in style and subject-matter is a metaphysical poet; but he is a greater poet in prose than in verse.
So much of his prose is before the reader, and its rare quality is
so immediately apparent, that to comment upon it would be
almost superfluous. He says in one of the Meditations:

We must disrobe ourselves of all false colours, and unclothe
our souls of evil habits; all our thoughts must be infant-like
and clear; the powers of our soul free from the leaven of this
world, and disentangled from men's conceits and customs.[2]

'Infant-like and clear'! There could be no more perfect description of Traherne's prose at its best, for it has the sweet

[1] *Poems of Felicity*, ed. Bell, p. B 3.   [2] 3rd Cent. p. 155.

gravity, the freshness, the wonder, the intense perception of childhood, to whom all things appear

> herrlich wie am ersten Tag

or, in Shelley's beautiful paraphrase,

> The world's unwithered countenance
> Is bright as on Creation's day.

The same qualities often appear in his poetry, but he only rarely succeeds in condensing the trailing clouds of glory which envelop his world into the concentrated emotion of a perfect poem. The famous Meditation beginning 'The corn was orient and immortal wheat' is followed by a poem that is diffuse and misty in comparison with his jewelled and dancing prose.[1] As Coleridge said of Thomson, he is a great rather than a good poet: the spirit is often finer than its expression, and it is only rarely that we find 'the best words in the best order'. We are often pulled up by clumsy inversions and by words and phrases that are essentially prosaic. Consider, for example, the second stanza of *Amendment*:

> That we should make the Skies
> More Glorious far before thine Eys,
> Then Thou didst make them, and even Thee
> Far more thy Works to prize,
> As usd they be,
> Then as they're made; is a Stupendious Work,
> Wherin thy Wisdom Mightily doth lurk.[2]

'As usd they be' is both harsh and unidiomatic; nothing can be said in favour of 'stupendious' and 'mightily'; and the only justification for 'lurk' is that it rhymes with 'work'. Indeed, there is here too much evidence of 'work'—the best poetry is more like play; for in matters of style, as distinct from the experience conveyed by style, it is the result, not the process, which should first arrest our attention. Too often in reading Traherne's poetry it is the creaking of the machine that makes us pause. Consider also the sixth stanza:

> Thy Soul, O GOD, doth prize
> The Seas, the Earth, our Souls, the Skies,
> As we return the same to Thee;
> They more delight thine Eys,
> And Sweeter be,
> As unto Thee we Offer up the same,
> Then as to us, from Thee at first they came.

---

[1] 3rd Cent. 3, p. 4.   [2] *Poetical Works*, ed. Wade, p. 51.

Phrases such as 'the same', 'the which', used in such a way that
they draw unnecessary attention to themselves, are all too common. Often, too, poems in which there are flashes of real
genius become discursive and prosaic and lose themselves in
vain repetitions. Here are a couple of stanzas from *The Antici-
pation*—a poem in which he develops the paradox that God is
perfect and yet has wants and desires—wherein, to borrow a
remark of Mr. Garrod's, 'those who know what is what will
be able to distinguish which is which'.

> His Essence is all Act: He did, that He
> All Act might always be.
> His Nature burns like fire;
> His Goodness infinitly doth desire,
> To be by all possest;
> His Love makes others Blest.
> It is the Glory of his High Estate,
> And that which I for ever more Admire,
> He is an Act that doth Communicate.
>
> From all to all Eternity He is
> That Act: An Act of Bliss:
> Wherin all Bliss to all,
> That will receiv the same, or on him call,
> Is freely given: from Whence
> Tis Easy even to Sence,
> To apprehend That all Receivers are
> In Him, all Gifts, all Joys, all Eys, even all
> At once, that ever will, or shall appear.[1]

The poem *An Infant-Ey* contains the delightful stanza:

> O that my Sight had ever simple been!
> And never faln into a grosser state!
> Then might I evry Object still have seen
> (As now I see a golden Plate)
> In such an hev'nly Light, as to descry
> In it, or by it, my Felicity.

But the rest of the poem is in a style which an Augustan would
have described as 'grovelling', and of which the two following
stanzas may serve as an example:

> The visiv Rays are Beams of Light indeed,
> Refined, subtil, piercing, quick & pure;
> And as they do the sprightly Winds exceed,
> Are worthy longer to endure:
> They far out-shoot the Reach of Grosser Air,
> Which with such Excellence may not compare.

[1] *Poetical Works*, ed. Wade, p. 59.

> But being once debas'd, they soon becom
> Less activ than they were before; & then
> After distracting Objects out they run,
>   Which make us wretched Men.
> A simple Infant's Ey is such a Treasure
> That when 'tis lost, w'enjoy no reall Pleasure.[1]

An irritating habit of apostrophe sometimes makes the child-
ishness into which his childlikeness too often falls still more
childish and absurd:

> Ye living Gems, how Tru! how Near!
> How Reall, Useful, Pleasant! O how Good!
> How Valuable! yea, how Sweet! how Fair!
>   B'ing once well understood!
> A Gem retains its Worth by being intire,
> Sweet Scents diffus'd do gratify Desire.[2]

I have already remarked that, besides the general similarity
of their experiences, there are many curious and interesting
resemblances in detail between Wordsworth and Traherne.
The most remarkable of these, it seems to me, is the poem *On
leaping over the Moon*, where we may discern that same lack of
humour, that same innocent indifference to conventional associations, and that same intense conviction of the value of an
apparently trifling experience, given with all its details, yet
in such a way that their significance is far less for the reader
than for the poet, which made *Peter Bell* and certain of the
Lyrical Ballads appear so incongruous and incomprehensible to
their original public, and which still leave those poems hovering between the sublime and the ridiculous. Traherne records
two anecdotes of his brother's childhood—how he leapt over
the moon, that is to say, over its reflection in a stream, and how
in still earlier days he exclaimed that the moon had followed
him to town. Here are the last three stanzas:

> As much as others thought themselves to ly
>   Beneath the Moon, so much more high
>   Himself he thought to fly
>   Above the starry Sky,
>   As *that* he spy'd
>   Below the Tide.
> Thus did he yield me in the shady Night
>   A wondrous & instructiv Light,
> Which taught me that under our Feet there is,
>   As o'r our Heads, a Place of Bliss.

---

[1] *Poems of Felicity*, ed. Bell, p. 10.   [2] *The Odour*, ibid., p. 65.

To the same purpos; he, not long before
    Brought home from Nurse, going to the door
        To do som little thing
        He must not do within,
            With Wonder cries,
            As in the Skies
He saw the Moon, *O yonder is the Moon*
    Newly com after me to Town,
That shin'd at Lugwardin but yesternight,
    Where I enjoyed the self-same Light.

As if it had ev'n twenty thousand faces,
    It shines at once in many places;
        To all the Earth so wide
        God doth the Stars divide
            With so much Art
            The Moon impart,
They serv us all; serv wholy ev'ry One
    As if they served him alone.
While evry single Person hath such Store,
    'Tis want of Sense that makes us poor.[1]

But I have said enough about the defects of Traherne's
poetry. His best poems, though not distinguished by verbal
felicity, have a gentle radiance, a candour and an innocence,
that is all their own, as in *The Salutation*, the poem which opens
the collection prepared by his brother.

            These little Limbs,
        These Eys & Hands wch here I find,
    This panting Heart wherwith my Life begins;
        Where have ye been? Behind
    What Curtain were ye from me hid so long!
    Where was, in what Abyss, my new-made Tongue?

            When silent I
        So many thousand thousand Years
    Beneath the Dust did in a *Chaos* ly,
        How could I *Smiles*, or *Tears*,
    Or *Lips*, or *Hands*, or *Eys*, or *Ears* perceiv?
    Welcom ye Treasures wch I now receiv.

            I that so long
        Was *Nothing* from Eternity,
    Did little think such Joys as Ear & Tongue
            To celebrat or see:
    Such Sounds to hear, such Hands to feel, such Feet,
    Such Eys & Objects, on the Ground to meet,

    [1] *Poems of Felicity*, ed. Bell, p. 107.

New burnisht Joys!
Which finest Gold & Pearl excell!
Such sacred Treasures are the Limbs of Boys
In which a Soul doth dwell:
Their organized Joints & azure Veins
More Wealth include than the dead World conteins.

From Dust I rise
And out of Nothing now awake;
These brighter Regions wch salute mine Eys
A Gift from God I take:
The Earth, the Seas, the Light, the lofty Skies,
The Sun & Stars are mine; if these I prize.

A Stranger here,
Strange things doth meet, strange Glory see,
Strange Treasures lodg'd in this fair World appear,
Strange all & New to me:
But that they *mine* should be who Nothing was,
That Strangest is of all; yet brought to pass.[1]

[1] *Poems of Felicity*, ed. Bell, p. 1.

TABLE OF POEMS QUOTED IN FULL OR IN PART

JOHN DONNE
Songs and Sonets

3886   G g

HENRY VAUGHAN

INDEX